Carolina Celebrations	9
Appetizers	15
Beverages	37
Soups	45
Salads and Dressings	55
Breads and Spreads	77
Entrees: Poultry and Game	99
Seafood	118
Meats	130
Vegetables	153
Sweet Endings: Desserts	183
Cakes	192
Pies	209
Cookies and Candies	218
Children's Fun	225
Helpful Handfuls	235
Index	245

Recipes kept from our previous cookbook, SOUTHERN SAMPLES, have been noted with a cotton boll, a symbol of our region.

Our Story

In 1927, a group of dedicated and community-spirited young women from Marlboro County, South Carolina, organized what has become the Junior Charity League of Marlboro County, Inc. Through the seventy year history of the League over 1,750 women have generously served their community.

Many individuals and community projects have benefited from the dedication and perseverance of the Junior Charity League members. In the 1930's and 1940's, the League served as a welfare agency for the county. In addition to assisting with welfare programs, during the 1950's and 1960's the League raised funds for hospitals, clinics, libraries, and local public service organizations. From the 1970's to present day, profits from League endeavors have assisted those in unfortunate circumstances such as needy children, the elderly, victims of domestic and sexual abuse, and the terminally ill.

Through the devotion and dilligence of the Junior Charity League of Marlboro County over $200,000 has been raised and given to various local causes which have benefited the citizens of Marlboro County. To maintain the credibility of the object of the organization, a united effort towards charity and service, League members continue to assist those in need and look boldly to the future of continued community service.

The Carolinas are steeped in many traditions, including that of mothers and grandmothers passing favorite family recipes to their daughters and encouraging them to take active roles in serving their home communities.

These traditions meet in CAROLINA CUISINE where we share dozens of favorite recipes in an effort to support our charitable endeavors, especially helping needy children.

CAROLINA CUISINE offers new, sumptuous, loved and time-tested family recipes in eleven diverse sections and some repeated favorite recipes from SOUTHERN SAMPLES published n November, 1976, by our League during its 50th Anniversary year.

All proceeds from the sale of this cookbook will benefit children's charities of Marlboro County, South Carolina.

Indeed, CAROLINA CUISINE unites these traditions --- great cooking and dedicated caring in Marlboro County, NOTHIN' COULD BE FINER.

The Cookbook Committee

Chairperson
Elisabeth McNiel
Co-Chairman
Lee King

Recipes
Sharon Beaty - Chairperson
Susan Hinson
Rhonda McIntyre
Christi Meggs
Beth Odom
Mica Roller

Editing
Cindi McInnis - Chairperson
Virginia Fowler
Leslie LaBean
Elaine Seales
Jan Weaver

Design
Deanne Hinson - Chairperson
Cammy Miller
Jennie Weatherly

Treasurers
Janis Usher - Chairperson
Gray Covington

Marketing
Elizabeth Munnerlyn - Chairperson
Jimmy Carol Avent
Julie Calhoun
Heather Midgley
Rebekah Rogers

Technical Advisor
Dan McNiel

Other Junior Charity League of Marlboro County members
Kim Bundy
Donna Daniels
Sherrye Jackson

Contributors

Mrs. Glenn (Janice) Allen
Mrs. Benjamin F. (Sara Jane) Alston
Mrs. Hank (Gloria) Avent
Mrs. Mark S. (Jimmy Carol) Avent
Mrs. Billie M. Beaty
Miss Peggy Beaty
Mrs. Dudley C. (Sharon) Beaty, III
Mrs. Shirley H. Beeson
Mrs. William B. (Frances) Belcher
Mrs. William (Erlene) Bethea, Jr.
Mrs. James (Carole) Bowdre
Miss Joye Breeden
Mrs. Smith C. (Helen) Breeden
Mrs. James (Nancy) Brogdon
Mrs. John (Jane) Brooks
Mrs. N. J. (Bernice) Broomfield
Mrs. Richard (Mary Sue) Burnette
Mrs. Andy (Mary Alice) Burroughs
Mrs. Henry (Frances) Burroughs, Jr.
Mrs. Henry (Gerry) Capps
Mrs. Willliam (Anne) Caudill
Mrs. James (Fannie) Chappelear
Mrs. Tony (Becky) Clark
Mrs. Jack (Margaret) Corry
Ms. Inez Cottingham
Mrs. Rhett (Gray) Covington
Mrs. Willie (Tonnie) Craig, Jr.
Mrs. Eugene (Mary) Crosland
Mrs. Wade R. (Elaine) Crow
Mrs. John (Peggy) Culp
Mrs. Rob (Karen) Curran
Miss Katie Currie
Mrs. Thomas P. (Mary) Davis
Mrs. Oscar (Betty Hailey) Derrick
Mrs. William E. (Toni Ann) Dew
Mrs. A. A. (Katie Belle) Drake
Mrs. Julian (Harriett) Drake
Mrs. John P. (Ruby) Driscoll
Mrs. Harry R. (Mary Kay) Easterling
Mrs. William (Marvella) Easterling
Mrs. Scott (Shelly) Elston
Mrs. Marion M. (Cathy) Evans
Mr. Thomas Mayes Evatt
Ms. Jane Anne Feldner
Mrs. Ruth Fields
Mrs. Willadean W. Flowers
Mrs. Forrest (Betty Lou) Fowler
Mrs. Julian (Kay) Fowler
Mrs. Leith (Virginia) Fowler
Mrs. John (Nancy) Fritschner

Mrs. Doug (Karen) Funderburk
Mrs. J. Palmer (Henrietta) Gaillard, III
The late John T. Geisel
Mrs. John T. (Margaret) Geisel
Mrs. Ed (Kaye) Goldberg, IV
Mrs. J. Maxwell (Martha) Gregg
Mrs. Walter W. (Saress) Gregg
Ms. Pamela R. Hall
Mrs. Eugene (Winnie) Hamer
Mrs. Jack (Melba) Hamilton
Mrs. Wadie Cottingham Hardy
Mrs. Lawson (Sarah) Harmon
Mrs. Les (Joann) Hart
Mrs. James (Anna Margaret) Hartis
Miss Karen Hearne
Mrs. Stanley (Elizabeth) Hearne
Mrs. Reid (Deanie) Hensarling
Miss Louise Heriot
Mrs. Arlo (Judy) Hill
Mrs. Robert (Mildred) Hillstrand
Mrs. Curt (Deanne) Hinson
Mrs. Susan McNiel Hinson
Mrs. F. M. (Susan) Hinson, III
Miss Courtney Hodges
Mrs. J. P. (Virginia) Hodges
The late Mrs. K. B. (Bess) Hodges
Mrs. Pledger (Beverly) Hodges
Mrs. A. M. (Mary Frances) Hollingsworth
Mrs. Larry (Phoebe) Howard
Mrs. Ray A. (Betty) Howe
Mrs. Roy (Betty) Howell
Mrs. Howard (Lillian) Hyatt
Mrs. Atley (Sherrye) Jackson
Mrs. Walker (Sophia) Jackson
The late Mrs. Billy (Jane) Jennings
Mrs. Douglas (Libby) Jennings
Mrs. Douglas (Debbie) Jennings, Jr.
Ms. C. J. Jones
Mrs. Mark (Melissa) Joye
Mrs. Ralph (Emily) Kelly
Mrs. Brian (Dena) Kett
Mrs. Martin (Gladys) Kinard
Mrs. Maxie Kinard
Mrs. Gordon (Ruth) King
Mrs. Merritt (Lee) King, III
Mrs. Merritt (Hazel) King, Jr.
The late Miss Annie Kinney
Mrs. William L. (Peggy) Kinney, Jr.
Mrs. Kenneth (Nancy) Klug
Mrs. Tim (Leslie) LaBean

Contributors

Junior Charity League
Mrs. Ray (Linda) Lee
Mrs. Lon (Laura) Lester
Ms. Fran Lewis
Mrs. Steve (Katherine) Littlejohn
Mrs. R. Glenn (Edna Earle) Locke
Mrs. David K. (Cathy) Lynch
Miss Marie Mackey
Miss Alma Manning
The late Miss Janie Manning
Mrs. Trey (Mary) Martin
Mrs. J. T. (Betty) Martin, Jr.
The late Mrs. Charles R. (Mildred) May, Jr.
Mrs. Warren (Kelly) McAlpine
Mrs. Harvey (Barbara) McCants
Mrs. Charles (Mary Alice) McColl
Mrs. Aubrey (Alison) McCormick, Jr.
Mr. Duncan McInnis
Mrs. Duncan (Cindi) McInnis
Mrs. James (Anne) McInnis
Mrs. Fred (Joyce) McIntyre
Mrs. Marty (Rhonda) McIntyre
Mrs. Gilbert (Winkie) McLaurin
Mrs. Daniel E. (Elisabeth) McNiel
Mrs. R. L. (Janie) McNiel
Mrs. Henry (Lisa) McQuage
Mrs. Hubert (Christi) Meggs, Jr.
Mrs. Ethel Mercer
Mrs. Charles (Susan) Midgley
Mrs. Charles Paul (Heather) Midgley
Mrs. Lucius (Ella) Miles
Miss Cammy Miller
Mrs. DuPre (Mary) Miller
Mr. J. DuPre Miller
Mrs. Gene (Mildred) Moore
Mrs. Ron (Elizabeth) Munnerlyn
Mrs. Sara Ellen Munnerlyn
Mrs. Clyde (Grace) Murphy
Mrs. James (Jaylene) Myers
Mrs. John (Pam) Napier
Mrs. Larry (Mary K.) Newton
Mrs. John R. (Penny) Nobles
Mrs. Mackie (Laurie) Norton
Mrs. E. Michael (Terri) O'Tuel, III
Mrs. Harrison (Beth) Odom
Mrs. Mary Odom
Mrs. Frank (Teenie) Parks

Mrs. Sally M. Patterson
Mrs. Tom (Dottie) Pharr
Miss Ivy L. Pope
Mrs. E. LeRoy (Florence) Powell
The late Mrs. Brenda Liles Quick
Mrs. James (Nancy Ruth) Raines
Mrs. Donald (Marty) Rankin
Mrs. Norman (Kay) Rentz
Mrs. Benjy (Linda) Rogers
Mrs. Charles M.(Becky) Rogers
Mrs. Ray (June) Rogers
Mrs. V. Cullum (Catherine) Rogers
Mrs. William A. (Mary Hope) Rogers
Mrs. John I. (Carolyn) Rogers, III
Ms. Dempcy Rowe
Mrs. B. B. (Martha) Sanders, IV
Mrs. Tim (Elaine) Seales
Mrs. David (Betty) Searcy
Mrs. Frank (Libby) Shutt
Mrs Willard (Thelma) Sligh
Mrs. Ray (Lydia) Smith
Mrs. Tony (Jani) Taparo
Mrs. William G. (Mary) Tatum
Mrs. Eben (Martha) Taylor
Mrs. William (Ruth) Therrell
Mrs. Samuel (Adrienne) Thomas, III
Mrs. Phillip (Amy) Thomas, Jr.
Mrs. Robert E. (Lib) Thompson
Mrs. Steve (Beverly) Thompson
The late Tip-Top Inn Pawleys Island, SC
Mrs. James M. (Frances) Townsend
Mrs. Hal (Mary Lois) Trimmier
Miss Louise Tucker
Miss Susan Turpin
Mrs. Jimmy (Janis) Usher
Mrs. Charles (Janice) Vaughan, Jr.
Mrs. Carolyn Dudley Wallace
Mrs. Bill (Gloria) Ward
Ms. Hope Weatherly
Mrs. Jim (Jennie) Weatherly
Mrs. William J. (Edythe) Weatherly
Ms. Jan Weaver
Mrs. Johnny (Janette) Weaver
Mrs. Jackie (Virginia) Williamson
Mrs. Michael (Bonnie) Winburn

Special Acknowledgements

Those who have created, submitted, tested, tasted, and proofed recipes - without your help there would not be a cookbook.

In addition, the Junior Charity League of Marlboro County is indepted to the following people who have so unselfishly given of their talents, time, and financial assistance to make this cookbook possible:

Artists: Donald Wayne Chavis, Pauline Proctor McLean, John L. Weaver, Jr., Dana Throop Crosland, Kathleen Thornton English, Catherine McCall Rogers, Margaret Strong Singletary, Henry E. Avent, Domonica Covington, and Johnsie Choate Stidd.

Graphic Designer: Kelly A. Barnes, Electronic Prepress Specialist, Trac Printing and Graphics, Florence, South Carolina

Technical Advisor: Dan McNiel, who helped organize, compile and format the contents of this cookbook on computer.

Sponsors:

Corporate Donors
BellSouth
Bennettsville Auto Parts
Carolina First Bank
Causey's Hardware and Home Center
The Dairy Dream
Easterling Furniture, Inc.
Easterling & Hinson Carpet and
  Upholstery Cleaning
Fowler Home & Garden Center
Gold Kist Inc.
Hamilton Office Supply Company
Heilig-Meyers Furniture Company
The Ivy Shop
Jennings and Harris, Attorneys at Law
Jimmy Long Oil Company
Main Street Restaurant
Marlboro Herald-Advocate
McColl Gin Company
Meggs Ford , Inc.
Midgley Insurance and Realty Inc.
Pee Dee Eye Associates
Preston Moore Oil Company
Sanders Oil Company
Scotland Orthopedics, PA
Shiness Gift Shop
Townsend Cleaners
Wachovia Bank
Willamette Industries Inc. - Willcopy

Personal Donors
Dudley Beaty, Jr., O.D.
Walt Bogart, M.D.
Mr. and Mrs. William L. Kinney, Jr.
James C. McAlpine, M. D.
Mr. Hubbard W. McDonald, Jr.
Mr. and Mrs. Daniel E. McNiel
Mr. Ellis M. O'Tuel, IV
Mr. Mahlon Padgett, IV
Lisa Petty, D. C.
Miss Janice A. Rozier
Mrs. Maria T. Thomas
Hal Trimmer, Jr., O. D.

CAROLINA CELEBRATIONS

Painting by: Polly McLean

Pauline Proctor McLean
"Graceful Magnolia"

Pauline "Polly" Proctor McLean maintained a residence in Bennettsville for 51 years before moving in 1995 to a retirement center in Columbia. During those years she was active in numerous community activities including membership of First Presbyterian Church. She also participated in the St. Andrews Institute for Life-Long Learning program at Scotia Village retirement community in Laurinburg, North Carolina.

Mrs. McLean has excelled in art classes offered at St. Andrews Presbyterian College in Laurinburg, as well as having received private art instruction.

She is the widow of Hector McLean, the mother of two children and has several grandchildren.

New Year's Day Lunch

*Grilled Pork Tenderloin
*Quick Dried Beans
*Citrus Rice
Collards
*John's Island Cornbread
*Baked Custard

Super Bowl Gathering

*Ole' Dip
*Beer Cheese
*Mountain Pot Beans
*Marinated Cole Slaw
*Spicy Pimento Cheese Sandwiches
*Buster Bar

Easter Dinner

*Ham
Deviled Eggs
*Marinated Asparagus
*Brown Rice
*Copper Pennies
*Sour Cream Potato Salad
*Breakaway Bread
*Angel Bavarian Cake

Graduation Supper

*Tex Mex
*Grandma's Famous Lasagna
*Seven Layer Salad
French Bread
*Chocolate Sheet Cake

*This recipe is included in CAROLINA CUISINE: NOTHIN' COULD BE FINER.

Junior Charity League of Marlboro County, Inc.

Carolina Celebrations

Thanksgiving Dinner

Turkey
Rice and Giblet Gravy
*Irene's Cranberry Salad
*Glazed Sweet Potatoes
*Broccoli and Mushroom Casserole
Butter Beans
*Pumpkin Muffins
*Caramel Cake
*Tip - Top Pecan Pie

Christmas Morning Breakfast

*Breakfast Casserole
Grits
*Sherried Fruit
*Monkey Bread
Orange Juice and Coffee

Christmas Dinner

*"Eye of Round" Roast
*Wild Rice with Oysters
*Sunday Asparagus Casserole
Broiled Tomato Halves
Yeast Rolls
*Black Fruit Cake
*Coconut Layer Cake

Cocktail Buffet

*Polly's Whiskey Sour Punch
*Toasted Pecans
*Lemon Chicken Kabobs
*Cinnamon Roll-Ups
*A Different Cheese Ring
*Ham Delights
*Trawler Crab Dip with Crackers
*Coastal Shrimp Mold with Crackers
*Fruit with Fresh Fruit Dip
*Vegetables with Virginia's Vegetable Dip
*Charleston Squares
*Tangy Lemon Bars

*This recipe is included in CAROLINA CUISINE: NOTHIN' COULD BE FINER.

Teddy Bear Tea Party

*Party Punch
*Vegetable Pizza Bake
Peanut Butter and Jelly Sandwiches
*Ruth Kirkwood's Mints
*World's Best Sugar Cookies

Birthday Party

*Spoonburgers
*Circus Bagels
*Honey Crackle Popcorn
*Carrot Sticks and Virginia's Vegetable Dip
*Million Dollar Pound Cake and ice cream

Sunday Dinner at Grandma's

Fried Chicken
Rice and Gravy
*Macaroni and Cheese
String Beans
*Raspberry Salad
*Refrigerated Rolls
*Mary Kay and Margaret Ann's Chocolate Pie

Backyard Barbecue

*Banana Slush
*Dried Beef Dip
*Barbecued Chicken
*Baked Beans
Corn on the Cob
*Spaghetti Salad
*My Favorite Rolls
*Easy Cobbler
*Congo Bars

*This recipe is included in CAROLINA CUISINE: NOTHIN' COULD BE FINER.

Junior Charity League of Marlboro County, Inc.   13

Carolina Celebrations

Low Country Boil

*Pig's Boiled Peanuts
*Clam Chowder
*Low Country Boil
Tossed Green Salad
*Seven-Layer Cookies
*Lemon Sours

Tables for Four Luncheon

*Baked Sandwich
Fresh Fruit
*Pecan Muffins
*Elisabeth's Key Lime Pie

After the Hunt

*Duck
*Cheese Grits Casserole
String Beans
*Easy Biscuits
*Chocolate Surprise

Supper Club Fare

*Delicious Seafood Casserole
*Prize Winning Eggplant
Saffron Rice
*Orange Salad
*Catherine's Bran Muffins
*Cream Pie

Bridal Luncheon

*Mimosas
*Broccoli Quiche
*Fruit Compote
*Refrigerator Bran Muffins
*Lemonade Pie

---

*This recipe is included in CAROLINA CUISINE: NOTHIN' COULD BE FINER.

*A*PPETIZERS

Painting by: Buster Weaver

John J. Weaver, Jr.
"The Fiddler"

The late John J. "Buster" Weaver, Jr. was owner of Weaver's Building and Specialty Company, a general contracting firm in Bennettsville, South Carolina. He was married to the former Marion Brasington and was an active member of Thomas Memorial Baptist Church. Mr. Weaver was the father of three children: Carol Weaver Covington Ross, Johnny Weaver, and Steve Weaver.

A native of Bennettsville, Mr. Weaver attended the University of South Carolina in Columbia and served in the United States Navy as a member of the Sea Bees in World War II. In his later years, he spent most of time painting and gardening.

Two current members of the Junior Charity League of Marlboro County, Inc. are close family members of Mr. Weaver: Ms. Jan Weaver, his granddaughter, and Mrs. Rhett (Gray) Covington, his granddaughter-in-law.

Dried Beef Dip

Preparation time: 20 minutes **Oven temperature: 350**

1	8 ounce package cream cheese	2	tablespoons onion flakes
2	tablespoons milk	1/4	teaspoons pepper
1	4 ounce package dried beef	1/4	teaspoon garlic salt
1/2	cup sour cream	1/4	cup chopped pecans
1/4	cup chopped bell pepper		

- Cream together cream cheese and milk.
- Stir in dried beef (cut into small pieces).
- Blend in other ingredients except pecans.
- Top with pecans that have been sautéed in butter.
- Bake.
- Serve hot on crackers.

Mrs. Aubrey (Alison) McCormick, Jr., Laurinburg, NC

Magnolia Caviar

Yields: 6 cups **Cooking time: 30 minutes**
Prepare ahead

3	16 ounce cans black-eyed peas	1	clove garlic
1	large green bell pepper	1/3	cup red wine vinegar
1	large red bell pepper	2/3	cup olive oil
2	medium hot peppers	1	tablespoon dijon mustard
1	medium onion	1/4	teaspoon hot pepper sauce
1	4 ounce jar pimento		tortilla chips

- Drain peas.
- Finely chop all peppers, onion, pimento and garlic.
- Mix with peas.
- In separate bowl, whisk together vinegar, olive oil, and mustard.
- Mix well.
- Pour over pea mixture and add hot pepper sauce.
- Refrigerate.
- Drain before serving with tortilla chips.
- May be refrigerated for four to five days.

Mrs. Daniel E. (Elisabeth) McNiel, Bennettsville, SC

Regal Red Caviar Dip

May prepare a day ahead, wait to garnish at seving time
Preparation time: 30 minutes   **Prepare ahead**
Serves: 25

1	pint sour cream	3	teaspoons onion, grated
1	8 ounce package cream cheese, softened		hot pepper sauce, to taste
1	teaspoon lemon juice	1	ounce jar red caviar

- Blend together sour cream, cream cheese, lemon juice, onion and hot pepper sauce.
- Carefully fold in caviar, reserving a little for garnish. Do not crush eggs.
- Serve with crackers.

Mrs. Henry (Lisa) McQuage, Clio, SC

Cheese Ball

Make several days prior to party.

2	3 ounce packages cream cheese	4	tablespoons Accent flavor enhancer
6	ounces sharp cheddar cheese, grated	1	medium onion, finely chopped
		1½	cups pecans, chopped

- Place cream cheese in a bowl and let soften.
- Add the grated cheese, Accent, and onions.
- Mix thoroughly and shape into a ball.
- Roll cheese ball in pecans.
- Refrigerate.

Mrs. Gilbert (Winkie) McLaurin, Bennettsville, SC

Pineapple Cheese Ball (or Spread)

Serves: 6-8 people
Prepare ahead

Preparation: 10 minutes

2   8 ounce packages cream cheese
1/2 cup mild cheddar cheese, grated
1   small can crushed pineapple,
    drained

2   tablespoons green pepper,
    chopped
2   tablespoons onion, minced
    garlic salt to taste

Ball
• Mix together all ingredients.
• Roll into a ball and roll ball in chopped pecans.
• Serve with crackers.

Spread
• Mix together all ingredients.
• Spread on bread of choice for sandwiches.

Mrs. Samuel J. (Adrienne) Thomas, III, Bennettsville, SC

A Different Cheese Ring

A pretty holiday dish!
Preparation time: 30 minutes
Serves: 20-25

Prepare ahead

1   pound sharp cheddar cheese,
    grated
3/4 cup mayonnaise
1/2 teaspoon hot sauce
2   green onions, chopped

3/4 teaspoon garlic, minced (not
    dehydrated)
3/4 cup nuts, chopped (large
    pieces)
    strawberry preserves

• Blend all ingredients together and mold into desired shape on glass serving
  plate.
• Refrigerate overnight.
• Before serving, "frost" with strawberry preserves.
• Spread on wheat crackers.

Mrs. Michael (Bonnie) Winburn, Bennettsville, SC

Junior Charity League of Marlboro County, Inc.

Cheese Biscuits

Preparation time: 10-15 minutes   **Oven temperature: 350**

1   pound sharp cheese
4   sticks butter (do not substitute)
4   cups all-purpose flour

1   teaspoon salt
$^{1}/_{2}$ teaspoon cayenne pepper

- Let butter and cheese soften to room temperature.
- Cream thoroughly.
- Add flour, salt, and cayenne pepper.
- Roll out to about $^{1}/_{8}$ inch on floured board and cut into roll.
- Chill and slice.
- Bake.

Mrs. James (Fannie) Chappelear, Bennettsville, SC

Cheese Straws

This recipe was given to me by the late Lois Weatherly.

Serves: 10   **Preparation time: 1 hour**
Cooking time: 15 minutes or until crisp
Oven temperature: 325   **Prepare ahead**
Freezes well

3   sticks butter
1   pound sharp cheese
4   cups all-purpose flour

1   teaspoon red pepper
1   teaspoon salt

- Leave butter and cheese out to soften.
- Blend butter, cheese, flour, red pepper and salt together.
- Put in cookie press using the star insert.
- Press on ungreased cookie sheet.
- Bake.
- Cut in two inch strips when done.

Mrs. Benjamin F. (Sara Jane) Alston, Bennettsville, SC

Carolina Cuisine: Nothin' Could Be Finer

Edythe's Cheese Straws

This recipe can be divided into fourths to yield approximately 50 straws.

Yields: 300 straws
Cooking time: 15 minutes
Prepare ahead

Preparation time: 30 minutes
Oven temperature: 350
Freezes well

4   cups extra sharp cheese, grated
4   sticks butter, softened
4   cups all-purpose flour

1   teaspoon salt
$^1/_2$ teaspoon red pepper

- Mix all ingredients by hand to the consistency of biscuit dough.
- Use star cutter in cookie press and place straws on an ungreased cookie sheet.
- Bake.
- Do not allow to burn on bottom.

Mrs. William J. (Edythe) Weatherly, Bennettsville, SC

Beer Cheese

Serves a crowd. Best if made ahead of time.

2   10 ounce packages extra sharp cheese
2   cloves garlic

1   7 ounce bottle beer
$^1/_8$ teaspoon salt
     hot sauce to taste

- Grate cheese and garlic in a food processor.
- Add remaining ingredients until blended.
- The mixture will be soft but will harden in the refrigerator.
- Serve with crackers, celery sticks or radish roses.

Mrs. James (Carole) Bowdre, Bennettsville, SC

Lemon Chicken Kabobs

Serves: 20

Prepare 24 hours ahead

1½ pounds boned chicken breast, chunked
1½ cups peanut oil
⅓ cup lemon juice
2 tablespoons red wine vinegar
1 tablespoon fresh parsley, chopped
1 teaspoon salt

½ teaspoon marjoram
¼ teaspoon thyme
¼ teaspoon oregano
¼ teaspoon basil
¼ teaspoon pepper
1 clove garlic, minced
40 lemon wedges

- In blender, place oil, lemon juice, vinegar, parsley, salt, marjoram, thyme, oregano, basil, pepper and garlic.
- Blend on high speed about 30 seconds.
- Place chicken chunks in medium bowl.
- Pour marinade over chicken, cover and refrigerate 24 hours.
- Remove chicken from marinade and drain well.
- Thread 20 small skewers, alternating 3 chicken chunks and 2 lemon wedges on each.
- Place on prepared grill about 8 inches from heat.
- Cook about 4 minutes, turn and cook about 4 minutes more, watching constantly.
- Serve immediately or chill in refrigerator and serve cold.

Miss Karen Hearne, Mt. Pleasant, SC

Taparo's Hot Chili Cheese Dip

Serves: 6-8
Cooking time: 30 minutes
Prepare ahead

Preparation time: 10 minutes
Oven temperature: 350

1 8 ounce package cream cheese
1 10 ounce can chili
1 8 ounce package Monterey Jack cheese

1 8 ounce package cheddar cheese
tortilla chips

- Spread cream cheese in 9 x 13 casserole dish.
- Place chili on top of cream cheese.
- Finish with the Monterey Jack and cheddar cheese.
- Bake.
- Serve with tortilla chips.

Mrs. Tony (Jani) Taparo, Nashville, TN

Carolina Cuisine: Nothin' Could Be Finer

Cinnamon Roll-Ups

Cooking time: 5-8 minutes

Oven temperature: 350

1 loaf bread
1 8 ounce cream cheese, softened
1 stick margarine, melted

1 tablespoon cinnamon
1 cup sugar

- Remove crust from bread.
- Roll out bread until flat.
- Spread with softened cream cheese.
- Roll up bread slice, cut in half.
- Mix cinnamon and sugar; brush roll-ups with cooled melted margarine.
- Place in container and shake.
- Roll roll-ups in sugar and cinnamon.
- Bake at 350 degrees for 5-8 minutes on an ungreased pan until golden brown.

Mrs. Dudley C. (Sharon) Beaty, III, Bennettsville, SC

Kaye's Crab Dip

This is absolutely delicious!

Serves: 12
Cooking time: 30 minutes

Preparation time: 30 minutes
Oven temperature: 350

2 8 ounce packages cream cheese
1/2 cup mayonnaise
3-4 6 ounce cans crab meat (rinsed & drained)
2 tablespoons onion, minced

1 2 ounce package slivered almonds
lemon juice to taste
hot sauce to taste
dash Worcestershire sauce

- Pour lemon juice over crab and drain in colander.
- In mixing bowl, cream mayonnaise and cream cheese.
- Add minced onion, several dashes of hot sauce and Worcestershire sauce.
- Add crab to cheese mixture and top with almonds.
- Bake.
- Serve with crackers or bugles.

Mrs. Ed (Kaye) Goldberg, IV, Murrells Inlet, SC

Meeting Street Crab Dip

Serves: 4-6
Oven temperature: 425

Cooking time: 10 minutes

$^1/_4$	cup butter		$^1/_4$	teaspoon pepper
$^1/_4$	cup all-purpose flour		$^1/_4$	teaspoon sherry
1	cup half and half		1	pound white crab meat
1	teaspoon salt		$^3/_4$	cup cheddar cheese, shredded

- In a saucepan, melt butter, stir in flour, then half and half, salt, pepper, and sherry.
- Cook over very low heat, stirring constantly until it becomes a thick white sauce.
- Remove from heat and add crab meat.
- Pour mixture into buttered 10 x 6 x 2 baking dish.
- Sprinkle with cheese and bake.
- Serve with crackers.

Mrs. Merritt (Lee) King, III, McColl, SC

Trawler Crab Dip

Will keep in refrigerator for 1 week.
Serves: 10-12 people

Preparation time: 5-10 minutes

1	cup lump imitation crab meat		4	tablespoons French dressing
1	cup cheddar cheese, grated		$1^1/_4$	cups mayonnaise
1	teaspoon horseradish sauce			

- Break crab meat into small strips.
- Combine all ingredients and chill.

Mrs. Hubert (Christi) Meggs, Jr., Bennettsville, SC

Crab And Shrimp Delight

Misses Alma and Janie Manning operated a guest house at Cherry Grove Beach, SC for many years. Their meals were famous throughout the Carolinas.

Serves: 6 to 8   **Cooking time: 30 minutes**

1	10 ¾ ounce can cream of mushroom soup	1	pound crab meat
½	can of milk	½	teaspoon prepared mustard
1	pound shrimp		dash of salt and pepper
			dash of hot sauce
		1	teaspoon Worcestershire sauce

- Make the white sauce of soup and milk combination.
- Into this mix all other ingredients.
- Pour into a greased casserole.
- Sprinkle top generously with parmesan cheese.
- Bake until bubbly.

Miss Alma Manning and the late Miss Janie Manning, Clio, SC

Fresh Fruit Dip

Always refreshing and light!

1	7 ounce jar marshmallow creme	1	8 ounce container soft cream cheese

- Mix the above with mixer.
- Ready to serve with any fresh fruit (strawberries, grapes, pineapple, kiwi)

Mrs. Mackie (Laurie) Norton, McColl, SC

Ham Delights

Men love this!

Serves: 12   **Preparation time: 20 minutes**
Cooking time: 30 minutes   **Oven temperature: 325**
Prepare ahead   **Freezes well**

2	teaspoons poppyseed	1	12 ounce package sliced ham
2	sticks margarine, melted	2	15 ounce packages finger rolls
1	onion, grated	8	slices Swiss cheese
5	heaping teaspoons mustard		

- Combine the first four ingredients and bring to a boil.
- Slice each package of rolls in half.
- Spread the mixture on both sides of the rolls.
- Layer ham and Swiss cheese.
- Replace top of rolls.
- Bake, covered with foil.

Mrs. Dudley C. (Sharon) Beaty, III, Bennettsville, SC

Junior Charity League of Marlboro County, Inc.

Appetizers

Jalepeno Roll-Ups

Serves: 25
Prepare ahead

Preparation time: 30 minutes

4   10 inch flour tortillas
2   8 ounce packages cream cheese
1   package original ranch dressing
1   medium onion, chopped finely

6   ounces jalepeno peppers,
     finely chopped
2    $2^{1}/_{4}$ ounce cans black olives,
     chopped
2   ounces pimentos,chopped (optional)

- Soften cream cheese to room temperature.
- Mix softened cream cheese and package of original ranch dressing.
- Quarter mixture and spread over each tortilla shell.
- Sprinkle chopped onion, jalepeno peppers, and black olives over cream cheese mixture.
- Roll length-wise each tortilla shell.
- Place on flat pan and refrigerate for 2 hours.
- Slice each tortilla shell into $^{1}/_{4}$ inch slices.
- Approximately 10-15 pinwheels per tortilla.

Mrs. Lon (Laura) Lester, Bennettsville, SC

Mark's Mess

Serves: 8
Prepare ahead: 1 day

Preparation time: 15 minutes

1   14 $^{1}/_{2}$ ounce can shoepeg corn,
     drained
1   15 ounce can black beans
1   24 ounce jar mild salsa
1   medium tomato, finely chopped

1   medium green bell pepper, finely
     chopped
1   medium onion, finely chopped
     tortilla chips

- Mix all ingredients the night before serving.
- Refrigerate until ready to eat.
- Serve with tortilla chips.

Mrs. Mark S. (Jimmy Carol) Avent, Bennettsville, SC

Mexican Dip

Preparation time: 20 minutes
Prepare ahead

Cooking time: 15 minutes

1 1/2 pounds hamburger meat
1 small onion, chopped
1/8 teaspoon garlic salt

1/8 teaspoon black pepper
1 8 ounce box mild Mexican cheese

- Brown hamburger meat with onion.
- Add seasonings.
- Drain grease.
- Place in casserole dish and cut up cheese in chunks on top of meat mixture.
- Cook in microwave until cheese melts.
- Stir and serve hot with white corn tortilla chips.

Mrs. Tim (Leslie) LaBean, Bennettsville, SC

Marinated Mushrooms

Serves: 12

Prepare ahead: 4 hours

4 4 ounce cans whole mushrooms
1 1/2 cups vegetable oil
2 cloves garlic, sliced
2/3 cup vinegar

1 1/2 teaspoons salt
1 1/2 teaspoons thyme
1 teaspoon marjoram
2 pinches rosemary

- Mix all the ingredients and store in a covered container.
- Serve after 4 hours. These will keep indefinitely.

Mrs. Wade R. (Elaine) Crow, Bennettsville, SC

Stuffed Mushrooms

12 large fresh mushrooms or
1 1/3 cups canned mushrooms, drained
1 teaspoon onion, finely chopped
1 teaspoon butter, melted
1 2 1/4 ounce can deviled ham
1 teaspoon prepared mustard
1/4 teaspoon Worcestershire sauce
1/2 cup soft bread crumbs

- Remove mushroom stems.
- Chop stems and cook with onions in butter for a few minutes.
- Stir in ham, mustard, Worcestershire sauce, and crumbs.
- Put stuffing in crowns and place in oven on foil-lined cookie sheet until warm.

Mrs. Douglas (Libby) Jennings, Bennettsville, SC

Ole' Dip

Serves: 6
Oven temperature: 350
Cooking time: 20 minutes

1 9 ounce can bean dip
1 8 ounce cream cheese, softened
1 8 ounce package sour cream
1 12 ounce package cheddar cheese
1 12 ounce package grated jack cheese
chips of your choice

- Mix the bean dip, cream cheese and sour cream together.
- In an oblong dish, spread bean mixture, cheese, bean mixture, cheese.
- Bake.

Mrs. Jim (Jennie) Weatherly, Bennettsville, SC

Hot Cheese Olives

Yields: 65-70 olives
Cooking time: 12 minutes
Prepare ahead
Preparation time: 45 minutes
Oven temperature: 425
Freezes well

1/2 pound sharp cheese, grated
1/2 cup margarine
dash Worcestershire sauce
1 cup all-purpose flour
1/2 teaspoon salt
1 10 ounce bottle of pimento-stuffed green olives, drained

- Blend together: cheese, margarine, and Worcestershire sauce.
- Add flour and salt.
- When mixture is smooth, wrap each olive with a bit of the dough and place on cookie sheet.
- When cookie sheet is full, place in freezer until frozen.
- Bake in preheated oven. Serve hot.

Mrs. Lon (Laura) Lester, Bennettsville, SC

Onion Canapes

These are simple to prepare and a delicious appetizer. They can be served hot or cold.

Serves: 5 or 6
Cooking time: 3 or 4 minutes
Prepare ahead

Preparation time: 10 minutes
Oven temperature: 425

$^1/_2$ cup mayonnaise
$^1/_2$ cup Parmesan cheese

2 tablespoons onion, grated
saltine crackers

- Mix the mayonnaise, cheese, and grated onion.
- Spread generously on the crackers.
- Bake until bubbly and brown around the edges.

Mrs. Forrest (Betty Lou) Fowler, Bennettsville, SC

Hot Oyster Cocktail A La Belle Isle

Serves: 8 to 10
Cooking time: 10 minutes

Preparation time: 15 minutes

6 slices bacon
2 sticks butter
2 tablespoons lemon juice
2 tablespoons minced onion
2 tablespoons minced parsley
2 tablespoons Worcestershire
   sauce

1 teaspoon celery seed
1 quart oysters
   dash red pepper
   dash black pepper
   dash salt
   toast points

- Fry bacon, crumble and set aside.
- Add butter to bacon drippings in pan.
- Add the next five ingredients.
- Cook just until gills curl.
- Add crumbled bacon.
- Serve at once with toast points.

Mrs. Tom (Dottie) Pharr, Bennettsville, SC

Junior Charity League of Marlboro County, Inc.

Pig's Boiled Peanuts

Perfect for a large crowd.

Preparation time: 15 minutes
Prepare ahead

Cooking time: 1 hour or more
Freezes well

green peanuts, raw and freshly
pulled

salt
water

- Wash peanuts until water is mostly clear.
- Put in large pot, unshelled, cover with water.
- Add salt and boil until shells soften and nut inside is tender and also softened.
- Boiling usually takes an hour or more, depending on how "green" the peanuts are.
- For a 6 quart pot full of peanuts, use $2/3$ cup salt.
- For an 8 quart pot use $1^1/4$ cups salt.
- For a 14 quart pot use $1^1/2$ cups salt.
- May remain in brine for several hours or overnight.
- Pour off brine and store in ziplock heavy duty plastic bags in refrigerator.

Mrs. William L. (Peggy) Kinney, Jr., Bennettsville, SC

Barbecued Pecans

Preparation time: 35-45 minutes
Oven temperature: 300
Freezes well

Cooking time: 35-45 minutes
Prepare ahead

2   tablespoons butter or margarine
$1/2$ teaspoon seasoned salt
1 or 2 dashes hot sauce

1   pound ($4^1/2$ cups) pecan halves
3   tablespoons Worcestershire
sauce

- Put margarine or butter, salt and hot sauce in 12 x 8 x 2 inch baking dish.
- Place in oven until butter melts.
- Add pecans, stirring until all are coated.
- Line baking dish with foil for easy cleanup.
- Bake about 20 minutes, stirring occasionally.
- Sprinkle with Worcestershire sauce; stir again and continue baking another 15 minutes or until crisp.

Miss Louise Heriot, Bennettsville, SC

Toasted Pecans

Cooking time: 30 minutes　　　　**Oven temperature: 300**

1　quart pecans　　　　　　　　　　dash salt
1/2　stick margarine

- Preheat oven.
- Melt margarine in baking pan.
- Place nuts in pan.
- Stir until coated with margarine.
- Place in oven.
- Stir at end of each 10 minutes of baking.
- Salt lightly twice.

Mrs. Wadie Cottingham Hardy, San Pedro, CA

Pepper Jelly Mold

Can be seasonally appropriate by using red or green jelly.
Yields: 3 1/2 cups　　　　　　**Preparation time: 30 minutes**
May prepare ahead, up to two days before serving.

2　8 ounce packages cream　　　1　tablespoon unflavored gelatin
　　cheese, softened　　　　　　　1/4　cup cold milk
1　cup hot pepper jelly　　　　　1/2　cup boiling milk

- With a mixer, beat cream cheese until smooth.
- Add jelly.
- Blend well.
- Soften gelatin in cold milk, add boiling milk.
- Stir until dissolved.
- Combine with cream cheese mixture.
- Pour into 3 1/2 cup mold.
- Chill.
- Unmold and serve with crackers.

Mrs. Benjy (Linda) Rogers, Bennettsville, SC

Salmon Mousse

Very filling and goes a long way!
Yields: 6 cup mold   **Preparation time: 45 minutes**
Prepare ahead

1   16 ounce can salmon
2   envelopes unflavored gelatin
2   cups mayonnaise
$1/2$ cup chili sauce
2   tablespoons lemon juice
1   tablespoon Worcestershire
    sauce
$1/2$ teaspoon dried dill weed
$1/4$ teaspoon pepper

1   $6^1/2$ ounce can tuna, drained
    and finely flaked (reserve liquid)
4   hard cooked eggs, finely
    chopped
$1/2$ cup pimento-stuffed olives,
    finely chopped
$1/4$ cup finely chopped onion

- Drain salmon, reserving liquid.
- Add water to liquid, if necessary, to equal $1/2$ cup.
- Bone and finely flake salmon; set aside.
- In heatproof measuring cup, combine gelatin and reserved salmon liquid.
- Place cup in a saucepan of hot water and stir to dissolve gelatin.
- Transfer dissolved gelatin to mixing bowl; gradually blend in mayonnaise.
- Stir in chili sauce, lemon juice, Worcestershire sauce, dillweed, and pepper.
- Fold in flaked salmon, tuna, egg, chopped olive, and onion.
- Turn into 6 cup mold (fish mold preferred).
- Chill until firm. Serve with crackers (round buttery).

Mrs. Benjy (Linda) Rogers, Bennettsville, SC

Sausage Dip

$1^1/2$ pounds sausage
1   medium onion, chopped
2   8 ounce packages cream
    cheese, softened

1   8 ounce package sour cream
2   14 $1/2$ ounce cans tomatoes and
    green chiles

- Brown sausage and onion.
- Drain well on paper towels.
- Mix cream cheese and all other ingredients together.
- Simmer for $1^1/2$ to 2 hours.
- Great with tortilla chips.

Mrs. Martin (Gladys) Kinard, Bennettsville, SC

Carolina Cuisine: Nothin' Could Be Finer

Cocktail Sausages

Serves: 10 to 12
Cooking time: 4 hours
Freezes well

Preparation time: 15 minutes
Prepare ahead

½ cup bottled chili sauce
½ cup apricot preserves
1½ tablespoons lemon juice
1½ teaspoons prepared mustard

1 pound smoked cocktail
   sausages
1 16 ounce can chunk pineapple

- Combine all ingredients except pineapple in a crockpot.
- Heat until hot (3-4 hours).
- Add pineapple about 30 minutes before serving.
- May leave in crockpot while serving to keep warm.

Mrs. Andy (Mary Alice) Burroughs, Bennettsville, SC

Pie's Sausage Pinwheels

Yields: 2 dozen
Oven temperature: 375

Cooking time: 10 to 12 minutes
Prepare ahead

1 pound sausage

1 can dinner rolls, triangular shape

- Brown sausage and drain.
- Open rolls and spread dough into four rectangles.
- Sprinkle sausage over dough.
- Pat in place.
- Roll dough over sausage.
- Will have four rolls.
- Refrigerate several hours.
- Pre-heat oven.
- Slice the dough into rounds, ¼ inch thick.
- Bake on bottom rack for 10 minutes
- Move to top rack for final 2 minutes.

Mrs. Donald (Marty) Rankin, Bennettsville, SC

Shrimp Ball

Preparation time: 45 minutes
Freezes well

Prepare ahead

$^1/_2$ 10 $^3/_4$ ounce can condensed
    tomato soup
1 envelope plain gelatin
1 teaspoon salt
$^3/_4$ cup mayonnaise

1 6 ounce package cream cheese
$^1/_2$ cup celery, finely chopped
$^1/_4$ cup onion, grated
1 pound cooked shrimp (grated or
    broken into small pieces)

- Mix soup, gelatin, and salt.
- Heat enough to dissolve gelatin.
- Blend this with remaining ingredients.
- Form into ball (can be rolled in parsley flakes if desired).
- Chill overnight.
- Sprinkle with paprika when ready to use.

Miss Katie Currie, Bennettsville, SC

Coastal Shrimp Mold

2 cups cooked chopped shrimp
2 hard boiled eggs, grated
1 small onion, grated

1 $^1/_2$ cups salad dressing
2 envelopes unflavored gelatin

- Mix all of above.
- Congeal overnight.
- Serve with crackers.

Mrs. John (Peggy) Culp, Bennettsville, SC

Petite Toast Cups

Cooking time: 10 minutes

Oven temperature: 350

6 slices sandwich bread

- Remove crust.
- Cut each slice into 4 equal squares.
- Carefully press square into 2 inch muffin cup.
- Toast in oven.
- Cool and fill with with your favorite salad or spread.

Mrs. N.J. (Bernice) Broomfield, Bennettsville, SC

Carolina Cuisine: Nothin' Could Be Finer

Taco Dip

Delicious and so easy!
Serves: 12
Prepare ahead

Preparation time: 10 minutes

2   8 ounce packages cream cheese
1   8 ounce jar medium salsa
¹/₄ cup sliced black olives

¹/₄ cup green onion tops
¹/₄ cup sharp cheddar cheese, grated

- Microwave cream cheese until soft.
- Add salsa to cream cheese and mix throughly.
- Pour into festive serving dish.
- Top with black olives, green onion tops, and cheddar cheese.
- Serve with taco chips.

Mrs. Wade R. (Elaine) Crow, Bennettsville, SC

Tex Mex

Wonderful for a large crowd!
Serves: 15
Prepare several hours before serving

Preparation time: 30 minutes

2   medium size avocadoes
2   tablespoons lemon juice
¹/₂ teaspoon salt
¹/₄ teaspoon pepper
    dash garlic salt
1   cup sour cream
¹/₂ cup mayonnaise
1   envelope taco seasoning mix

2   10¹/₂ ounce cans plain or
    jalapeno bean dip
³/₄ cup chopped green onion
2   medium size tomatoes, seeded
    and chopped
³/₄ cup chopped ripe olives
2   cups sharp cheddar cheese,
    shredded
    Tortilla chips for dipping

- Peel, pit, mash avocadoes with lemon juice, salt, pepper, and garlic salt.
- Combine sour cream, mayonnaise, and taco mix.
- Spread bean dip on large shallow platter.
- Top with avocado mixture.
- Top with sour cream mixture.
- Sprinkle with onions, tomatoes, ripe olives.
- Cover with cheese.
- Refrigerate for several hours.
- Serve with tortilla chips for dipping.

Mrs. Norman (Kay) Rentz, Pickens, SC

Vegetable Pizza Bake

Very pretty on tray!
Cooking time: 8 to 10 minutes or until golden brown
Oven temperature: 350

2	cans refrigerated crescent dinner rolls	3/4	cup each red and green pepper, chopped
1	package original ranch dressing	3/4	cup cauliflower, chopped
1/2	cup mayonnaise	3/4	cup mushrooms, chopped
2	8 ounce packages cream cheese	1/2	cup onion, chopped
3/4	cup broccoli, chopped	1	cup cheddar cheese, shredded
3/4	cup carrots, shredded		

- Open rolls and place on cookie sheet or pizza pan to cover bottom of pan.
- Bake.
- Mix dressing, mayonnaise, and cream cheese until blended well and smooth.
- Spread mixture on baked rolls.
- Top with vegetables and cheese.
- Refrigerate for 2 hours before serving.

Mrs. Steve (Beverly) Thompson, Bennettsville, SC

Virginia's Vegetable Dip

Serves: 25
Prepare ahead

Preparation time: 15 minutes

1	cup mayonnaise	1/2	teaspoon Worcestershire sauce
1	teaspoon lemon juice	1/2	teaspoon red pepper sauce
1	teaspoon curry powder	1/4	cup chili sauce
1/2	teaspoon onion, finely minced		salt and pepper to taste

- Mix well.
- Serve with an assortment of raw vegetables.

Mrs. J.P. (Virginia) Hodges, Bennettsville, SC

Painting by: Dana Crosland

Dana T. Crosland

"Spivey's Beach"

Dana T. Crosland, an avid sportsman and lifelong resident of Marlboro County, attended local schools and began drawing at an early age. He successfully completed art classes at the University of South Carolina in Columbia, but considers himself to be a self-taught artist. Mr. Crosland's love to create art has continued throughout his life.

Among other interests, he was a charter member of the Marlboro Rescue Squad and the Marlborough Historical Society. His community activities also include being associated with the Boy Scouts of America. Mr. Crosland is presently enjoying an active retirement from the United States Postal Service and is a current member of the Marlboro County Historic Preservation Commission.

He is married to the former Cornelia McCall Freeman, and has one daughter and one grandson.

Banana Slush

Serves: 15
Freezes well

Prepare ahead

4   cups sugar
6   cups water
1   46 ounce can pineapple juice
1   46 ounce can orange juice

5   mashed bananas
$^1/_2$ cup fresh lemon juice
5   quarts ginger ale

- Bring sugar and water to a boil.
- Cool.
- Pour into 5 quart freezer container.
- Stir in next 4 ingredients.
- Remove from freezer several hours before serving.
- This will be slushy.
- Put into glass and pour ginger ale over it.

Mrs. Ray A. (Betty) Howe, Bennettsville, SC

Bloody Marys for a Crowd

Serves: 16 to 18
Prepare ahead

Preparation time: 5 minutes

2   46 ounce cans tomato juice
1   pint Vodka
4   tablespoons Worcestershire
    sauce
6   tablespoons fresh lemon juice
1   teaspoon salt

$^1/_4$ teaspoon pepper
$^1/_4$ teaspoon hot pepper sauce
    dash of celery salt
    celery stalks, for garnish
    ice cubes

- Mix all ingredients in a gallon jug.
- Shake well and refrigerate for several hours.
- Serve over ice with celery stalks as garnish.

Mrs. David K. (Cathy) Lynch, Bennettsville, SC

Junior Charity League of Marlboro County, Inc.

Champagne Punch

Serves: 25 **Preparation time: 20 minutes**

2	25.4 ounce bottles sparkling white grape juice, chilled	1	6 ounce can frozen lemonade concentrate (thawed and undiluted)
2	2 liter bottles ginger ale, chilled		red maraschino cherries for garnish
1	32 ounce bottle white grape juice, chilled		

- Pour all ingredients in punch bowl and mix well.
- Make an ice ring with punch and cherries.
- Add a red cherry to each punch cup before pouring in punch.

Mrs. A.M. (Mary Frances) Hollingsworth, Fayetteville, NC

Instant Hot Chocolate

1	box (8 quarts) instant dry milk	1	8 ounce non-dairy creamer
16	ounces dry instant chocolate drink mix	1/2	cup powdered sugar or more to taste

- Mix together.
- Use 1/3 cup with each cup of hot water.

Mrs. Carolyn Dudley Wallace, Bennettsville, SC

Adelaide's Instant Russian Tea

This recipe was given me by the late Adelaide Sellers of Chesterfield, a well-known baby nurse who stayed with many newborns and their families in the area.

1 cup dry instant orange drink mix	½ teaspoon ground cinnamon
⅔ cup granulated sugar	½ teaspoon ground clove
⅓ cup instant tea with lemon and sugar (increase to ⅔ cup if more flavor is desired)	

- Mix well and store in covered glass container.
- Use a heaping spoonful per cup of boiling water.

Mrs. William L. (Peggy) Kinney, Jr., Bennettsville, SC

Pawley's Island Daiquiris

Wonderful! Often requested!
Serves: 4
Freezes well

Preparation time: 5 minutes

6 ounces frozen pink lemonade or limeade	4 teaspoons sugar or 2 packets sweetener
1 cup fresh or frozen strawberries or peaches	ice
6 ounces light white rum	

Optional: 1 small scoop lime sherbet

- In blender place lemonade (or limeade, if no fruit is used), fruit, sugar or sweetener, rum, and ice to fill container.
- Use lime sherbet with limeade, if no fruit is available.
- Blend on highest level until all ice has been crushed.
- Add more ice so that container will become filled with frozen mixture.
- Blend again until crushed.
- Pour into individual glasses and enjoy.

Mrs. William L. (Peggy) Kinney, Jr., Bennettsville, SC
Mrs. Daniel E. (Elisabeth) McNiel, Bennettsville, SC

Mimosas

Delicious beginnings for a Sunday brunch.
Preparation time: 5 minutes   **Serves: 15**
Prepare ahead

2   700 milliliter bottles of champagne   2   quarts orange juice
                                                  strawberries for garnish (optional)

- Combine champagne and orange juice in a gallon container.
- Served chilled with a strawberry as garnish.

Mrs. Hubert (Christi) Meggs, Jr., Bennesttsville, SC

Cheerwine Punch

Children love this because it is sweet, and the pineapple juice is nutritious for them. Stains from Cheerwine are hard to remove from carpet so it might be best to serve this at outdoor functions.
Serves: 25

1   3 liter bottle of Cheerwine (or the equivalent using 2-liter bottles)
1   46 ounce can pineapple juice

- Mix together.

Miss Louise Tucker, Salisbury, NC

Party Punch

Serves: 12-15

1   cup water   1   cup orange juice, chilled
1   cup sugar   2   quarts ginger ale, chilled
1   cup grape juice, chilled

- Bring water and sugar to boil.
- Let boil 3 minutes.
- In punch bowl add grape juice, orange juice and water/sugar mixture.
- Stir.
- Add ginger ale right before serving.

Mrs. Jim (Jennie) Weatherly, Bennettsville, SC

Sparkling Punch

Yields: 125 servings

6	46 ounce cans pineapple juice	3	1 quart bottles sparkling grape
3	2 liter bottles ginger ale		juice or champagne
6	6 ounce cans frozen lemonade, thawed	1	pint fresh strawberries

- Chill and combine as needed to serve.
- Make 2 ice molds of pineapple juice, lemonade and strawberries the day before.

Mrs. Julian (Harriett) Drake, Blenheim, SC

Rum Divine

Wonderful at holiday time! A great gift!

1	quart vanilla ice cream, softened	2	teaspoons nutmeg
1	pound butter, softened (DO NOT SUBSTITUTE!)	2	teaspoons cinnamon
1/2	pound brown sugar	1	jigger rum or bourbon per serving boiling water
1/2	pound 10X confectioners sugar		

- Mix all ingredients except rum/bourbon and water, in plastic container, cover and refreeze.
- When ready to serve, put 1 1/2-2 teaspoons ice cream mixture in mug.
- Add 1 jigger rum/bourbon.
- Fill mug with boiling water.
- Stir, drink, and enjoy.

Mr. Thomas Mayes Evatt, Sullivans Island, SC

Russian Tea

Great for a reception!
Serves: 30-35   **Preparation time: 30 minutes**

3	quarts water	6	ounces orange juice
1/4	ounce cloves (whole)	8	ounces lemon juice
8	tea bags	1	16 ounce can pineapple juice
		3	cups sugar

- Boil water, cloves and tea bags.
- Let steep for ten minutes and strain.
- Add orange juice, lemon juice, pineapple juice, and sugar.
- Bring to a boil and stir.
- Refrigerate until needed.
- Heat and serve.

Mrs. Steve (Katherine) Littlejohn, Columbia, SC

Junior Charity League of Marlboro County, Inc.

Christmas Spritzer

Easily doubled for a crowd!
Serves: 10   **Preparation time: 5 minutes**

1   12 ounce can frozen cranberry
    juice concentrate
1   750 milliliters white zinfandel
1   liter club soda

cherries
orange slices

- Combine first two ingredients.
- Before serving add club soda.
- Garnish with cherries and orange slices.

Mrs. Charles Paul (Heather) Midgley, Bennettsville, SC

Allbritain Plantation Wassail

Great for the holidays!
Serves: 15   **Preparation time: 5 minutes**
Cooking time: 10 minutes

2   quarts apple juice
3   cups pineapple juice
2   cups orange juice
1   cup lemon juice

1   cup sugar
1   tablespoon whole cloves
    several sticks cinnamon

- Tie spices in cheesecloth or place in stainless steel tea ball to be removed before serving.
- Boil all ingredients together.
- Serve warm.

Mrs. R.L. (Janie) McNiel, Hamer, SC

Polly's Whiskey Sour Punch

Always a hit at cocktail parties!
Yields: 100 ounces   **Preparation time: 10 minutes**
Prepare ahead

1   12 ounce frozen lemonade concen-
    trate
1   6 ounce frozen orange juice
    concentrate
30 ounces water

24 ounces whiskey
1   liter ginger ale
    orange slices
    cherries with stems

- Mix all ingredients and serve over ice.
- Garnish with orange slices and cherries.

Mrs. Daniel E. (Elisabeth) McNiel, Bennettsville, SC

Soups

Painting by: Ting English

Kathleen Thornton English
"St. Mark's Lighthouse"

Kathleen "Ting" Thornton English, a native of Pachuta, Mississippi, lived in several locales before settling for 35 years in Pittsburgh, Pennsylvania. While in Pittsburgh, she was a founder of the Whitehall Art League and served as its president for two years. She studied under several well - known local artists and was an art exhibitor with several prize winning shows.

A resident of Bennettsville for seven years, Mrs. English has been an active community member by participating in the Marlboro Players, "Paint for Fun" hobby group, and First United Methodist Church. She presented an individual art exhibit at the Marlboro County Public Library in 1993.

Mrs. English and her husband, Tom, have two children: Kathy English Wetzel, and Tommy English. They have six grandchildren and three great-grandchildren.

Avgholemono (Chicken-Egg-Lemon) Soup

Broth may be made by boiling a chicken flavored with an onion and celery...(This makes it better!) If you are in a hurry use the canned chicken broth.

Serves: 3-4 **Preparation time: 30 minutes**
Cooking time: approximately 20 minutes

2	cups water	3	eggs
2	cans chicken broth		juice of 2 lemons
1/2	cup enriched macaroni product or rice		salt to taste

- Bring water and broth to boil.
- Add enriched macaroni product or rice and cook until tender.
- Remove one cup of broth and set aside to cool.
- Beat eggs until well blended.
- SLOWLY add juice of lemons to the eggs.
- Then slowly add the cup of broth while stirring at all times.
- Remove broth from burner and add the egg-lemon mixture to broth while stirring slowly.
- Turn heat down on burner.
- Return soup to burner that has been lowered and keep stirring for 3 to 4 minutes.
- Serve while hot and enjoy.

Mrs. Gordon (Ruth) King, Bennettsville, SC

Chicken Stew

Skim milk and half of the butter may be used to reduce the fat.

Serves: 8 **Preparation time: 1/2 hour**
Cooking time: 1 hour

1	chicken, cut into pieces	1	large can evaporated milk
1	quart water	2	cups regular milk
1	stick butter		3 - 4 drops hot sauce
1	large onion, chopped		

- Boil chicken in water with salt and pepper until done.
- After chicken has cooled, skin and de-bone.
- Put 1 quart chicken broth in large pot with butter and onion.
- Cook until onion is done, about 30 minutes.
- Add chicken to pot and heat until boiling rapidly.
- Add both kinds of milk and turn heat off.
- Milk will curdle if left over high heat.
- Add hot sauce.
- Serve with saltine crackers.

Mrs. Andy (Mary Alice) Burroughs, Bennettsville, SC

Junior Charity League of Marlboro County, Inc.

Clam Chowder

No salt needed when using fresh clams.

2	cups potatoes, diced	2	tablespoons Worcestershire Sauce
2	cups onion, chopped	1	teaspoon hot sauce
1/2	cup celery, chopped	1/4	pound butter
1	medium bell pepper, chopped	1	quart ground clams
1	quart canned tomatoes	6	slices bacon

- Fry bacon and set aside.
- Cook potatoes, onions, and celery in small amount of water.
- Cook clams for a short while before adding them to other ingredients.
- Put all together and simmer for at least an hour.
- Add fried bacon to bowls of chowder when serving.

The late Mrs. Billy (Jane) Jennings, Bennettsville, SC

Fresh Corn Chowder

Serves: 4
Cooking time: 15 minutes
Freezes well

Preparation time: 25 minutes
Prepare ahead

4	medium potatoes, peeled and cubed	1	medium green pepper, chopped
1	cup water	10	ears corn, cooked and cut off cob
1/4	teaspoon salt	2 1/2	cups milk
6	strips bacon, cooked and diced	1	cup half and half
2	tablespoons bacon drippings		salt and pepper, to taste
1	medium onion, chopped		

- Combine potatoes, water, and salt.
- Cover and cook until tender.
- Sauté onions in bacon drippings.
- Add pepper and cook until tender.
- Add potatoes, corn, bacon, milk, and cream.
- Season with salt and pepper.
- Cook until warm.

Mrs. David K. (Cathy) Lynch, Bennettsville, SC

Mountain Pot Beans

Great on a cold winter day served with cornbread!

Serves: 10-12   **Preparation time: 20 minutes**
Cooking time: 1 hour

1 pound ground beef	1 16 ounce can pork and beans
1/2 pound bacon	1 16 ounce can pinto beans
1 cup onions, chopped	1 16 ounce can red kidney beans
1 cup ketchup	1 16 ounce can water
1/2 cup brown sugar	1 teaspoon Worcestershire Sauce
	1 teaspoon hot sauce

- Fry bacon, drain well and set aside.
- Brown ground beef and drain well.
- Crumble bacon into ground beef.
- Add the next 9 ingredients.
- Bring to a boil and let simmer for 1 hour.

Mrs. Dudley C. (Sharon) Beaty, III, Bennettsville, SC

Lentil and Brown Rice Soup

A favorite soup of all ages, because of the rice/lentil combination.

Serves: 8-10   **Preparation time: 1 hour**
Freezes well

5 cups of chicken broth, or more	1 tablespoon minced garlic (optional)
3 cups of water, or more	1/2 teaspoon crumbled dried basil
1 1/2 cups lentils, picked over and rinsed	1/2 teaspoon crumbled oregano
1 cup long-grain brown rice	1/2 teaspoon crumbled thyme
1 35 ounce can tomatoes, drained (save the juice), and chopped	1 bay leaf
	1/2 cup minced fresh parsley
3 carrots, halved lengthwise and cut crosswise into 1/4 inch pieces	red wine or cider vinegar (optional)
	salt, if desired, to taste
1 cup onion, chopped	freshly ground pepper to taste
1/2 cup celery, chopped	

- In a large, heavy Dutch oven or stock pot combine the broth, water, lentils, rice, tomatoes, reserved tomato juice, carrots, onion, celery, garlic, basil, oregano, thyme and bay leaf.
- Bring to a boil, reduce the heat, cover the pan, and simmer the soup, stirring it occasionally until lentils and rice are both tender, about 1 hour.
- Discard bay leaf.
- Stir in parsley, salt and pepper.
- If necessary thin the soup with additional hot broth or water.
- Some may want the soup to have a little more "zip" to it, so pass the vinegar and let each individual put in the desired amount.
- Children prefer this soup usually without vinegar.

Mrs. John (Pam) Napier, Pawleys Island, SC

Junior Charity League of Marlboro County, Inc.

Fresh Mushroom Soup

Very Good!
Serves: 6-8
Cooking time: 1 hour
Freezes well

Preparation time: 45 minutes
Prepare ahead

1½	pounds fresh mushrooms	1	teaspoon fresh dillweed, chopped
3	teaspoons olive oil	½	teaspoon paprika
1	cup onions, chopped	1	teaspoon tomato paste
1	carrot, chopped	½	cup sherry
2	teaspoons minced garlic	2	teaspoons lemon juice
3½	cups chicken broth	¼	cup parsley, chopped
⅓	cup barley		dash black pepper

- Chop the mushrooms and set aside about 1 cup.
- Heat 2 teaspoons of the olive oil, sauté onions, carrot, and garlic.
- Add broth, barley, dill, paprika, and tomato paste.
- Cover and simmer about 10 minutes.
- Add mushrooms and ¼ cup sherry.
- Cover and cook on low about 50 minutes.
- Add lemon juice, parsley, and pepper.
- Sauté remaining mushrooms in the other 1 teaspoon olive oil 3 to 4 minutes.
- Add ¼ cup sherry.
- Simmer about 10 minutes.
- Use as garnish.

Mrs. Smith C. (Helen) Breeden, Bennettsville, SC

French Onion Soup

Serves: 4
Cooking time: 35 minutes

Preparation time: 20 minutes

6	large Vidalia onions, sliced	10¾ ounces water
1½	cups butter	French bread slices
1	teaspoon all-purpose flour	Mozzarella cheese, grated
2	ounces dry white wine	Parmesan cheese, grated
1	10¾ ounce can beef bouillon	

- Sauté onions in butter.
- Stir in flour.
- Add wine, bouillon, and water.
- Cook 30 minutes.
- Toast French bread slices.
- Cover with soup.
- Sprinkle with Mozzarella and Parmesan cheeses.
- Broil until cheese bubbles.

Mrs. David K. (Cathy) Lynch, Bennettsville, SC

50   Carolina Cuisine: Nothin' Could Be Finer

Pawleys Island Frogmore Stew

Note: You need a big pot! Serve with slaw and rolls.

Serves: 10 - 12

Preparation time: 1 1/2 - 2 hours

1   bag crab boil
2-3 large onions
6   celery stalks
    salt and pepper to taste

2   packages kielbasa sausage
24+ new potatoes
12+ small corn ears
1-2 pounds shrimp

- Fill a big pot of water $2/3$ full and add crab boil, onions, celery, salt, and pepper.
- Bring to a boil and boil for 10 - 15 minutes.
- Add sausage and potatoes and boil 20 minutes.
- Add corn and boil 15 minutes or longer.
- Add shrimp and boil 3 minutes, or until they are pink.
- Drain in a large colander and serve.

Mrs. Johnny (Janette) Weaver, Pawleys Island, SC

Potato Soup

Serves: 4
Cooking time: 20 minutes
Freezes well

Preparation time: 20 minutes
Prepare ahead

3   large potatoes, peeled and cubed
1   large onion, chopped
$1/2$ stick butter
    salt and pepper, to taste

2   cups half and half cream
6   cups water
    milk

- Cook potatoes, onion, butter, salt, pepper, and water for 15 minutes.
- Pour half of the water off.
- May beat soup until creamy while adding cream or just add cream to lumpy soup.
- Heat to serve.
- Add milk to obtain desired consistency.

Mrs. David K. (Cathy) Lynch, Bennettsville, SC

Creamy Potato Soup

Instant mashed potatoes are great for thickening gravies, stews and sauces. Plus, it will not lump.

Serves: 6 to 8
Cooking time: 45 to 60 minutes

Preparation time: 20 minutes
Prepare ahead

1¹/₂ quarts water
1-2 celery ribs, finely chopped
1 small onion, finely chopped
2 tablespoons margarine or butter

1 10³/₄ ounce can cream of chicken soup
6-8 medium potatoes, diced
salt and pepper to taste

- Cook water, celery ribs, potatoes, salt, pepper, and onion until tender.
- Add margarine and chicken soup.
- Heat thoroughly.
- Serve with crackers or French bread.

Mrs. John T. (Margaret) Geisel, Bennettsville, SC

Cheesy Baked Potato Soup

Serves: 6 to 8

Preparation time: 35 minutes

3 large baking potatoes, cubed
2¹/₂ cups water
1 tablespoon chicken bouillon
1 cup ham, cooked (optional)
3-4 slices bacon
¹/₂ small onion, chopped

¹/₄ cup margarine
¹/₄ cup all-purpose flour
1¹/₂ cups milk
¹/₄ teaspoon paprika
¹/₄ teaspoon pepper
2 cups grated cheddar cheese

- Cook potatoes, chicken bouillon, and ham in 2¹/₂ cups of water for 15 minutes.
- Fry bacon and sauté onion.
- Add bacon and onion to potatoes.
- In a saucepan, melt margarine over low heat.
- Add flour and cook 1 minute, stirring constantly.
- Gradually add milk.
- Cook this mixture over medium heat until thickened and bubbly.
- Stir in paprika, pepper and grated cheese.
- Drain ¹/₂ of the water from the potatoes.
- Stir cheese sauce into potatoes.
- Serve immediately.
- Crumble bacon on top when serving.

Mrs. Hubert (Christi) Meggs, Jr., Bennettsville, SC

Spaghetti Soup

This is a very thick soup, but delicious! Can double nicely and reheats well.

Serves: 4 to 6
Cooking time: 1 hour

Preparation time: 30 minutes
Freezes well

¹/₂	pound ground round
¹/₂	pound pork sausage
1	clove garlic, chopped
1	onion, chopped
1	4 ounce jar pimento (optional)

1	6 ounce can pitted olives, drained
1	28 ounce can tomatoes, broken up
1	cup beef broth
6	ounces dry spaghetti
1	10 ounce package frozen peas
³/₄	pound cheddar cheese, grated

- Brown meats in a skillet.
- Add garlic and onion and cook until soft.
- Drain.
- In a large pot, cook spaghetti and drain.
- Add pimentos (optional), olives, tomatoes, and broth.
- Add meats, garlic, and onion from skillet.
- Cover and simmer on low for approximately 45 minutes to one hour.
- Add peas and cheese and simmer 15 minutes longer.

Mrs. Scott (Shelly) Elston, Portland, OR

Turkey Soup

Serves: 6
Cooking time: 45 minutes

Preparation time: 20 minutes

1¹/₂	pounds ground turkey
1	large onion, chopped
1	small bunch celery, chopped
2	pounds carrots, thinly sliced
1¹/₂	sticks margarine
1	cup uncooked rice

6	cups water
4	teaspoons chicken bouillon
1	14 ¹/₂ ounce can chicken broth
	Italian herb seasoning (enough to lightly cover)
	pepper to taste

- Put first five ingredients in soup pot.
- Lightly sauté until turkey is no longer red.
- Add other ingredients and cook until carrots are tender, about 45 minutes.

Mrs. Wadie Cottingham Hardy, San Pedro, CA

Junior Charity League of Marlboro County, Inc.   53

Becky's Vegetable Soup

Preparation time: 15 minutes **Cooking time: 30 minutes**

1	46 ounce can vegetable juice	2	10 ounce packages frozen mixed vegetables
1	10¾ ounce can condensed cream of onion soup	2	onions, diced
1	10¾ ounce can condensed cream of celery soup	1-3	pounds lean ground beef, browned and drained
3	beef bouillon cubes		water

- In a large pot mix and heat vegetable juice and soups.
- Add bouillon and at least 2 soup cans of water (more if desired).
- Bring to a boil and simmer 30 minutes making sure bouillon cubes are dissolved.

Mrs. Charles M. (Becky) Rogers, Bennettsville, SC

Vegetable Soup

This makes a large quantity of soup.

Stock:
1 pound stew beef
2 tablespoons butter
3 quarts water
1 cup celery leaves
2 teaspoons salt
2 carrots, sliced
2 onions, sliced

- Brown beef in butter.
- Add water, celery leaves, salt, carrots and onions.
- Simmer 2 hours and strain.
- Set this stock aside.

Soup:
¼ cup butter
2 cups carrots, diced
2 cups onions, diced
2 cups celery, diced
2 cans tomatoes
2 cups potatoes, cubed
1 package frozen beans
1 teaspoon salt

- Heat the butter.
- Add carrots, celery, and onions.
- Cook for 5 minutes, stirring constantly.
- Add stock, tomatoes, potatoes, beans, meat, and salt.
- Simmer for several more hours.

The late Mrs. Brenda Liles Quick, Bennettsville, SC

Carolina Cuisine: Nothin' Could Be Finer

Salads & Dressings

Painting by: Ting English

Kathleen Thornton English
"Barn in the Snow"

Kathleen "Ting" Thornton English, a native of Pachuta, Mississippi, lived in several locales before settling for 35 years in Pittsburgh, Pennsylvania. While in Pittsburgh, she was a founder of the Whitehall Art League and served as its president for two years. She studied under several well - known local artists and was an art exhibitor with several prize winning shows.

A resident of Bennettsville for seven years, Mrs. English has been an active community member by participating in the Marlboro Players, "Paint for Fun" hobby group, and First United Methodist Church. She presented an individual art exhibit at the Marlboro County Public Library in 1993.

Mrs. English and her husband, Tom, have two children: Kathy English Wetzel, and Tommy English. They have six grandchildren and three great-grandchildren.

Sparacino's Antipasto Salad

Serves: 10-12
Cooking time: 10 minutes

Preparation time: 45 minutes
Prepare ahead

1	pound shell pasta
1/8	pound provolone cheese
1/4	pound salami
1/8	pound pepperoni
1/2	green pepper, chopped
1/2	small onion, chopped
3	stalks celery, sliced
1	small can black olives, sliced and drained
1	small jar green olives, sliced and drained

2   small tomatoes chopped
    feta cheese
Dressing:
3/4   cup oil
1/2   cup vinegar
1 1/2 teaspoons salt
1   teaspoon oregano
1   teaspoon pepper
1 1/2 teaspoons sugar

- Prepare dressing and refrigerate.
- Boil pasta and drain.
- Rinse pasta with cool water and drain.
- Combine pasta with next nine ingredients.
- Toss with dressing.
- Let chill in refrigerator overnight.
- Take out 30 minutes before serving.
- Toss well and sprinkle with feta cheese.

Mrs. Duncan (Cindi) McInnis, Clio, SC

Apricot Salad

Serves: 8-10

1   8 ounce can pineapple
1/2 cup sugar
1   8 ounce package cream cheese
1   6 ounce package apricot gelatin
1   cup ice water

1   cup celery, chopped
1/2 cup pecans, chopped
1   8 ounce whipped topping

- Bring pineapple (with juice) and sugar to boil.
- Stir in cream cheese until dissolved.
- Add gelatin and stir until dissolved.
- Let cool.
- Add 1 cup ice water, celery and pecans.
- Blend in whipped topping.
- Chill until firm.

Mrs. Julian (Harriet) Drake, Blenheim, SC

Junior Charity League of Marlboro County, Inc.

Carbo's "Ashland Farms" Salad

Great for ladies' luncheon.

Serves: 6
Cooking time: 10-15 minutes
Prepare ahead

Preparation time: 20-30 minutes
Oven temperature: 400

4	tablespoons sugar	2	tablespoons sugar
4	tablespoons rice wine vinegar	2	tablespoons butter or margarine
1	teaspoon freshly ground black pepper	1	tablespoon scallions, chopped
$^1/_2$	cup salad oil (80% vegetable; 20% olive oil)	6	strawberries (medium diced)
$^1/_2$	cup pecans, chopped		mixed baby lettuces
			strawberries (sliced lengthwise to garnish) optional

- Heat first three ingredients over low heat until sugar is melted.
- Emulsify with salad oil.
- Toss pecans in 2 tablespoons sugar with 2 tablespoons butter and roast until caramelized.
- Toss greens, vinaigrette, cooled pecans, scallions, and chopped strawberries.
- Divide into equal proportions and garnish with sliced strawberries.

Mrs. Rob (Karen) Curran, Atlanta, GA

Congealed Asparagus Salad

Serves: 8-10

Prepare ahead

$^3/_4$	cup sugar	1	small jar pimento, chopped
$1^1/_2$	cups water	2	tablespoons lemon juice
$^1/_2$	cup white vinegar	2	teaspoons grated onion
2	envelopes unflavored gelatin	$^1/_2$	cup pecans, chopped
$^1/_2$	teaspoon salt	1	10 $^1/_2$ ounce can cut asparagus, drained
1	cup celery, chopped		

- Combine sugar, 1 cup water and vinegar.
- Bring to a boil.
- In separate container dissolve gelatin in remaining $^1/_2$ cup water.
- Add to sugar mixture.
- Cool, add remaining ingredients and pour in molds or glass dish.
- Refrigerate to set.

Mrs. Ray A. (Betty) Howe, Bennettsville, SC

Delicious Bean Salad

Good with any meat!

3^1/$_2$ cups French style green beans, drained
3^1/$_2$ cups English peas, drained
1 cup onion, chopped
1 cup celery, diced

1 green bell pepper, chopped
1 small jar pimentos, chopped
1 cup vinegar
1 cup sugar
^{1}/$_2$ cup salad oil

- Place first six ingredients in mixing bowl.
- Mix vinegar, sugar, and oil.
- Stir until sugar dissolves.
- Pour over vegetables.
- Store in refrigerator.
- Will keep two weeks or longer.

Mrs. Stanley (Elizabeth) Hearne, Blenheim, SC

Black Bean Salad

Serves: 4-6
Prepare ahead

Preparation time: 15 minutes

1 15 ^{1}/$_2$ ounce can black beans
8 ounces smoked turkey strips
1 3 ounce jar cocktail onions, drained
^{1}/$_3$ cup purple onion, chopped

2 tablespoons parsley, chopped
2 tablespoons olive oil
^{1}/$_2$ teaspoon pepper
salt to taste

- Lightly mix beans, turkey, cocktail onions, and purple onion.
- Add parsley, olive oil, pepper, and salt to bean mixture.
- Marinate 4 hours or overnight.

Mrs. Eugene (Mary) Crosland, Bennettsville, SC

Salads and Dressings

Junior Charity League of Marlboro County, Inc.

Blueberry Salad

Serves: 12
Prepare ahead

Preparation time: 30 minutes

2   small boxes black cherry gelatin
1½ cups boiling water
1   can blueberries, drained
1   8 ounce can pineapple, crushed and
     drained
¾ -1 cup of pecans, chopped
     juice of 1 lemon
     dash of salt

Topping:
¼   cup sugar
½   teaspoon vanilla
1   3 ounce package cream cheese
1   8 ounce carton sour cream
     dash of salt

- Place all of the ingredients in an 11 x 7 dish.
- Then cream together topping and spread over top.
- This is usually prepared the day before in order for it to congeal.

Mrs. James (Anne) McInnis, Bennettsville, SC

Broccoli Salad

Serves: 6-8
Preparation time: 30 minutes

1   head broccoli, finely chopped
½   cup celery, finely chopped,
     (optional)
½   cup raisins
½   cup pecans, finely chopped
½   cup onion, finely chopped

6   slices of bacon, cooked crisp and
     crumbled
Dressing:
¼   cup sugar
⅛   cup vinegar
¼   cup mayonnaise

- After all vegetables have been prepared, place them along with the raisins and nuts in a bowl.
- In another bowl, mix dressing ingredients together well and pour over vegetables.
- Mix well.
- Just before serving add crumbled bacon and mix again.

Mrs. Andy (Mary Alice) Burroughs, Bennettsville, SC
Mrs. B. B. (Martha) Sanders, IV, Bennettsville, SC

Broccoli Salad Supreme

Serves: 6-8   **Preparation time: 25 minutes**

1	large bunch fresh broccoli	1/2	cup raisins
1/2	pound bacon, fried crisp and crumbled	1	cup sliced fresh mushrooms
		1	cup mayonnaise
1/2	medium red onion, chopped	1/4	cup sugar
1	cup sunflower seeds	2	tablespoons cider vinegar

- Cut broccoli florets and tender stalks into bite size pieces.
- Place first six ingredients in a large bowl.
- Mix mayonnaise, sugar, and vinegar.
- Pour over broccoli mix and toss gently.
- Serve immediately.

Mrs. James (Jaylene) Myers, Bennettsville, SC

Picnic Broccoli Salad

Serves: 4-6   **Preparation time: 20-30 minutes**

1	bunch fresh broccoli, chopped	1	cup celery, chopped
1	7 ounce jar stuffed olives, chopped	1/2	cup onions, chopped
3	hard boiled eggs, chopped		mayonnaise

- Mix ingredients with enough mayonnaise to bind.

Mrs. Stanley (Elizabeth) Hearne, Blenheim, SC

Crisp Broccoli Salad

Serves: 4-6   **Preparation time: 15 minutes**
Prepare ahead

1	head broccoli	Dressing:
1	purple onion	1/2 cup mayonnaise
1	small package sliced almonds	3 tablespoons sugar
1	cup sharp cheese, grated	2-3 tablespoons red wine vinegar
8	strips bacon	

- Separate broccoli into florets.
- Coarsely chop purple onion.
- Cook bacon and break into pieces.
- Combine broccoli, onion, almonds, cheese, and bacon; toss with the dressing.
- Let the salad sit in the refrigerator several hours or overnight before serving.

Mrs. John I. (Carolyn) Rogers, III, Bennettsville, SC

Junior Charity League of Marlboro County, Inc.

Betty's Chicken Salad

Serves: 8

Prepare ahead

4 cups cooked chicken, diced
1 cup celery, diced
1/3 cup onions, chopped
2 ounces pimento, sliced
1/4 cup almonds, toasted
1 cup green or red seedless grapes, halved

3 tablespoons lemon juice
1 teaspoon salt
1/2 teaspoon pepper
1/3 cup mayonnaise
lettuce leaves

- Mix together.
- Chill.
- Serve on lettuce leaf.

Mrs. Ray A. (Betty) Howe, Bennettsville, SC

Chicken Salad with Fruit

Serves: 8-10

4 cups cooked chicken, chopped
2 cups celery, thinly sliced
2 tablespoons onion, minced
3/4 cup mayonnaise
1/4 cup whipping cream
1 tablespoon lemon juice

1/2 teaspoon salt
dash white pepper
lettuce leaves
1/2 cup slivered almonds, toasted
2-3 cups cantaloupe balls
seedless green grapes

- Combine chicken and celery.
- Combine next 6 ingredients.
- Stirring well; add to chicken mixture and toss well.
- Chill.
- Serve salad on lettuce leaves.
- Sprinkle with toasted almonds and garnish with melon balls and grapes.

Mrs. Merritt (Lee) King, III, McColl, SC

Low Salt Chicken Salad

A very healthy dish.
Serves: 2-3　　　　　　　　　　　　**Preparation time: 45 minutes**

1　cup cooked chicken, chopped
1　crisp apple, chopped
1　tablespoon celery, finely chopped
1/2　small onion, finely chopped

2　tablespoons green pepper, finely
　　chopped
2　tablespoons salt-free mayonnaise

- Add apple, celery, onion, and green pepper to chicken.
- Stir in mayonnaise.
- May use to stuff tomatoes or just on a bed of lettuce with a dash of paprika for color.

Mrs. J. Maxwell (Martha) Gregg, Bennettsville, SC

Crook's Corner's Curried Chicken Salad

Served in 'Crook's Corner', Chapel Hill, North Carolina
Serves: 6-8　　　　　　　　　　　**Prepare ahead**

2 1/2　cups cooked chicken breast, cubed
1　cup celery, chopped
1/2　cup scallions, chopped
1/2　cup slivered almonds, toasted
1　cup white seedless grapes

Dressing:
3/4　cup mayonnaise
1　tablespoon Dijon mustard
1　tablespoon curry powder
　　dash of tabasco
　　salt and pepper to taste

- Mix ingredients and dressing thoroughly.
- Chill before serving.

Mrs. Eugene (Winnie) Hamer, Monroe, NC

Spicy Chicken Salad

Serves: 6-8

Prepare ahead

4	tablespoons soy sauce	1	teaspoon sugar
1	tablespoon minced garlic	2	tablespoons vinegar
1	teaspoon ginger	1	tablespoon sesame oil
2	tablespoons crunchy peanut butter	$^1/_2$	teaspoon salt
1	tablespoon hot red pepper oil		cashews to taste
$^1/_2$	teaspoon pepper		

- Cook chicken, skin, and cube.
- Mix above ingredients, except cashews.
- Add chicken, dressing, and cashews.

Mrs. Warren (Kelly) McAlpine, Hickory, NC

Congealed Corn Beef Salad

Great for ladies luncheons!

Serves: 10

Prepare ahead

1	can corn beef, mashed well	1	tablespoon ketchup
3	boiled eggs, well chopped	1	cup mayonnaise
1	cup celery, chopped finely	2	envelopes unflavored gelatin
1	tablespoon Worcestershire sauce	$^1/_4$	cup water
$^1/_2$	teaspoon salt	$^3/_4$	cup boiling water
1	lemon, juiced		

- Mix first eight ingredients.
- Dissolve gelatin packets in $^1/_4$ cup water.
- Add $^3/_4$ cups boiling water to gelatin water.
- Add other ingredients-mix well.
- Refrigerate overnight in glass loaf pan.

Mrs. Hal (Mary Lois) Trimmier, Bennettsville, SC

Irene's Cranberry Salad

Good with chicken or turkey and at Christmas.

Serves: 10-12
Prepare ahead

Preparation time: 30 minutes

1   6 ounce package raspberry gelatin
1   3 ounce package cream cheese, softened
1   16 ounce can whole cranberry sauce
1   8 ounce can crushed pineapple

1   cup nuts, chopped finely
3   tablespoons sugar
1   cup boiling water
     lettuce leaves

- Mix cream cheese and dry gelatin until well blended.
- Add 1 cup boiling water, mix well.
- Blend cranberry sauce, pineapple, nuts, and sugar into first mixture.
- Put in 10 x 5 inch glass dish.
- Chill in refrigerator until set.
- Serve on lettuce leaf on salad plate.

Mrs. John T. (Margaret) Geisel, Bennettsville, SC

Creamy Frozen Salad

Serves: 12
Prepare ahead

Preparation time: 10 minutes
Freezes well

1   3 ounce package cream cheese
1/2   cup mayonnaise
1   cup pineapple preserves
1/2   cup golden raisins

1/2   cup maraschino cherries, drained
1/2   cup nuts, chopped
2   cups frozen dessert topping, thawed

- Bring cream cheese to room temperature.
- Mix with mayonnaise until smooth.
- Add preserves, raisins, cherries, and nuts.
- Blend well.
- Fold in thawed dessert topping and freeze covered in 9 x 12 inch glass dish.

Mrs. Pledger (Beverly) Hodges, Bennettsville, SC

Fruit Compote

Great for luncheons!
Serves: 8

1 16 ounce can peaches, undrained & chopped
2 15¼ ounce cans pineapple chunks, undrained
2 bananas, sliced
1 apple, cored & cubed

4 cups fresh fruits such as cantaloupe, strawberries, kiwi, grapes, or blueberries, chopped
1 3½ ounce package instant vanilla pudding mix
2 tablespoons orange liqueur

- Combine liquids from canned fruits and mix with pudding mix.
- Blend in fruits.
- Add liqueur.
- Cover and refrigerate overnight.
- Put in apples and bananas the day of serving.
- Serve with slotted spoon.

Mrs. Billie M. Beaty, Bennettsville, SC

John's Fruit Compote

A wonderful breakfast dish.

2 pink grapefruit
2 naval oranges
2 apples, red or yellow delicious
1 15½ ounce can pineapple (tidbits or crushed) with juice

½ cup orange juice
2 bananas (optional)

- Peel and remove membrane from grapefruit and oranges.
- Core apples and cut in bite size pieces.
- Leave skin on for color.
- Add pineapple, including juice.
- Combine all fruit in large bowl.
- Mix well.
- Add orange juice, chill and serve.
- Bananas may be added before serving.

The late John T. Geisel, Bennettsville, SC

Hearts of Palm Salad

Serves: 6
Prepare 3-4 hours ahead

Preparation time: 10 minutes

1   14 ounce can hearts of palm, drained

1   15 1/4 ounce can pineapple chunks, drained

1   2 ounce jar pimentos, diced (may use more, according to taste)

4   ounces of bottled poppy seed dressing

- Cut hearts of palm in rounds about one inch thick.
- Mix with other ingredients and refrigerate for three or four hours before serving.
- Fresh pineapple may be substituted for canned.
- Line the serving bowl with lettuce.

Mrs. DuPre (Mary) Miller, Bennettsville, SC

Orange Salad

Serves: 10-12
Prepare ahead

Preparation time: 10 minutes

2   cups water, boiling

1   6 ounce package lemon gelatin

1   6 ounce can frozen orange juice

1   20 ounce can crushed pineapple, not drained

1   11 ounce can mandarin oranges, drained

- Heat 2 cups water to boiling; mix with gelatin to dissolve.
- Add 1 can frozen orange juice, stirring until completely blended.
- Add crushed pineapple and oranges.
- Mix thoroughly.
- Put in refrigerator to congeal for 8 hours or overnight.

Mrs. Howard (Lillian) Hyatt, Bennettsville, SC

Junior Charity League of Marlboro County, Inc.

Macaroni Salad

Serves: 15-20

1	pound macaroni, cooked and drained	1	cup vinegar
1	large purple onion, chopped	1	teaspoon salt
1	large green pepper, chopped	1	teaspoon black pepper
4	medium carrots, shredded	2	cups mayonnaise
1	14 ounce can condensed milk	3/4	cup sugar

- Combine the first five ingredients.
- Combine the next five ingredients.
- Mix all together and refrigerate overnight.
- Mixture will thicken overnight.

Mrs. Gilbert (Winkie) McLaurin, Bennettsville, SC

Mandarin Orange Salad

Serves: 9
Prepare ahead

Preparation time: 15 minutes

1	3 ounce package orange gelatin	1	cup juice combined from oranges and pineapple
1	cup boiling water		
1	11 ounce can mandarin oranges	3/4	cup whipped dessert topping
1	8 ounce can crushed pineapple	3/4	cup salad dressing
			juice of one lemon

- Dissolve gelatin in 1 cup of boiling water.
- Add 1 cup of juice from oranges and pineapple.
- Add water to juices to bring to 1 cup, if necessary.
- Cut oranges in half; add to gelatin.
- Add pineapple.
- Congeal in 8 x 8 pan..
- Top with whipped dessert topping, salad dressing, and lemon juice, which have been combined.

Mrs. Frank (Libby) Shutt, Bennettsville, SC

Sour Cream Potato Salad

Serves: 12

7 medium potatoes, peeled, cooked, and chopped	1 cup mayonnaise
1/3 cup Italian dressing (creamy Italian)	1 1/2 tablespoons horseradish mustard
3/4 cup celery, sliced	1/2 cup sour cream
1/3 cup onions, sliced	salt and celery seed to taste
4 hard-boiled eggs	1/3 cup cucumbers, peeled and diced

- Pour Italian dressing over warm cooked potatoes.
- Chill 2 hours.
- Add everything except cucumbers.
- Chill.
- Add cucumbers just before serving.
- Reserve 1 egg yolk and slice over top.

Mrs. James (Carole) Bowdre, Bennettsville, SC

Pretzel Salad

Serves: 12-15   **Prepare ahead**

2 cups crushed pretzels	1 8 ounce carton whipped topping
3/4 cup butter, melted	1 6 ounce package strawberry gelatin
4 tablespoons sugar	2 cups boiling water
1 8 ounce package cream cheese	1 pint (or more) frozen strawberries
1 cup sugar	

- Mix the first three ingredients together and pat in bottom of a 9 x 13 pan.
- Bake for 8 minutes at 350 degrees.
- Do not over-bake.
- Cool completely.
- Combine cream cheese and sugar until light and fluffy.
- Fold whipped topping into cream cheese mixture.
- Spoon mixture on top of cooled pretzels.
- Put in refrigerator and prepare gelatin mixture by dissolving gelatin in 2 cups boiling water.
- Add frozen strawberries.
- Put this mixture in refrigerator and when completely thickened, but not completely congealed, put on top of whipped topping mixture, keep chilled until ready to serve.

Mrs. Marty (Rhonda) McIntyre, Bennettsville, SC

Raspberry Salad

Serves: 12-14

2	3 ounce packages cherry gelatin	2	8 ounce packages frozen raspberries, slightly thawed
5	cups crushed pineapple		
	juice from pineapple plus enough water to make 3 cups liquid	2	bananas, mashed
		2	16 ounce cartons sour cream

- Dissolve gelatin in 3 cups liquid (heated).
- Cool until syrupy.
- Add rest of ingredients, except sour cream.
- Pour half of mixture in shallow dish.
- Let set.
- Spread sour cream over congealed half.
- Then carefully spoon or pour remaining gelatin mixture over sour cream layer.
- Place in refrigerator until set.
- Can be molded as bells, stars, etc.

Mrs. R. L. (Janie) McNiel, Hamer, SC

Seashell Salad

Serves: 24   **Prepare ahead**

1	pound medium seashell macaroni	1	3 ounce jar green olives, sliced
1/2	pound provolone cheese, diced	3	tablespoons chopped onion
1/4	pound salami, diced		Dressing:
2	green peppers, diced	1	teaspoon dried oregano
3	stalks celery, diced	1	teaspoon salt
3	tomatoes, diced-optional	1/2	cup vinegar
1	6 ounce can black olives, sliced	3/4	cup vegetable oil

- Cook seashell macaroni.
- Mix dressing ingredients in blender.
- When macaroni is tender, drain and pour dressing over hot shells.
- When this has cooled, add in remaining ingredients.
- Chill 24 hours.

Mrs. John (Pam) Napier, Pawleys Island, SC

Seven Layer Salad

Prepare ahead

1/2	head lettuce	1/2	cup grated cheese
1	cup mayonnaise	1/2	cup English peas, drained
1	package original ranch dressing	1	tablespoon sugar
1/4	cup spring onions, finely chopped	1/4	cup bacon bits
1/4	cup celery, finely chopped		light dusting of Parmesan cheese

- Mix mayonnaise with ranch dressing package.
- Place lettuce on bottom of dish.
- Seal with mayonnaise mixture.
- Layer the other ingredients in order.
- Chill for one hour and serve.

Mrs. Marty (Rhonda) McIntyre, Bennettsville, SC

Marinated Cole Slaw

Prepare at least a day before serving.

1	medium cabbage, shredded	3/4	cup vegetable oil
1	bell pepper, chopped	1	teaspoon salt
1	red pepper or pimento, chopped	1/2	teaspoon turmeric
1	cup sugar	1	medium onion (chopped)
3/4	cup white vinegar		

- Combine cabbage, red and green peppers, and onion.
- Set aside.
- Combine sugar, vinegar, oil, salt, and turmeric and boil for 1-2 minutes.
- Pour over cabbage.
- Keep refrigerated.

Mrs. Martin (Gladys) Kinard, Bennettsville, SC

Macaroni-Shrimp Salad

Easy to prepare!
Serves: 10   **Preparation: 1 hour**
Prepare ahead

1¹/₂ pounds shrimp, cleaned and boiled
3³/₄ cup corkscrew macaroni
1   6 ounce package frozen Chinese pea
    pods (or 1-10 ounce package peas)
¹/₂ cup water chestnuts, sliced

2   tablespoons parsley
1¹/₂ tablespoons pimento, diced
¹/₈ teaspoon salt
¹/₈ teaspoon pepper
¹/₂-1 cup mayonnaise

- Prepare shrimp and set aside.
- Boil macaroni and set aside; let cool.
- Combine all ingredients and toss lightly until well coated.
- Chill 6 hours.

Mrs. Douglas (Debbie) Jennings, Jr., Bennettsville, SC

Spaghetti Salad

Refreshing for a summer picnic!

1   8 ounce box spaghetti
6   green onions
2   bell peppers
2   tomatoes

2   cucumbers
1   16 ounce bottle of Italian dressing
2   1.5 ounce envelopes powdered
    Italian seasoning mix

- Cook spaghetti until tender, then drain.
- Run cold water over spaghetti to cool.
- Drain.
- Cut up onions, peppers, tomatoes, and cucumbers into a large salad bowl with cooked spaghetti.
- Pour in bottle of dressing and powdered mix.
- Fold lightly until mixed.

Mrs. Howard (Lillian) Hyatt, Bennettsville, SC

Marinated Steak Salad

Serves: 8-10
Prepare ahead

Preparation time: 45 minutes

8-10 ounces sirloin steak (grilled and thinly sliced)
1   6 ounce jar marinated artichoke hearts
1   2¼ ounce can sliced ripe olives

8   ounces fresh sliced mushrooms
1   basket cherry tomatoes (quartered)
1   16 ounce bottle Italian dressing
salad greens
bleu cheese

- Layer above ingredients and pour one bottle Italian dressing all over.
- Refrigerate 6 to 8 hours.
- When ready to serve toss with mixture of salad greens (curly leaf, Romaine, etc.)
- Serve bowl of crumbled bleu cheese on the side to sprinkle on top.

Mrs. Norman (Kay) Rentz, Pickens, SC

Better-than-Ever Tomato Aspic

Serves: 12
Prepare ahead

Preparation time: 30 minutes

1   6 ounce package lemon gelatin
4   cups tomato juice
3   tablespoons vinegar
1   teaspoon salt
dash hot pepper sauce
1   tablespoon onion flakes
1   tablespoon lemon juice
1   tablespoon parsley flakes

Optional:
1   cup, separately or in combination
sliced stuffed green olives
small cooked, cleaned shrimp
shredded raw cabbage
chopped celery
chopped bell pepper
diced pimentos

- Dissolve gelatin in 2 cups hot tomato juice. Add remaining juice and other ingredients, mixing well.
- Chill until firm in 9 x 13 pan or glass casserole, tube pan or molds.
- Serve on lettuce with topping of mayonnaise (may substitute bleu cheese dressing).

Mrs. William L. (Peggy) Kinney, Jr., Bennettsville, SC

Salads and Dressings

Junior Charity League of Marlboro County, Inc.

Tomato Refresher

Perfect for good, fresh summer tomatoes!
Serves: 8
Prepare ahead
Preparation time: 15 minutes

2	small green peppers, diced	¼	cup vinegar
⅔	cup diced celery	¼	cup sugar
2	small onions, diced	1	cup cold water
1	tablespoon salt	6	medium tomatoes, sliced
¼	teaspoon pepper		

- Combine the first eight ingredients, and pour over the tomatoes.
- Cover and chill three to four hours.
- Can be prepared 24 hours before serving.
- Drain some of the liquid before placing in the serving dish.

Mrs. DuPre (Mary) Miller, Bennettsville, SC
Mrs. Ron (Elizabeth) Munnerlyn, Bennettsville, SC

Marinated Vegetable Salad

Serves: 8

1	15 ounce can green beans, French cut, drained		Dressing:
1	15 ounce can English peas, drained	¼	cup sugar
4	stalks celery, chopped	1	tablespoon salt
1	green pepper, chopped	½	cup salad oil
1	small jar pimentos, diced	¾	cup vinegar
1	small onion, chopped	1	tablespoon water

- Prepare the vegetables.
- Prepare the dressing.
- Pour over vegetables.
- Marinate in refrigerator overnight. Drain before serving.

Mrs. Donald (Marty) Rankin, Bennettsville, SC

Poppy Seed Dressing

Yields: 3½ cups

1½	cups sugar	2	teaspoons salt
2	teaspoons dry mustard	⅔	cup vinegar

- Mix and then add the following:

3	tablespoons onion juice	2	cups salad oil
3	tablespoons poppy seed		

- Add slowly, beating constantly.
- Beat until thick.

The late Mrs. Charles R. (Mildred) May, Jr., Bennettsville, SC

Bleu Cheese Dressing

Prepare ahead

8 ounces bleu cheese	2 tablespoons sugar
2 cups mayonnaise	2 cups sour cream
¼ cup vinegar	1 teaspoon garlic powder

- Crumble a small amount of bleu cheese and set aside.
- Mix all ingredients in a bowl until smooth and fluffy.
- Add rest of bleu cheese.
- Use small amount of bleu cheese on top of dressing before serving.
- Best if you chill 12 hours or more.

Mrs. Willie (Tonnie) Craig, Jr., Bennettsville, SC

French Dressing

¾ cup salad oil	2 teaspoons salt
⅔ cup vinegar	1 teaspoon Worcestershire sauce
⅔ cup sugar	1 cup chili sauce
2 small onions, grated	1 square bleu cheese
2 cloves garlic, grated	

- Beat first 7 ingredients in mixer or blender for 1 minute.
- Add chili sauce and crumble bleu cheese into mixture.
- Mix well for 30 seconds.
- Store in refrigerator.
- Dressing makes 1 pint.

Mrs. Wade R. (Elaine) Crow, Bennettsville, SC

Pat's Salad Dressing

coarse ground black pepper	½ cup salad oil
⅓ cup vinegar	4 tablespoons Parmesan cheese
¼ cup water	garlic salt

- Put first four ingredients in a cruet.
- Cover Parmesan cheese with garlic salt.
- Shake vigorously.

Mrs. E. Michael (Terri) O'Tuel, III, Bennettsville, SC

Junior Charity League of Marlboro County, Inc.

Tangy Slaw Dressing

Serves: 6
Prepare ahead

Preparation time: 20 minutes

1	medium cabbage, shredded	3	tablespoons cooking oil
1	teaspoon salt	1/3	cup vinegar
1/2	teaspoon dry mustard	1/2	teaspoon grated onion (or dry onion flakes)
2	tablespoons sugar		
1	teaspoon celery salt	1	tablespoon pimento, chopped
1/4	teaspoon black pepper	1/4	cup bell pepper, chopped

- Shred cabbage and set aside in mixing bowl.
- In a jar with a lid, mix the next 10 ingredients.
- Shake well before pouring over cabbage.
- Toss well.
- Best if chilled before serving.

Mrs. Henry (Frances) Burroughs, Jr., Conway, SC

Quick Salad Dressing

Serves: 6-8
Preparation ahead

Preparation time: 5 minutes

8 tablespoons mayonnaise
1/3 cup wine vinegar

3 tablespoons ketchup

- Blend all ingredients together.
- Great for tossed salad.

Mrs. James (Anna Margaret) Hartis, Bennettsville, SC

Blender French Dressing

Yields: 1 1/2 cups

1/3 cup ketchup
1/4 cup vinegar
1/4 cup sugar

1/2 cup vegetable oil
1 teaspoon salt
1 teaspoon grated onion

- Mix all ingredients in blender.
- Chill.

Mrs. Sara Ellen Munnerlyn, Bennettsville, SC

Breads & Spreads

Painting by: Buster Weaver

John J. Weaver, Jr.
"Thomas Memorial Baptist Church"

The late John J. "Buster" Weaver, Jr. was owner of Weaver's Building and Specialty Company, a general contracting firm in Bennettsville, South Carolina. He was married to the former Marion Brasington and was an active member of Thomas Memorial Baptist Church. Mr. Weaver was the father of three children: Carol Weaver Covington Ross, Johnny Weaver, and Steve Weaver.

A native of Bennettsville, Mr. Weaver attended the University of South Carolina in Columbia and served in the United States Navy as a member of the Sea Bees in World War II. In his later years, he spent most of time painting and gardening.

Two current members of the Junior Charity League of Marlboro County, Inc. are close family members of Mr. Weaver: Ms. Jan Weaver, his granddaughter, and Mrs. Rhett (Gray) Covington, his granddaughter-in-law.

Cannoli Bagels

Serves: 2

Preparation time: 15 minutes

1 cup ricotta cheese
1/4 teaspoon vanilla extract
1 tablespoon plus 1 teaspoon
  confectioners sugar
1 tablespoon citron, chopped (or
  mixed assorted fruits, chopped, used
  for fruitcakes)

1/4 cup semisweet chocolate chips
1 cinnamon-raisin bagel, halved
1 tablespoon pistachio nuts or slivered
  almonds, chopped

- Mix cheese in blender or food processor for a few seconds until creamy.
- Scrape cheese into a small mixing bowl.
- Add vanilla extract and sugar, mixing well.
- To cheese mixture, add citron, or other fruit, and chocolate chips; blend well.
- Spread half of the mixture on each bagel half and sprinkle with chopped nuts or almonds.

Mrs. Mark S. (Jimmy Carol) Avent, Bennettsville, SC

Pineapple - Cream Bagels

Serves: 2

Preparation time: 15 minutes

1/2 cup cream cheese or ricotta cheese
2 teaspoons dark brown sugar
1/4 cup pecans, finely chopped

1 pineapple ring, chopped and well
  drained
1 bagel, halved
2 whole pineapple rings, well drained

- Whip cheese until creamy.
- Combine with brown sugar, pecans, and chopped pineapple.
- Mix well and spread onto bagel halves.
- Top each with whole pineapple ring and serve.

Mrs. Mark S. (Jimmy Carol) Avent, Bennettsville, SC

Nimmy's Bagel Spread

Yields: 1 cup

Preparation time: 15 minutes

1   4 ounce package cream cheese,
    softened
1¹/₂ tablespoons honey
¹/₈ cup golden raisins

1   medium carrot, peeled and grated
¹/₄ cup walnuts, chopped
4   bagels (your choice), halved

- Mix cream cheese and honey.
- Stir in raisins, carrot, and walnuts.
- Spread on bagel halves and serve.

Mrs. Mark S. (Jimmy Carol) Avent, Bennettsville, SC

Strawberries-and-Cream Bagel Slimmers

Great tasting and good for you, too!

Serves: 2

Preparation time: 10 minutes

³/₄ cup strawberries
¹/₂ cup part skim ricotta cheese
¹/₂ teaspoon granulated sugar

1   bagel, halved and toasted
    fresh mint (optional)

- Mash ¹/₄ cup strawberries.
- Mix strawberries with Ricotta cheese and sugar, blend well.
- Spread each toasted bagel half with mixture.
- Slice remaining strawberries and place on top of ricotta cheese.
- Garnish with mint leaves, if desired.
- Serve open face.

Mrs. Mark S. (Jimmy Carol) Avent, Bennettsville, SC

Breads and Spreads

Carolina Cuisine: Nothin' Could Be Finer

Banana-Wheat Quick Bread

Serves: 8
Cooking time: 60-70 minutes

Preparation time: 10 minutes
Oven temperature: 325

1¼ cup all-purpose flour
½ cup whole wheat flour
1 cup sugar
1 teaspoon baking soda
1 teaspoon salt
1½ cups (3) mashed bananas

2 tablespoons orange juice
¼ cup margarine, softened
¼ teaspoon lemon juice
1 egg
½ cup raisins or chopped nuts

- Preheat oven.
- Grease and flour loaf pan.
- Blend all ingredients.
- Beat 3 minutes.
- Bake.

Mrs. Tim (Elaine) Seales, Bennettsville, SC

Beer Bread

Great Tasting!
Serves: 8-10
Cooking time: 45 minutes

Preparation time: 5 minutes
Oven temperature: 350

3 cups self-rising flour
3 tablespoons sugar

1 12 ounce can beer

- Mix all ingredients together until firm.
- Place in a well-greased bread (loaf) pan.
- Bake.

Mrs. Hubert (Christi) Meggs, Jr., Bennettsville, SC

Easy Biscuits

So Easy!
Yields: 20 2-inch biscuits
Cooking time: 8-12 minutes
Freezes well

Preparation time: 10 minutes
Oven temperature: 425

$^1/_2$ cup vegetable oil
$^1/_2$ cup milk

2 cups self-rising flour

Substitution 1:
$^1/_4$ cup canola oil
$^3/_4$ cup skim milk
2 cups self-rising flour

Substitution 2:
$^1/_3$ cup canola oil
$^2/_3$ cup skim milk
2 cups self-rising flour

- Combine ingredients.
- Roll out on floured surface and cut to desired size.
- Bake until lightly browned.

Mrs. Charles (Janice) Vaughan, Jr., Bennettsville, SC

Blueberry Pancakes for Two

Yield: 10 pancakes
Cooking time: 2 minutes each side

Preparation time: 15 minutes

1 cup sifted all-purpose flour
3 teaspoons baking powder
$^1/_8$ cup sugar
$^1/_2$ teaspoon salt

1 egg
1 cup milk
3 tablespoons oil
$^1/_2$ cup blueberries

- Sift together flour, baking powder, sugar, and salt.
- Beat egg, stir in milk and oil.
- Combine with dry ingredients and beat to a smooth batter.
- Add well drained, thawed blueberries.
- Drop by tablespoons or pour from pitcher onto hot, ungreased griddle.
- Bake until underside is golden brown and top is bubbly.
- Turn and bake other side.
- Serve with butter and syrup.

The late John T. Geisel, Bennettsville, SC

82   Carolina Cuisine: Nothin' Could Be Finer

Catherine's Bran Muffins

Yields: 6-8 muffins
Cooking time: 15 to 20 minutes
Prepare ahead

Preparation time: 10 minutes
Oven temperature: 400
Freezes well

1 cup flour	1 $1/4$ cups all bran cereal
$1/2$ cup sugar	1 cup milk
$2 1/2$ teaspoons baking powder	1 egg
$1/2$ teaspoon baking soda	$1/4$ cup vegetable oil
$1/2$ teaspoon salt	

- Preheat oven.
- Combine first 5 ingredients.
- Set aside.
- Pour milk over bran and let stand 5 minutes until softened.
- Add egg, oil, beating until blended.
- Add flour mixture, stirring just until combined.
- Do not over mix.
- Fill greased $2 1/2$ inch muffin pans $2/3$ full.
- Bake.

Mrs. V. Cullum (Catherine) Rogers, Bennettsville, SC

Refrigerator Bran Muffins

This batter will keep in the refrigerator for several weeks. Just bake as needed.
Cooking time: 20 minutes   **Oven temperature: 400**

1 cup bran flakes	$2 1/2$ cups all-purpose flour, sifted
1 cup boiling water	2 cups bran
$1/2$ cup shortening	$1/2$ teaspoon salt
1 cup sugar	$2 1/2$ teaspoons soda
2 eggs	
1 pint buttermilk	

- Mix bran flakes and boiling water. Let stand.
- Cream shortening, sugar, eggs, and buttermilk.
- Add bran mixture, flour, bran, salt, and soda.
- Bake in greased muffin pans.

Mrs. Ron (Elizabeth) Munnerlyn, Bennettsville, SC

Breads and Spreads

Junior Charity League of Marlboro County, Inc.

Breakaway Bread

Recipe may be halved and baked in one pan.

Serves: 16
Oven temperature: 350
Preparation time: 30 minutes

Cooking time: 30 minutes
Prepare day before

2	packages yeast	1^1/$_2$	teaspoons salt
1	cup warm water	2	eggs, beaten
1	cup boiling water	6	cups all-purpose flour
1	cup shortening	1	stick margarine, melted
^{1}/$_2$	cup sugar		

- Dissolve yeast in warm water and set aside.
- In large bowl, pour boiling water over shortening and dissolve (or heat water and shortening in microwave until dissolved).
- Add sugar, salt, eggs, flour, and dissolved yeast and mix well with regular beater or electric mixer-dough hooks not necessary.
- Cover with plastic wrap and refrigerate overnight.
- Next day roll dough and cut with biscuit cutter.
- Dip each biscuit in melted margarine and stack in two greased bundt pans.
- Let rise 2-3 hours.
- Bake.

Mrs. John (Jane) Brooks, John's Island, SC

Cheese Danish

Very Good!

Serves: 12
Cooking time: 25 minutes

Preparation time: 25 minutes
Oven temperature: 350

2	packages crescent rolls	1	teaspoon vanilla extract
2	8 ounces cream cheese, softened	1	egg yolk, save white
^{2}/$_3$	cup sugar	^{1}/$_2$	teaspoon almond extract

- Mix cheese, sugar, vanilla, and egg yolk with wooden spoon until mixed well.
- Place 1 package of crescent rolls into 13 x 9 dish which has been sprayed with non stick cooking spray.
- Pinch edges together.
- Spread cheese mixture on top.
- Place second can of rolls on top, seal seams.
- Brush top of rolls with egg white.

Mrs. A. M. (Mary Frances) Hollingsworth, Fayetteville, NC

Cinnamon Flop

Yields: 2 9-inch pies
Cooking time: 30 minutes
Prepare ahead

Preparation time: 20 minutes
Oven temperature: 375

1 cup sugar
1 tablespoon butter
1 cup milk
   pinch salt
2½ cups all-purpose flour

2½ teaspoons baking powder
Topping:
   butter
   cinnamon
   brown sugar

- Preheat oven.
- Cream butter, gradually adding sugar.
- Sift salt, flour, and baking powder together.
- Add alternately with milk to butter and sugar mixture.
- Put in 2 9-inch pie tins and sprinkle liberally with brown sugar and cinnamon.
- Press bits of butter into cakes.
- Bake until firm to touch.

Mrs. Benjamin F. (Sara Jane) Alston, Bennettsville, SC

Corny Corn Bread

Yields: 12-18 one inch pieces
Cooking time: 25 to 30 minutes
Freezes well

Preparation time: 15 to 20 minutes
Oven temperature: 350

2 eggs, beaten
½ cup oil
1 cup sour cream
1 cup creamed corn

1 cup corn meal
3 teaspoons baking powder
   salt to taste
   pepper if desired

- Mix eggs, oil, sour cream, corn, and corn meal.
- Add baking powder, salt, and pepper.
- Stir well.
- Place in muffin tins and bake.

Mrs. Willard (Thelma) Sligh, Bennettsville, SC

Crook's Corner's Black Pepper Cornbread

Served in "Crook's Corner", Chapel Hill, North Carolina.

Oven temperature: 450   **Cooking time: 20-25 minutes**

$1/2$ cup flour	$1^3/4$ cups buttermilk
$1/8$ cup sugar (2 tablespoons)	$2^1/2$ tablespoon melted butter
$1/2$ teaspoon baking soda	1 large egg
1 tablespoon baking powder	$1/4$ teaspoon coarse black pepper or
$1/4$ teaspoon salt	fresh cracked peppercorns
1 cup corn meal	

- Preheat oven.
- Butter a 9 x 2 inch round cake pan.
- Coat with 2 tablespoons corn meal.
- Sift flour, sugar, soda, baking powder, and salt into mixing bowl.
- Sift in 1 cup of cornmeal.
- Beat the buttermilk, egg, and melted butter.
- Fold the dry flour mixture into the liquid mixture, using a few quick strokes.
- Do not over mix.
- Pour in pan.
- Sprinkle with pepper.
- Bake until golden brown and bread is pulling away from pan.

Mrs. Eugene (Winnie) Hamer, Monroe, NC

John's Island Corn Bread

A light, delicious corn bread.

Serves: 8-10   **Preparation time: 15 minutes**
Cooking time: 25 minutes   **Oven temperature: 450**
Freezes Well

$1/4$ cup sugar	$1^1/4$ cups flour
1 cup margarine	6 teaspoons baking powder
2 eggs, well beaten	1 teaspoon salt
$1^3/4$ cups corn meal	$1^1/4$ cups milk

- Cream margarine and sugar, add eggs.
- Sift corn meal, flour, baking powder, and salt.
- Add sifted mixture into creamed mixture, alternating with milk.
- Bake in greased 10 x 14 pan.
- Cut into squares.

Mrs. John R. (Penny) Nobles, Bennettsville, SC

Carolina Cuisine: Nothin' Could Be Finer

Mexican Corn Bread

Very good and colorful!
Serves: 10
Cooking time: 30-45 minutes
Freezes well

Preparation time: 30 minutes
Oven temperature: 350

1 cup self-rising corn meal	1 11 ounce can creamed corn
1/4 cup self-rising flour	2 eggs, beaten
1/2 teaspoon baking powder	1 1/2 cups green bell pepper, finely chopped
1/2 teaspoon salt	
3/4 cup buttermilk	1 teaspoon hot pepper, finely chopped
1/2 cup canola oil	3/4 cup grated sharp cheddar cheese
1 medium onion, finely chopped	

- Mix corn meal, flour, baking powder, and salt; then sift together.
- Add buttermilk and oil with dry ingredients in medium mixing bowl.
- Add onion, corn, eggs, peppers, and cheese.
- Mix well and pour in 9 x 13 baking pan.

- Variation: for hotter cornbread-use 2 teaspoons hot pepper, 1 cup grated sharp cheddar cheese, and 1 1/2 cup finely chopped onion.

Mrs. Willard (Thelma) Sligh, Bennettsville, SC

Ginger Sandwich Spread

1 8 ounce package cream cheese
6 ounces ginger marmalade

1/2 cup chopped nuts
mayonnaise to mix well

- Mix and spread.

Mrs. J. Palmer (Henrietta) Gaillard, III, Charleston, SC

Breads and Spreads

Junior Charity League of Marlboro County, Inc.

Raisin and Nut Spread

1 cup sugar	1 cup mayonnaise
1 egg, beaten well	1 cup raisins
1 lemon, juiced	1/4 stick margarine
1 cup nuts, chopped	

- Combine and cook sugar, egg, and lemon juice until thick.
- Remove from heat.
- Add raisins and margarine.
- Cool.
- Add nuts and mayonnaise.

Mrs. J. Palmer (Henrietta) Gaillard, III, Charleston, SC

Honey Muffins

Yields: 12 muffins　　　　　　　　**Cooking time: 15-20 minutes**
Oven temperature: 375

- 1/2 cup honey
- 1/2 cup orange juice
- 1/3 cup margarine, melted
- 2 eggs, beaten
- 1 cup all-purpose flour
- 1/4 cup sugar (or 3 packets of artificial sweetener)
- 1 teaspoon baking soda
- 2 teaspoons baking powder
- 1 teaspoon vanilla extract (optional)

- Mix honey, orange juice, margarine, eggs, and vanilla.
- In another bowl, mix flour, sugar, baking powder, and baking soda.
- Stir liquid into dry mixture until well blended.
- Bake in muffin pans until golden brown.

Mrs. Ruth Fields, Bennettsville, SC

Another Version of "Hot Kentucky Brown"

Serves: 6
Cooking time: 10 minutes

Preparation time: 15 minutes

6	slices bread, lightly toasted	6	slices of Swiss cheese, thinly sliced
6	deli slices smoked turkey	1	1 ounce envelope Bernaise Sauce
1	bunch fresh asparagus OR		
1	8 ounce package frozen asparagus, steamed and cooled		

- Make Bernaise sauce according to package directions.
- Add turkey slices on top of bread slices followed by 3-4 asparagus stalks and cheese.
- Broil until cheese is slightly melted.
- Add Bernaise sauce and broil 2-3 minutes more.
- Serve hot.

Mrs. Mary Odom, Bowling Green, KY

Marmalade Sandwich Spread

Yields: 4 dozen sandwiches
Cooking time: 10 minutes

Preparation time: 30 minutes
Prepare ahead

2	cups dark raisins, finely chopped	2	eggs
1	cup pecans, finely chopped	2	cups sugar
	rind of 2 lemons, grated	2	cups mayonnaise

- Mix all ingredients and place in double boiler.
- Cook for 10 minutes.
- Mixture will be transparent.
- Cool and spread for sandwiches.

Mrs. Daniel E. (Elisabeth) McNiel, Bennettsville, SC

Breads and Spreads

Orange Cranberry Bread

A delicious holiday dish!

Serves: 10-12
Cooking time: 50-60 minutes
Freezes well

Preparation time: 30 minutes
Oven temperature: 350

2 cups all-purpose flour, sifted	2 cups cranberries
1 cup sugar	1 orange (use juice and grated rind)
1/2 teaspoons baking soda	2 tablespoons cooking oil
1 1/2 teaspoons baking powder	1 egg, well beaten
1 teaspoon salt	1/2 cup walnuts, chopped(optional)

- Slice cranberries in half.
- Sift dry ingredients together.
- Combine juice, oil, rind, and enough water to make 3/4 cup.
- Mix dry and wet ingredients enough to dampen.
- Fold in cranberries and nuts.
- Spread mixture into a greased 9 x 5 x 3 bread pan, sides slightly higher.
- Bake until toothpick comes out dry.

Miss Cammy Miller, Bennettsville, SC

Pear Bread

Preparation time: 30 minutes
Oven temperature: 325

Cooking time: 1 hour 15 minutes

3 cups all-purpose flour	1/2 cup raisins
1 teaspoon soda	3/4 cup vegetable oil
1/4 teaspoon baking powder	3 eggs, slightly beaten
1 teaspoon salt	2 cups sugar
2 teaspoons ground cinnamon	2 teaspoons vanilla extract
1 1/2 cup pecans, chopped	2 1/2 cups pears, peeled and grated

- Mix the first 7 ingredients in a large bowl.
- Make a well in the center of the mixture.
- Combine the last five ingredients and add to dry ingredients, stirring just until moistened.
- Spoon mixture into 2 greased 8 1/2 x 4 1/2 x 3 loaf pans.
- Bake until bread tests done.
- Cool 10 minutes before removing from pans.

Mrs. William (Erlene) Bethea, Jr., McColl, SC

Breads and Spreads

Carolina Cuisine: Nothin' Could Be Finer

Pecan Muffins

Yield: 12 Muffins
Cooking time: 20-25 minutes

Preparation time: 35 minutes
Oven temperature: 350

1 cup light brown sugar	$^1/_3$ cup butter, melted
$^1/_2$-1 cup pecans, chopped	2 eggs
$^1/_2$ cup self-rising flour	

- Mix all ingredients with a spoon in a bowl.
- Spoon into muffin tins lined with paper baking cups, filling half full.
- Bake.

Mrs. Steve (Katherine) Littlejohn, Columbia, SC

Pumpkin Muffins

Yield: 12 muffins
Cooking time: 45 minutes

Preparation time: 16 to 18 minutes
Oven temperature: 375

2 cups all-purpose flour, sifted	$^1/_3$ cup butter, softened
2 teaspoons baking powder	$^3/_4$ cup brown sugar
$^1/_2$ teaspoon salt	$^1/_4$ cup molasses
$^1/_2$ teaspoon ginger	2 eggs, beaten
$^1/_2$ teaspoon nutmeg (ground)	1 cup canned pumpkin
$^1/_8$ teaspoon cloves (ground)	$^1/_2$ cup milk
$^1/_3$ cup raisins	

- Sift together flour, baking powder, salt, and spices.
- Add raisins after coating with flour.
- Cream sugar, butter, and molasses.
- Add milk, eggs, and pumpkin.
- Blend well.
- Stir in dry ingredients, blending only until flour disappears.
- Fill greased muffin pans full.
- Bake.

Mrs. Lawson (Sarah) Harmon, Bennettsville, SC

Breads and Spreads

Junior Charity League of Marlboro County, Inc.

Spicy Pimento Cheese

Preparation time: 15 minutes

1 pound sharp cheddar cheese
$^1/_2$ cup mayonnaise
$^1/_2$ cup salad dressing

1 4$^1/_2$ ounce can chopped green chilies
1 4 ounce jar chopped pimento
pepper to taste

- Grate cheese and combine well with remaining ingredients.
- Serve with crackers for appetizer or on bread for sandwich.

Mrs. James (Jaylene) Myers, Bennettsville, SC

Melt in Your Mouth Rolls

Yields: 36 rolls
Cooking time: 10-15 minutes
Prepare ahead

Preparation time: Several hours
Oven temperature: 350
Freezes well

1 package dry yeast
$^3/_4$ teaspoon salt
3 tablespoons water
2 tablespoons shortening

3 tablespoons sugar
1 egg
1 cup milk
3 cups all-purpose flour

- Dissolve yeast and salt in hot water (not boiling water).
- Cream shortening and sugar, beat in egg, add milk, then dissolved yeast mixture.
- Work in the flour.
- Let rise at least 1 hour in a greased bowl, covered.
- Roll out and cut with biscuit cutter.
- Let rise another hour.
- These should be placed in greased pan and covered with cheese cloth.
- Bake.

Mrs. V. Cullum (Catherine) Rogers, Bennettsville, SC

Mayonnaise Rolls

Preparation time: 7 minutes
Oven temperature: 375

Cooking time: 15 minutes

2 cups self-rising flour
$^1/_4$ cup mayonnaise

1 cup milk

- Mix ingredients in bowl.
- Place in greased muffin tin.
- Bake.

Mrs. Tim (Leslie) LaBean, Bennettsville, SC

My Favorite Rolls

Yields: 60 rolls
Cooking time: 15 minutes
Prepare ahead

Preparation time: 30 minutes
Oven temperature: 400
Freezes well

1	cup lukewarm water	1	cup boiling water
2	envelopes yeast	2	large eggs, beaten
3/4	teaspoon sugar	6	cups bread flour
1	cup shortening	2	teaspoons salt
3/4	cup sugar		

- In a 2 cup measuring cup or bowl, mix lukewarm water, yeast, and 3/4 teaspoon sugar; stir well.
- Beat shortening and 3/4 cup sugar in large mixing bowl with electric mixer.
- Add boiling water, beating well until dissolved.
- Add yeast mixture and eggs, the flour and salt, stirring with a spoon instead of mixer when it gets too thick.
- Cover bowl and place in refrigerator several hours or overnight.
- Three hours before serving, roll dough on floured surface 1/2 inch thick and cut with a 2 inch round cutter.
- Place in greased pans with sides of rolls barely touching.
- Cover and let rise (not in refrigerator) 2 hours.
- Remove covers and bake.
- May use (5) 8 x 8 aluminum pans (12 rolls to a pan) instead of 2 large ones.
- Variation: mix 1/2 cup sugar and 1 stick butter or oleo and dip each one in this as they are placed them in the pans.

Mrs. J. Maxwell (Martha) Gregg, Bennettsville, SC

Nancy's Little Rolls

No butter needed on the table with these!

Yields: 40 rolls
Cooking time: 20 minutes
Prepare ahead

Preparation time: 10 minutes
Oven temperature: 350
Freezes well

2	cups baking mix	16	ounces sour cream
1	stick margarine, melted		

- Mix all ingredients and place in mini-muffin pans.
- Fill cups about 1/2 full.
- May be frozen after baked and reheated in foil.

Mrs. Daniel E. (Elisabeth) McNiel, Bennettsville, SC

Breads and Spreads

Junior Charity League of Marlboro County, Inc.

Refrigerated Rolls

Preparation time: 3½ hours
Oven temperature: 375
Cooking time: 20 minutes

2 packages dry yeast	3 tablespoons shortening
2 cups warm water	1 egg, slightly beaten
½ cup sugar	6½ cups flour
1½ teaspoon salt	

- Sprinkle yeast over water.
- Add sugar, salt, shortening, egg, and flour.
- Beat until smooth.
- Shape into ball.
- Place in greased bowl.
- Turn once and cover with a damp cloth.
- Let rise until double in size — about 1½ hours.
- Punch down.
- Cover and refrigerate 2 hours.
- Shape into oval shaped rolls about 1½ inches long.
- Place in greased pan about ¼ inch apart.
- Let rise.
- Bake.

Mrs. F. M. (Susan) Hinson, III, Bennettsville, S.C.

Shrimp Sandwiches

1 can of shrimp, drained	salt
3 boiled eggs	pepper
2 tablespoons onion, minced	2 tablespoons pickles, chopped
dash garlic salt	mayonnaise

- Mix all ingredients well in blender.
- Add 3 or 4 drops red food coloring and blend until shrimp are colored.
- Spread sandwiches.

Mrs. Sally M. Patterson, Murrells Inlet, SC

Breads and Spreads

Carolina Cuisine: Nothin' Could Be Finer

Baked Sandwich

Wonderful for a ladies' luncheon!

Serves: 10-12
Cooking time: 1 hour
Prepare ahead

Preparation time: 40 minutes
Oven temperature: 350 degrees
Freezes well

16	slices bread (crust removed)	$^3/_4$	teaspoon salt
	butter	$^3/_4$	teaspoon pepper
2	cups sharp cheese, grated	2	tomatoes, sliced
$^3/_4$	pound bacon, diced	6	eggs
1	cup onion, diced	3	cups milk
$^3/_4$	cup celery, diced	$1^1/_2$	teaspoons prepared mustard
6	tablespoons green pepper, diced		

- Spread butter on each slice.
- Arrange 8 slices of buttered bread down in a 4 quart casserole dish.
- Cover with 1 cup of sharp grated cheese.
- Brown together the next 6 ingredients and pour over buttered bread and cheese.
- Arrange 8 tomato slices on top of bacon mixture.
- Cover with 8 more slices of bread.
- Beat together eggs, milk, and mustard; pour over bread.
- Add 1 cup grated cheese.
- Refrigerate overnight.
- Bake.
- Slice before serving.

Mrs. Shirley H. Beeson, Little River, SC

Squash Bread

Two 16 ounce cans of squash can be used if fresh squash is unavailable.

Serves: 8
Cooking time: 30 minutes
Freezes well

Preparation time: 30 minutes
Oven temperature: 375

5-6	cups yellow squash, cooked and chopped	1	12 ounce carton small curd cottage cheese
4	large eggs, slightly beaten	1	12 ounce box cornbread mix
1	cup milk	1	stick margarine, melted
1	teaspoon salt		

- Combine squash, eggs, milk, salt, and cottage cheese.
- Stir in cornbread mix.
- Pour into greased 3 quart casserole dish.
- Pour margarine over top.
- Bake.

Mrs. Marion M. (Cathy) Evans, Bennettsville, SC

Junior Charity League of Marlboro County,Inc.

"Star" Loaves

Yields: 2 large loaves or 3 small loaves
Cooking time: 30 minutes
Prepare ahead

Preparation time: 15 minutes
Oven temperature: 350
Freezes well

1   6 ounce box instant coconut
    pudding
1   18.5 ounce butter pecan cake mix
1/2 cup oil

3   large eggs
1/4 cup poppy seeds
1   cup warm water
1   cup pecans

- Mix all ingredients together in a large mixing bowl, adding eggs one at a time.
- Pour into loaf pans.
- Bake.

Mrs. Ed (Kaye) Goldberg, IV, Murrells Inlet, SC

Sticky Buns

Yield: 24 buns
Oven temperature: 350

Cooking time: 25 minutes

24 yeast rolls (frozen)
1/2 cup sugar
1 1/2 teaspoons cinnamon
1/2 cup brown sugar

1   3.5 box butterscotch cook and serve
    pudding
3/4 cup margarine, cut into chunks
1/2 cup pecans, chopped

- Place frozen yeast rolls in bottom of 9 x 13 baking pan.
- Sprinkle with mixture of sugar and cinnamon.
- Sprinkle nuts, brown sugar, dry pudding, chopped margarine over all.
- Cover with towel and put in oven overnight.
- Next morning remove pan from oven.
- Preheat and cook.
- Remove and invert on cookie sheet.
- Let cool 10 minutes.

Mrs. Clyde (Grace) Murphy, Bennettsville, SC

Carolina Cuisine: Nothin' Could Be Finer

Sweet Potato Bread

A traditional Thanksgiving bread!
Oven temperature: 350-375

8-10 medium sweet potatoes, baked and
    mashed
2¹/₂ sticks margarine or butter, softened
3   cups sugar
1   teaspoon nutmeg

1   teaspoon cinnamon
³/₄ cup self-rising flour
1   teaspoon vanilla extract
    pinch salt

- Mash potatoes and add other ingredients.
- Grease and flour a 13 x 9 inch pan.
- Spread mixture 1 inch thick in pan.
- Cook until brown.
- Cool and cut into squares.

Mrs. William (Toni Ann) Dew, Latta, SC

Sweet Potato Biscuits

A recipe my grandmother taught me.
Yield: 4 dozen
Cooking time: 10-15 minutes
Prepare ahead

Preparation time: 30 minutes
Oven temperature: 450
Freezes well

3   medium sweet potatoes or 8 sweet
    potato patties
2   cups all-purpose flour
4   level teaspoons baking powder
1   cup sugar

¹/₂ teaspoon salt
¹/₄ cup all vegetable shortening
1   egg
¹/₄ cup milk

- Boil and mash whole potatoes or mash patties.
- Sift salt, flour, and baking powder.
- Add potatoes to flour mixture in large bowl.
- Cut in shortening.
- Mix to a light dough with egg and milk.
- Roll and cut.
- Place in cold oven to rise as oven heats.
- Bake.
- Serve as soon as done—these will not brown on top but will on bottom.
- Dough may be mixed in bread maker following manufacturer's instructions for correct order of adding ingredients.

Mrs. Daniel E. (Elisabeth) McNiel, Bennettsville, SC

Breads and Spreads

Junior Charity League of Marlboro County,Inc.

Vegetable Sandwich Spread

Yields: 80-100 sandwiches

Prepare ahead

3   carrots
1   bell pepper
1   onion
1   cucumber

1   8 ounce package cream cheese
½   cup mayonnaise
    pinch salt

- Grate all vegetables and drain well.
- Add cream cheese, mayonnaise, and a pinch of salt.
- Mix together and refrigerate.
- Spread on bread.

Mrs. Maxie Kinard, Bennettsville, SC

Zucchini Nut Bread

Yield: 2 loaves
Cooking time: 55-60 minutes
Freezes well

Preparation time: 30 minutes
Oven temperature: 350

3   eggs
2   cups sugar
2   cups zucchini, peeled and grated
1   cup oil
3   teaspoons vanilla
3   cups all-purpose flour

1   teaspoon salt
1   teaspoon baking soda
¼   teaspoon baking powder
3   teaspoons cinnamon
1   cup pecans, chopped

- Beat eggs till light and fluffy on low speed of mixer.
- Add sugar, oil, zucchini, and vanilla.
- Combine well.
- Combine flour, salt, baking soda, baking powder, and cinnamon.
- Stir into other mixture.
- Stir in nuts.
- Pour into well-greased loaf pans.

Mrs. Norman (Kay) Rentz, Pickens, SC

Carolina Cuisine: Nothin' Could Be Finer

ENTREES

Drawing by: Catherine Rogers

Catherine McCall Rogers
"Out on the Porch"

Catherine McCall Rogers, a Marlboro County native, began painting after her seventieth birthday. She has taken both drawing and painting classes at St. Andrews Presbyterian College in Laurinburg, North Carolina and Lees-McRae College in Banner Elk, North Carolina to help foster her talent.

Mrs. Rogers, the widow of V. Cullum Rogers, is the mother of five adult children: Cullum, Charles, Richard, Catherine, and Mary. She has five grandchildren. Mrs. Rogers is an active member of First Presbyterian Church in Bennettsville.

Barbecued Chicken

Serves: 6
Cooking time: 2 hours, 20 minutes
Prepare ahead

Preparation time: 20 minutes
Oven temperature: 350

2½ pounds favorite chicken pieces, cut
    to frying size
1 ½ teaspoon salt
2 medium onions, sliced
½ cup butter
2 tablespoons vinegar
1 tablespoon Worcestershire sauce
2 teaspoons salt

    pinch of red pepper
3 teaspoons brown sugar
½ teaspoon paprika
½ teaspoon chili powder
¼ teaspoon black pepper
1 cup ketchup
1 cup hot water

- Preheat oven.
- Lightly grease large casserole or roaster.
- Arrange chicken in bottom of casserole and sprinkle with salt.
- Place onions on top of chicken and dot with butter.
- Combine remaining ingredients and mix well.
- Pour over chicken.
- Bake uncovered for 2 hours.
- Remove cover and bake for 20 minutes at 375 degrees.

Mrs. David K. (Cathy) Lynch, Bennettsville, SC

Entrees

Junior Charity League of Marlboro County, Inc.

Charleston Chicken Casserole

Great for dinner parties!

Serves: 8-10
Cooking time: 25 minutes
Prepare ahead

Preparation time: 30 minutes
Oven temperature: 350
Freezes well

2   10 ounce boxes frozen chopped
    broccoli, slightly cooked
3   cups white rice, cooked
3   cups chicken, cooked and diced
2   10³/₄ ounce cans cream of chicken
    soup
1   cup mayonnaise
1   teaspoon lemon juice

¹/₄   teaspoon curry powder
1¹/₂ cups sharp cheddar cheese, grated
1¹/₄ cups bread cubes or crumbs
2   tablespoons butter, melted
¹/₃   cup white wine, optional
2   14 ounce cans artichoke hearts,
     optional

- Layer 12 x 9 x 2 casserole with broccoli, rice, and chicken. Blend soup, mayonnaise, lemon juice, curry powder, and wine (optional); pour over chicken. Sprinkle with cheese. Toss bread with butter; arrange over cheese. At this point casserole may be covered and refrigerated for later use. Allow to return to room temperature before baking.
- Variation: Instead of broccoli and rice, use drained and quartered artichoke hearts. Layer chicken over artichokes. Proceed with original directions.

Mrs. Roy (Betty) Howell, Charleston, SC

Chicken Bog

A truly Southern main dish!

1   large hen
2   chicken bouillon cubes
2   medium onions, chopped
1   pound loose hot pork sausage,
    uncooked

¹/₄   teaspoon hot pepper sauce
4   cups rice
     salt and pepper to taste
     water

- Salt and pepper hen and boil in large pot with bouillon cubes and enough water to nearly cover chicken.
- Cook covered until chicken is well done.
- Remove chicken from broth and let cool, then debone.
- Cool broth and remove grease from top.
- Discard grease and use broth to cook chicken bog.
- Use broth and enough water to make 8 cups of liquid.
- To the liquid add sausage crumbled up, chopped onions, hot pepper sauce, and salt to taste.
- Bring to boil and add rice and chicken.
- Stir and cook covered on low for 20 minutes, not opening pot.

Mrs. Henry (Gerry) Capps, Bennettsville, SC

Rolled Chicken Breast

A Bennettsville favorite!

Serves: 8
Cooking time: 65 minutes

Preparation time: 20 - 30 minutes
Oven temperature: 350

8	chicken breasts, boneless
3/4	stick of butter or margarine,melted
8	slices Melba toast

1/2	cup Parmesan cheese
3/4	teaspoon salt

- Grind Melba toast in blender and mix with Parmesan cheese and salt.
- Dip chicken in butter.
- Roll breast, dredge in crumb mixture.
- Place in baking pan or dish - do not allow pieces to touch.
- Bake for 45 minutes covered with foil, then 20 minutes uncovered.

Mrs. A. A. (Katie Belle) Drake, Orangeburg, SC

Chicken and Broccoli Casserole

Serves: 10 - 12
Oven temperature: 350

Cooking time: 40 minutes

2	9 ounce packages frozen broccoli spears
6	chicken breasts, halved, cooked, skinned and cut into chunks
2	10 3/4 ounce cans cream of chicken soup
1/2	cup milk

1	teaspoon lemon juice
3/4	cup mayonnaise
1/2	teaspoon curry powder
1	cup sharp cheese, grated
1/2	cup stuffing mix
1/2	cup bread crumbs
2	tablespoons margarine, melted

- Cook broccoli by package directions and drain.
- Arrange in a greased 3 quart (9 x 13) casserole.
- Spread chicken on top of broccoli.
- Combine next six ingredients and pour over broccoli and chicken.
- Combine stuffing mix, bread crumbs, and melted margarine.
- Sprinkle over top.
- Bake.

Mrs. Benjy (Linda) Rogers, Bennettsville, SC

Entrees

Junior Charity League of Marlboro County, Inc.

Crisp Chicken Casserole

Serves: 4 - 6 servings
Cooking time: 45 minutes
Prepare ahead

Preparation time: 30 minutes
Oven temperature: 350

1   10³/₄ ounce can cream of celery
    soup
1   10³/₄ ounce can cream of chicken
    soup
¹/₂ cup water
1   cup mayonnaise
2   cups chicken, cooked and chopped

2   cups rice, cooked
1   small onion, chopped
1   8 ounce can water chestnuts,
    drained and sliced
2   cups corn flakes, crushed
¹/₂ stick butter, melted

- Mix soups with water and mayonnaise; then add the next 4 ingredients; mix well.
- Place in buttered casserole dish.
- Combine crumbs and butter and spread over mixture.
- Bake.

Mrs. Timothy (Leslie) LaBean, Bennettsville, SC

Deluxe Chicken Casserole

Serves: 8 - 10 servings
Cooking time: 15 minutes

Preparation time: 30 minutes
Oven temperature: 400

1¹/₂ cups chicken, cooked and diced
2   teaspoons onion, finely chopped
¹/₂ cup pecans, chopped
1¹/₂ cups rice, cooked
1   10³/₄ ounce can cream of chicken
    soup
1   cup celery, sliced

¹/₄ teaspoon cayenne pepper
¹/₂ teaspoon black pepper
1   tablespoon lemon juice
³/₄ cup mayonnaise
¹/₄ cup water
3   hard boiled eggs, diced
2   cups potato chips, crushed

- Mix all ingredients, except mayonnaise, water, eggs, and chips.
- Combine mayonnaise and water, then add to previous mixture.
- Gently fold in eggs.
- Place in 9 x 13 greased casserole and top with chips.
- Bake until bubbly.

Mrs. Larry (Phoebe) Howard, Bennettsville, SC

Entrees

104   Carolina Cuisine: Nothin' Could Be Finer

Easy Chicken Casserole

A delicious and simple main course.

Serves: 6
Cooking time: 50 minutes
Prepare ahead

Preparation time: 1 hour
Oven temperature: 350

4	chicken breasts
2	10¾ ounce cans chicken broth
2	10¾ ounce cans cream of chicken soup
¼	cup margarine
1	8 ounce package herbed stuffing mix

- Boil chicken until tender, debone.
- Layer herbed stuffing mix in 9 x 13 baking pan, then mix chicken broth and cream of chicken soup together in a large bowl.
- Pour a layer of soup over the dressing mix and layer chicken over the dressing mix.
- Repeat until all ingredients have been used, ending with seasoning mix sprinkled on top.
- Pat with small amount of margarine.
- Do not cover.
- Bake.

Mrs. John P. (Ruby) Driscoll, Bennettsville, SC

Chicken and Chip Bake

Serves: 6 - 8
Oven temperature: 425

Cooking time: 15 minutes

2	cups chicken, cooked and cubed
½	cup blanched toasted slivered almonds
½	teaspoon salt
2	teaspoons onion, grated
1	cup mayonnaise
1	cup potato chips, crushed
2	cups celery, chopped
½	teaspoon monosodium glutamate
2	tablespoons lemon juice (or to taste)
½	cup cheese, shredded

- Combine all ingredients except cheese and chips.
- Pile lightly into baking casserole.
- Sprinkle cheese and chips over all.
- Bake.

Mrs. J. Maxwell (Martha) Gregg, Bennettsville, SC

Chicken Crunch

Serves: 4
Cooking time: 20 minutes

Preparation time: 15 minutes
Oven temperature: 400

4	chicken breasts, skinned and boned	2	tablespoons all-purpose flour
1	10³/₄ ounce can cream of chicken soup	1¹/₂	cups herbed seasoned stuffing, finely crushed
¹/₂	cup milk	2	tablespoons margarine, melted

- In a shallow dish, combine ¹/₃ cup of the soup and ¹/₄ cup of the milk; set aside.
- Lightly coat each piece of chicken with the flour, then the soup-milk mixture, then the stuffing.
- In baking dish (or on baking sheet) arrange the chicken.
- Drizzle the margarine over the chicken.
- Bake.
- Combine remaining soup and milk and heat to use as "gravy" for rice or potatoes.

Mrs. Charles Paul (Heather) Midgley, Bennettsville, SC

Chicken Delights

Yields: 16 pieces
Cooking time: 15 minutes
Prepare ahead

Preparation time: 20 minutes
Oven temperature: 350
Freezes well

2	cups chicken, cooked and chopped	2	tablespoons margarine
2	tablespoons onions, chopped	1	3 ounce package cream cheese
2	tablespoons milk	2	8 ounce packages crescent rolls

- Mix ingredients and put on flattened rolls. Wrap putting corners over ingredients (about one tablespoon per roll).
- Put on baking sheet and freeze before you put in freezer bags or bake.

Mrs. Harry R. (Mary Kay) Easterling, Bennettsville, SC

Entrees

Carolina Cuisine: Nothin' Could Be Finer

Easy Chicken Divan

Serves: 6
Oven temperature: 350
Freezes well.

Cooking time: 25 - 30 minutes
Prepare ahead

2   10 ounce packages frozen broccoli
    (or two bunches fresh, cooked)
3-4 chicken breasts, cooked and boned
    (or 2 cups chicken, cooked and
    cubed)
1   10 ³/4 ounce can cream of chicken
    soup

1   cup mayonnaise
1   teaspoon lemon juice
¹/2 teaspoon curry powder
¹/2 cup sharp cheddar cheese, shredded
¹/2 cup soft bread crumbs mixed with 1
    tablespoon butter, melted

- Cook broccoli in boiling salted water until tender.
- Drain.
- Arrange in greased 12 x 8 baking dish.
- Place chicken on top of broccoli.
- Blend soup, mayonnaise, and curry.
- Pour over chicken.
- Sprinkle cheese over all.
- Top with buttered crumbs.
- Bake.

Mrs. James (Carole) Bowdre, Bennettsville, SC

Jean and Allen's Chicken Divan

Serves: 6 - 8
Cooking time: 30 minutes
Prepare ahead

Preparation time: 45 minutes
Oven temperature: 350
Freezes well

2- 3 pounds chicken breasts
2   10 ounce package frozen broccoli
    spears
1   10³/4 ounce can cream of celery
    soup

1   10³/4 ounce can cream of chicken
    soup
¹/2 cup chicken stock
1   cup mayonnaise/salad dressing
1   teaspoon lemon juice
2   cups sharp cheddar cheese, grated

- Boil chicken breasts.
- Pull meat from the bone.
- Prepare the broccoli according to package directions.
- Drain the broccoli and place it in 13 x 9 x 2 casserole dish.
- Cover with chicken.
- Combine soups, stock, mayonnaise and lemon juice.
- Pour over chicken.
- Cover with grated cheese and bake.

Mrs. Duncan (Cindi) McInnis, Clio, SC

Junior Charity League of Marlboro County, Inc.

Chicken and Dumplings

Serves: 8
Prepare ahead

Preparation time: 1 hour

1   fryer, cut up
1   large onion, chopped
5   tablespoons chicken bouillon

3   tablespoons flour, for thickening
1   12 ounce package dumpling noodles
    salt and pepper to taste

- Boil chicken, onion, and bouillon in large pot; when chicken is done, remove from broth and let cool, if in a hurry, put in freezer for a few minutes, debone and set aside.
- Bring broth to a boil and add noodles, cook for 5 minutes and add thickenings (3 tablespoons flour to 2/3 cup cold water, mixed until smooth) to noodles. Boil 5 minutes more, stirring constantly. Add chicken, turn off heat, and serve.

Mrs. Ray (Linda) Lee, Bennettsville, SC

Quick Chicken and Dumplings

Serves: 2 - 3
Cooking time: 20 minutes

Preparation time: 5 minutes
Prepare ahead

1²/₃ cups reduced fat biscuit mix
¹/₂   teaspoon dried rosemary
1¹/₂ teaspoon fresh parsley, chopped or
¹/₂   teaspoon dried parsley

²/₃   cup skim milk
2   16 ounce cans fat-free ready to serve
     chicken broth
1   10 ounce can white chicken in water

- Combine first 3 ingredients in a large bowl; make a well in center of mixture.
- Add milk, stirring just until moistened.
- Bring chicken broth to a boil in a large Dutch oven over medium- high heat.
- Drop biscuit mixture by tablespoonfuls into broth, cook uncovered 10 minutes.
- Cover, reduce heat, and simmer 10 minutes.
- Add chicken and cook 1 minute.
- Sprinkle with parsley.
- Serve immediately.

Mrs. Harrison (Beth) Odom, Bennettsville, SC

Chicken and Dumpling Casserole

Serves: 8
Cooking time: 30 minutes
Freezes well

Preparation time: 35 minutes
Oven temperature: 350

1   chicken stewed (or 4 chicken breasts)
1   12 ounce package dumpling noodles
1   8 ounce sour cream
1   10³/₄ ounce can cream of chicken soup

1   10³/₄ ounce can cream of mushroom soup
1¹/₂ cups bread crumbs
1   stick margarine, melted

- Cook chicken.
- Chop chicken (removing all skin and bones).
- Boil dumplings in chicken broth until tender.
- Mix together chicken, dumplings, sour cream, and soups.
- Pour into a large casserole dish.
- Top with bread crumbs.
- Pour melted margarine over crumbs.
- Bake until bubbly.

Ms. Pamela R. Hall, Bennettsville, SC

French-Italian Chicken

Can use chicken tenderloins and serve as an appetizer.

Serves: 8
Cooking time: 30 minutes

Preparation time: 5 minutes
Prepare ahead

8   chicken breasts, skinned and deboned
1   16 ounce bottle French dressing

1   16 ounce bottle Italian dressing

- Pierce chicken with a fork.
- Place chicken in a bowl or dish.
- Mix dressings and pour over chicken.
- Cover and marinate chicken overnight in refrigerator.
- Grill until done.

Mrs. Rhett (Gray) Covington , Bennettsville, SC

Country Style Chicken Kiev

Elegant yet so easy!

Serves: 8
Cooking time: 50 minutes

Preparation time: 25 minutes
Oven temperature: 350

8	chicken breasts, skinned and boned	1½	sticks butter
1	cup bread crumbs	1	tablespoon parsley, chopped
⅔	cup Parmesan cheese	2	tablespoons green onion tops
1	teaspoon garlic salt	¼	cup sherry
1	teaspoon basil		
1	teaspoon oregano		

- Combine bread crumbs, cheese, and spices in flat dish.
- Melt butter.
- Dip chicken in butter, covering well.
- Roll chicken in crumb mixture, covering well.
- Place in lightly greased, shallow baking dish or pan.
- Bake for 40 minutes.
- To remaining butter, add parsley, onion tops and sherry.
- Microwave for 2 minutes, then pour over chicken breasts.
- Return to oven and bake 10 minutes more.
- More butter may be needed, perhaps another half stick.

Mrs. Wade R. (Elaine) Crow, Bennettsville, SC

Chicken Parmesan

Preparation time: 10 minutes
Oven temperature: 350

Cooking time: 1 hour, 15 minutes

8	chicken breast halves	½	cup Parmesan cheese
1	stick margarine, melted	¾	teaspoon salt
½	cup Italian bread crumbs	½	teaspoon black pepper

- Mix all dry ingredients.
- Roll chicken in margarine, then in dry mix.
- Place chicken in baking dish.
- Bake covered for 45 minutes.
- Uncover and bake for 30 minutes longer.

Mrs. Tim (Leslie) LaBean, Bennettsville, SC

Entrees

Carolina Cuisine: Nothin' Could Be Finer

No-Peek Chicken

Serves: 5
Cooking time: 2 1/2 hours

Preparation time: 15 minutes
Oven temperature: 350

1   cup rice, uncooked
1   10³/₄ ounce can celery soup
1   10³/₄ ounce can mushroom soup

1   1.3 ounce package onion soup mix
1   chicken, cut up
¹/₄   cup water

- In 9 x 13 pan, mix rice and soup, spreading over bottom of pan.
- Lay chicken on top and sprinkle with dry onion soup mix.
- Seal with foil and place in oven.
- Don't peek!

Mrs. Harrison (Beth) Odom, Bennettsville, SC

Chicken Pie

Serves: 8
Cooking time: 45 minutes
Prepare ahead

Preparation time: 15 minutes
Oven temperature: 350

3   pounds chicken, deboned and cooked
2   boiled eggs, diced
1   10³/₄ ounce can mushroom soup
1   10³/₄ ounce can cream of chicken soup

1   cup self-rising flour
1   stick margarine, melted
1   teaspoon baking powder
1   cup chicken broth

- Combine first four ingredients and mix well.
- Mix flour with melted margarine - add baking powder and chicken broth.
- Pour over the chicken mixture.
- Bake.

Mrs. Ray (Lydia) Smith, Bennettsville, SC

Entrees

Junior Charity League of Marlboro County, Inc.

Big Sis' Chicken Pie

Serves: 6 - 8
Cooking time: 45 minutes
Prepare ahead

Preparation time: 1 hour
Oven temperature: 350
Freezes well: if cooked

1   chicken (or 4 breasts), cooked and cut up
$^1/_2$ stick margarine
1   10$^3/_4$ ounce can cream of mushroom soup

1   10$^3/_4$ ounce can cream of chicken soup
1$^1/_2$ cups chicken broth
1$^1/_2$ cups all-purpose baking mix
$^3/_4$ cup milk

- Coat 2-quart casserole dish with non-stick cooking spray.
- Place chicken in dish.
- Melt margarine and drizzle over chicken.
- Mix soups and $^2/_3$ cup chicken broth; pour over chicken.
- Mix baking mix and remaining broth and milk.
- Spread over casserole.
- Bake.

Mrs. Susan McNiel Hinson, Bennettsville, SC

Chicken Pot Pie

Cooking time: 30 minutes

Oven temperature: 400

$^1/_2$ package frozen mixed vegetables (or more), cooked and drained
1   whole chicken, cooked and deboned
1   stick butter

1   cup self-rising flour
1   cup buttermilk
1   10$^3/_4$ ounce can cream of chicken soup
1   cup (or more) chicken broth

- Coat 9 x 13 dish with non-stick spray.
- Layer chicken in bottom of sprayed dish.
- Make a batter of butter, flour, and buttermilk.
- Pour over layered chicken.
- Mix and heat cream of chicken soup and chicken broth.
- Add vegetables to soup and broth.
- Pour this mixture over chicken and batter.
- Bake.

Mrs. Mackie (Laurie) Norton, McColl, SC

Piper's Chicken Pie

Serves: 10 - 12 people
Cooking time: 40 - 45 minutes
Prepare ahead

Preparation time: 45 minutes
Oven temperature: 400

3 cups chicken, cooked and cut into bite-sized pieces
2 cups potatoes, cubed
1 cup celery, in small pieces
1/2 cup onion, in small pieces
1 10 ounce package frozen peas and carrots

3/4 stick margarine
3/4 cup flour
salt and pepper to taste
water as needed
1 10 count can refrigerated biscuits

- Cook vegetables separately.
- Reserve cooking water and broth.
- Melt margarine, stirring in flour to brown slightly.
- Add vegetable broth and water as needed.
- Stir as the mixture cooks and thickens to a medium consistency.
- In a large mixing bowl, mix meat, vegetables and sauce.
- Pour into a slightly buttered 13 x 9 x 2 inch baking dish.
- Divide biscuits and arrange on top of pot pie.
- Bake until mixture is bubbly and brown.
- Watch biscuits and near end you may need to cover with foil to prevent over browning.

Mrs. William (Anne) Caudill, Laurinburg, NC

Chicken Pot Pie Casserole

Compliments are always given.
Serves: 8 to 10
Oven temperature: 325

Cooking time: 1 hour
Prepare ahead

1 3-4 pound chicken, cooked and cut up
1 10³/₄ ounce can cream of celery soup

1 10³/₄ ounce can cream of onion soup
1 cup chicken stock
1 small can mixed vegetables

- Mixed together in 9 x 12 casserole.

Topping:
1 stick of butter, melted
1 cup self-rising flour

1 tablespoon baking powder

- Pour topping over chicken mixture.
- Can add: boiled eggs or 1 small can mixed vegetables.

Mrs. Billie M. Beaty, Bennettsville, SC

Junior Charity League of Marlboro County, Inc.

Kay's Poppy Seed Chicken

This recipe came from Kay Rentz, a former Bennettsville resident we all miss.

Serves: 10

Preparation time: 30 minutes

Cooking time: 40 - 60 minutes

Oven temperature: 350

Prepare ahead

8-10	chicken breast halves	1	sleeve round, buttery crackers, crushed
4-6	tablespoons chicken broth	1	stick butter, melted
2	8 ounce sour cream	2	tablespoons poppy seeds
2	10³/₄ ounce cans cream of chicken soup		salt and pepper to taste
2	tablespoons lemon juice		

- Cook and remove chicken from bones, place in greased 9 x 13 pan.
- Sprinkle with chicken broth.
- Mix sour cream, chicken soup, lemon juice, salt and pepper, and pour over chicken.
- Mix crackers, butter, and poppy seeds, spread over top.
- Bake.

Mrs. John R. (Penny) Nobles, Bennettsville, SC

Rosemary Chicken

Serves: 4

Preparation time: 15 minutes

Cooking time: 25 minutes

Oven temperature: 500

Prepare ahead: 1 day

3	tablespoons lime juice	¹/₂	teaspoon salt
¹/₄	cup vegetable oil	¹/₄	teaspoon black pepper
2	tablespoons scallions, chopped	4	chicken breast halves
1	tablespoon fresh parsley, chopped		fresh rosemary and lime slices for garnish
1¹/₂	teaspoons fresh rosemary OR		
¹/₂	teaspoon dried rosemary		

- Mix lime juice, oil, scallions, parsley, rosemary, salt, and pepper in casserole.
- Add chicken and turn to coat.
- Marinate overnight in refrigerator.
- Broil 15 minutes per side or grill 25 minutes per side, turning once.
- Sprinkle with fresh rosemary and arrange lime slices on top before serving.

Mrs. Hank (Gloria) Avent, Sewickley, PA

Soy Chicken

Serves: 6
Cooking time: 1½ hours
Prepare ahead

Preparation time: 5 minutes
Oven temperature: 350

1 small (2-2 ½ pound) chicken OR
6 chicken breasts, cut up
½ medium onion, finely chopped

2 teaspoons dry mustard
1 10 ounce bottle low sodium soy
   sauce

- Mix onion, mustard, and soy sauce in pan and boil 5 minutes.
- Pour over chicken and marinate overnight.
- Place chicken in uncovered pan with marinade and bake.

Mrs. Julian (Harriett) Drake, Blenheim, SC

Stir-Fried Chicken with Vegetables

Serves: 4
Cooking time: 30 minutes

Preparation time: 30 minutes

1 tablespoon cooking oil
1 small onion, chopped
4 cups mixed raw vegetables, cut into
   bite-size pieces (Examples: carrots,
   broccoli, cauliflower, green pepper)

2 cups chicken, cooked and diced

- Heat skillet over medium-high heat.
- Add oil.
- Sauté onion until limp.
- Add vegetables, stirring constantly to cook evenly and avoid sticking.
- When vegetables have wilted slightly, add chicken.
- Stir constantly for 3-4 minutes.
- Remove skillet from heat and cover.
- Let sit for 4-5 minutes to heat through.
- Serve hot.

Mrs. Jackie (Virginia) Williamson, Bennettsville, SC

Swiss Chicken Casserole

Serves: 4 - 6
Cooking time: 50 minutes

Preparation time: 5 - 10 minutes
Oven temperature: 350

6-8 chicken breasts, skinned and
  deboned
6 slices Swiss cheese
1 10³/₄ ounce can cream of chicken
  soup, undiluted

¹/₄ cup milk
2 cups herb-seasoned stuffing mix
¹/₄ cup butter or margarine, melted

- Arrange chicken breasts in a lightly greased 8 x 11 baking dish.
- Top with cheese.
- Combine soup and milk; stir well.
- Spoon soup mixture over chicken.
- Sprinkle with stuffing mix.
- Drizzle butter over stuffing.
- Cover and bake.

Mrs. Jack (Margaret) Corry, Bennettsville, SC
Mrs. Hubert (Christi) Meggs, Jr., Bennettsville, SC
Mrs. Mackie (Laurie) Norton, McColl, SC

Chicken Tetrazzini

Serves: 6
Cooking time: 30 minutes
Prepare ahead

Preparation time: 1 hour
Oven temperature: 350
Freezes well

1 whole 3 to 3¹/₂ pound fryer
  water, salt, and pepper to taste
1 large onion
1 stalk celery
1 8 ounce box thin spaghetti

Sauce:
1 10 ³/₄ ounce can cream of
  chicken soup
10³/₄ ounces milk
2 cups cheese crackers, crushed

- Cook fryer in enough water to cover.
- Boil until falling off bone.
- Debone and dice in bottom of 13 x 9 casserole dish.
- Chop onions and celery into the broth the chicken was cooked in and cook until tender.
- Layer onions and celery on top of chicken.
- Break spaghetti into chicken broth.
- Cook until tender.
- Layer on top of celery and onion.
- In small saucepan heat soup and milk.
- Pour over spaghetti.
- Put crumbled cheese crackers on top. Bake uncovered.

Mrs. Doug (Karen) Funderburk, Bennettsville, SC

Texas Pile-Up

Great for a large crowd. Looks pretty, too!
Wonderful Tex-Mex dish which is delicious and inexpensive.

16-20 chicken strips, skinned
3 15 ounce cans black beans
2 large tomatoes, diced
1 10 ounce bag saffron rice, cooked
1 16 ounce sour cream
1 green onion, diced

16 ounces sharp cheddar cheese, shredded
1 6 ounce can black olives, chopped
1 16 ounce jar mild salsa
   tortilla chips

- Cook chicken until tender. (May bake in salsa for zesty taste, double ounces of salsa if so desired, reserving half.)
- Remove chicken from heat.
- Layer rice, black beans, chicken, tomatoes, onions, black olives, cheese, sour cream, and salsa.
- Serve and enjoy.

Mrs. Mark S. (Jimmy Carol) Avent, Bennettsville, SC

Duck

Serves: 4
Cooking time: 3 hours

Preparation time: 15 minutes
Oven temperature: 325

2 wild ducks (Mallard, Pintails, etc.)
2 apples, quartered
2 medium onions, quartered
4 stalks celery, halved
4 strips of fat back or bacon
1 quart orange juice
4 tablespoons Worcestershire sauce

4 tablespoons soy sauce
1/2 cup red wine
   salt
   pepper
1 medium-size roaster with rack and air vents

- Wash ducks thoroughly after cleaning.
- Salt cavity freely with salt and then stuff, alternating with apples, onions, and celery.
- Put in roaster.
- Sprinkle salt and pepper on breast.
- Place bacon strips on breast.
- Mix wine, orange juice, and sauces together and pour in roaster.
- Bottom of roaster should be covered with almost one inch of liquid.
- Cover and cook with vents open for 2 1/2 hours.
- Remove lid and cook 1/2 hour longer uncovered.

Mr. J. DuPre Miller, Bennettsville, SC

Junior Charity League of Marlboro County, Inc.

Smoked Fowl

Serves: 8
Cooking time: 4 hours

Preparation time: 15 minutes

4	Cornish hens	Liquid for pan:
4	slices bacon, halved	1 quart orange juice
1	onion, quartered	1 cup inexpensive wine
1	apple, quartered	1 12 ounce can beer
2	stalks celery, halved	several peppercorns
	salt	2 tablespoons Worcestershire sauce
	pepper	2 tablespoons soy sauce
		enough water to fill pan of smoker

- Prepare hens (or other fowl) and salt cavity heavily.
- Stuff, alternating with onions, celery, and apples.
- Close cavity.
- Salt and pepper the breast of fowl.
- Cover breast with bacon.
- Mix liquid ingredients and place in pan. Use full pan and smoke for 4 hours or until legs move easily.
- Use hickory or mesquite chips on coals.

Mr. J. DuPre Miller, Bennettsville, SC

Chesapeake Bay Crab Cakes

Never turn crab cakes twice!

Serves: 4
Cooking time: 10 minutes

Preparation time: 20 minutes

1	pound crab meat	$1/2$ teaspoon salt
2	tablespoons onion, chopped	dash black pepper
2	tablespoons butter	dash red pepper
1	egg, beaten	$1/2$ cup dry bread crumbs
$1/2$	teaspoon dry mustard	

- Pick over crab meat.
- Sauté onion in butter.
- Combine crab meat with onion, egg, mustard, salt, and peppers.
- Shape into cakes; roll each cake in bread crumbs.
- Fry on both sides, about 3 - 4 minutes each side.
- Drain well before serving.

Mrs. Tom (Dottie) Pharr, Bennettsville, SC

Crab Imperial

Serves: 4
Cooking time: 20 minutes

Oven temperature: 350

1/3 cup onion, chopped
1/4 cup green pepper, chopped
3 tablespoons all-purpose flour
1/2 teaspoon dry mustard
1 cup skim milk
2 tablespoons lemon juice
1 1/2 teaspoons Worcestershire sauce
1/4 teaspoon black pepper

1 2-ounce jar diced pimento, drained
1 pound fresh lump crab meat, drained
3 tablespoons reduced calorie mayonnaise
2 tablespoons onion flavored melba toast, crumbled

- Coat pan with non-stick spray and place over medium heat until hot.
- Add onion and green pepper; sauté until tender.
- Sprinkle flour and dry mustard over vegetables, tossing gently to coat.
- Gradually stir in skim milk, bring to a boil and cook one minute or until thick and bubbly.
- Remove from heat.
- Stir in lemon juice and next three ingredients.
- Gently stir in crab meat and mayonnaise.
- Spoon 3/4 cup into four individual serving dishes.
- Top with 1 1/2 teaspoon Melba toast crumbs.
- Place on baking sheet and bake until thoroughly heated.
- Garnish with lemon wedges or slices.

Miss Karen Hearne, Mt. Pleasant, SC

Imitation Crab Meat Casserole

Serves: 8 - 10
Cooking time: 20 minutes
Prepare ahead

Preparation time: 1 - 1 1/2 hours
Oven temperature: 350

1/2 pound mushrooms, sliced
1/2 stick margarine
2 tablespoons flour
2 cups half and half or milk
1/2 cup cooking sherry
1 pound imitation crab meat, chopped

1/4 teaspoon salt
1/4 teaspoon black pepper
1 8 ounce egg noodles, cooked and drained
1/2 cup parmesan cheese

- Sauté mushrooms in margarine.
- Add flour and stir.
- Add half and half or milk and stir while cooking until thickened.
- Add sherry, salt and pepper to taste, and crab meat.
- Add egg noodles, which were salted while cooking and then drained well.
- Pour into greased 9 x 13 pan and sprinkle with Parmesan cheese.
- Bake.

Mrs. Jimmy (Janis) Usher, Bennettsville, SC

Junior Charity League of Marlboro County, Inc.

Crab Casserole

Serves: 6 - 8
Cooking time: 20 minutes

Preparation time: 15 minutes
Oven temperature: 350

1	pound fresh crab meat (white is preferable)
1	8 ounce package cream cheese
	Worcestershire sauce

	sherry
	garlic powder
2	tomatoes
	sliced Swiss cheese

- Pick crab meat well to remove shell.
- Mix crab meat and cream cheese well.
- Add Worcestershire, sherry, and garlic powder to taste.
- Place crab mixture in lightly greased casserole dish.
- Peel tomatoes and slice semi-thickly.
- Place tomato slices on crab meat and top with cheese slices.
- Bake until cheese is melted and slightly browned.

Mrs. Wade R. (Elaine) Crow, Bennettsville, SC

Cheese and Crab Meat

Serves: 10

Preparation time: 8 - 10 minutes

2	tablespoons butter
2/3	cup onion, finely chopped
1/2	cup green pepper, chopped
1	cup celery, diced
1	cup milk
1	cup light cream

2	3 ounce packages blue cheese, crumbled
1	cup ripe olives, sliced and pitted
4	6 ounce packages frozen crab meat, thawed and drained
1	teaspoon paprika
2	tablespoons parsley, chopped

- In hot butter, sauté onion, green pepper, and celery, stirring over medium heat until vegetables are tender, 8 to 10 minutes.
- Remove from heat.
- In top of double boiler, add milk, cream and cheese.
- Heat until cheese is melted and the mixture is smooth, stirring occasionally.
- Add cheese to vegetables along with olives and crab meat, stirring until well mixed.
- Heat mixture slowly, stirring until hot, about 20 minutes.
- Serve in heated chafing dish.
- Sprinkle with paprika.
- Circle edge with parsley.
- Serve in pastry shells.

Mrs. David K. (Cathy) Lynch, Bennettsville, SC

Chesapeake Crab Quiche

Serves: 8
Cooking time: 40 - 45 minutes

Preparation time: 15 minutes
Oven temperature: 350

$^1/_2$ cup mayonnaise
2   tablespoons flour
2   eggs, beaten
$^1/_2$ cup milk

$1^2/_3$ cups crab meat (claws)
8   ounces Swiss cheese, grated
$^1/_3$ cup onion, sliced
1   9 inch pie crust (baked)

- Combine mayonnaise, flour, eggs, and milk.
- Mix well.
- Stir in crab meat, cheese, and onion.
- Pour into pie crust.
- Bake.

Mrs. Tom (Dottie) Pharr, Bennettsville, SC

Deviled Crab

Serves: 4
Cooking time: 30 minutes

Preparation time: 20 minutes
Oven temperature: 400

$^1/_4$ pound butter, reserving some for
    buttered crumbs
1   pound crab meat
3   tablespoons mayonnaise

1   teaspoon dry mustard
1   teaspoon Worcestershire sauce
1   cup buttered bread crumbs
    paprika

- Melt butter.
- Mix crab meat, mayonnaise, dry mustard, and Worcestershire sauce.
- Add butter to crab mixture.
- Put in shells or ramekins, cover with buttered crumbs and paprika.
- Bake.

Mrs. Tom (Dottie) Pharr, Bennettsville, SC

Entrees

Mrs. "C's" Crab Meat and Shrimp Casserole

Serves: 6
Cooking time: 45 minutes
Prepare ahead

Preparation time: 30 minutes
Oven temperature: 350

1	medium green pepper, chopped	$^1/_8$	teaspoon pepper
1	medium onion, chopped	1	teaspoon Worcestershire sauce
1	cup celery, chopped	$^3/_4$	cup mayonnaise
$^1/_2$	pound crab meat	$^1/_2$	cup tangy mustard-mayonnaise
1	pound shrimp, cleaned and boiled		sauce
$^1/_2$	teaspoon salt		bread crumbs, buttered

- Combine ingredients and top with buttered bread crumbs.
- Bake in greased casserole.

Mrs. Julian (Kay) Fowler, Bennettsville, SC

Heavenly Flounder or Sole

Serves: 3 - 4
Cooking time: 20 minutes

Preparation time: 35 minutes
Oven temperature: Broil

3-4 filets of flounder or sole	3	tablespoons mayonnaise
2-3 lemons	3	tablespoons green onions, chopped
$^1/_4$ cup butter, softened	4	drops hot sauce
$^1/_2$ cup Parmesan cheese		

- Heat broiler.
- Place fish in oven proof dish.
- Cover fish with lemon juice and soak for $^1/_2$ hour.
- Pour off lemon juice.
- Broil close to heat until fish flakes easily with a fork.
- Do not overcook.
- Remove from heat and pour off any liquid in pan.
- Mix remaining ingredients and spread on fish.
- Return fish to broiler and cook until bubbly and brown.
- Watch carefully.

Mrs. John (Pam) Napier, Pawleys Island, SC

Pawleys Island Frogmore Stew

Great when served with slaw and rolls.

Serves: 10 - 12   **Preparation time: 1$^{1}/_{2}$ - 2 hours**

1	bag crab boil	2	packages kielbasa sausage
2-3	large onions		enough new potatoes to serve 12
6	celery stalks	12+	small corn ears
	salt and pepper to taste	1-2	pounds shrimp

- Fill a big pot of water $^{2}/_{3}$ full and add crab boil, onions, celery, salt, and pepper.
- Bring to a boil and boil for 10 - 15 minutes.
- Add sausage and potatoes and boil 20 minutes.
- Add corn and boil 15 minutes or longer.
- Add shrimp and boil 3 minutes, or until they are pink.
- Drain in a large colander and serve.

Mrs. Johnny (Janette) Weaver, Pawleys Island, SC

Low Country Boil

Great for a crowd!

Serves: Crowd   **Preparation time: 1$^{1}/_{2}$ hours**

Cooking time: 1$^{1}/_{2}$ hours

3	new potatoes per person		shrimp
1	teaspoon vinegar per pound shrimp	$^{1}/_{2}$	pound cooked smoked sausage per person
$^{1}/_{2}$	teaspoon hot sauce per pound shrimp	2	onions per person
1	teaspoon red pepper per 4 pounds shrimp	1	ear corn per person, shucked
1	teaspoon black pepper per 4 pounds	$^{1}/_{2}$	pound shrimp per person, in shell

- Fill a large pot about $^{3}/_{4}$ full of water.
- Add potatoes and all spices.
- Bring to a boil and cook 5 minutes.
- Add sausage and boil for 5 minutes.
- Add corn and boil 5 minutes.
- Check all ingredients for doneness.
- Add shrimp and boil until shells begin to separate from the shrimp.
- Turn off heat and let stand for a few minutes.

Mrs. Tom (Dottie) Pharr, Bennettsville, SC

Oyster Pie

This dish was served by the Junior Charity League of Marlboro County members at the Doctor's Dinner for many years.

Cooking time: 30 minutes   **Oven temperature: 350**

1/2 pound saltine crackers	milk
1 pint oysters	Worcestershire sauce
butter	salt and pepper

- Grease casserole dish with butter.
- Cover bottom of dish with cracker crumbs.
- Dot with butter.
- Then add a layer of oysters.
- Sprinkle with salt and pepper and Worcestershire.
- Repeat with crumbs, oysters, etc.
- Top with crumbs.
- Pour milk over this so that the milk reaches the top of the
- crumbs.
- Bake.

Junior Charity League of Marlboro County, Bennettsville, SC

M.M.'s Oyster Pie

Serves: 10   **Preparation time: 15 minutes**
Cooking time: 50 minutes   **Oven temperature: 350**

1 1/2	pints standard oysters	1	teaspoon Worcestershire sauce
2	cups milk	1/2	teaspoon salt
2	eggs, beaten	1/4	teaspoon pepper
1	8 ounce box oyster crackers or saltine crackers	3	tablespoons margarine

- Break enough crackers in a 2 quart casserole to cover the bottom of the dish.
- Place some of the oysters (about one-third) on top of saltines.
- Dot with margarine.
- Repeat layers of crackers, oysters, and margarine until there are three layers.
- Crumble saltines on top of casserole.
- Mix together beaten eggs, milk, Worcestershire sauce, salt, and pepper.
- Pour over casserole mixture, being sure milk mixture covers casserole contents.
- Dot with margarine.
- Bake.

Miss Marie Mackey, Bennettsville, SC

Salmon Croquettes

Serves: 6
Cooking time: 20 - 30 minutes

Preparation time: 30 minutes

1	16 ounce can salmon, retain juice
1/4	pound cracker crumbs
2	eggs
1	stalk celery, finely chopped
1	onion, finely chopped
2	heaping tablespoons mayonnaise or salad dressing
	cornmeal
	oil or bacon grease

- Mix first 6 ingredients together.
- Put some cornmeal in palm of hand.
- Spoon into the meal a tablespoon of the salmon mixture.
- Form an egg - shaped croquette, well coated with meal.
- Repeat until all the croquettes are formed.
- Brown very slowly on all sides in oil or bacon grease.

Mrs. Richard (Mary Sue) Burnette, Bennettsville, SC

Seafood Casserole

This recipe is flexible as to amounts. I vary the quantity of shrimp and crab according to the amount I have and the number I want to serve. A little extra rice and vegetable/tomato juice may be added to "stretch" it.

Serves: 8
Cooking time: 30 minutes
Prepare ahead

Preparation time: 30 minutes
Oven temperature: 350
Freezes well

1	cup celery, chopped	2	cups rice, cooked
1	cup vegetable/tomato juice	1/2	cup green pepper (chopped)
1	cup mayonnaise		salt and pepper to taste
1	cup (or one can) crab meat	1	cup unseasoned herbed stuffing mix
2	cups shrimp, cooked		almonds (optional)

- Mix all ingredients, except stuffing mix, in large bowl.
- Place in 2 quart buttered baking dish.
- Top with stuffing mix crumbs that have been mixed with a tablespoon of melted butter, top with almonds (if desired).
- Bake.

Mrs. William A. (Mary Hope) Rogers, Bennettsville, SC

Delicious Seafood Casserole

Cooking time: 30 minutes   **Oven temperature:** 350

1/2 green pepper, chopped	1 teaspoon Worcestershire sauce
1 onion, chopped	1/2 teaspoon salt
1 cup celery, chopped	1/2 teaspoon pepper
1 6 1/2 ounce can crab or lobster meat	butter
1 pound shrimp, cooked and cut up	1 cup bread crumbs
1 cup mayonnaise	

- Combine all ingredients except crumbs, put in greased casserole.
- Crumbs can be mixed in or sprinkled on top.
- Dot top of casserole with butter.
- Bake.

Mrs. R. L. (Janie) McNiel, Hamer, SC

Creamed Shrimp

A good party or luncheon dish.
Serves: 6

6 English muffins or toast points	1 5 ounce can shrimp, drained and rinsed
1 10 3/4 ounce can cream of shrimp soup	1 cup frozen or canned peas and onions, cooked
1/3 cup milk	
1/4 teaspoon dillweed	

- Toast English muffins or bread for toast points.
- Combine soup, milk, and dillweed; heat over low heat until sauce simmers.
- Add shrimp, peas, and onions; heat thoroughly.
- Spread over muffins or toast points.

Mrs. Henry (Frances) Burroughs, Jr., Conway, SC

Easy Shrimp Casserole

Serves: 6
Cooking time: 50 minutes
Prepare ahead

Preparation time: 30 minutes
Oven temperature: 350

2 10³/₄ ounce cans mushroom soup
1 cup sour cream
¹/₂ cup onions, sliced
1 medium tomato, diced
1 cup extra sharp cheese

1 8 ounce package medium egg noodles, cooked
1+ pounds raw shrimp, peeled and deveined

- Preheat oven.
- Mix all ingredients.
- Place in a 9 X 12 casserole.
- Cook 40 minutes covered and 10 minutes uncovered.

Mrs. Benjamin F. (Sara Jane) Alston, Bennettsville, SC

Garides Tourkolimano (Greek Shrimp)

Delicious and spicy!
Serves: 4
Cooking time: 15-20 minutes

Preparation time: 20 minutes

2 pounds large raw shrimp, peeled and deveined
¹/₂ cup lemon juice
¹/₂ cup butter, whipped
1 clove garlic, minced
1 cup green onion tops, chopped

3 large tomatoes, peeled and cut into wedges
1 teaspoon oregano
salt and pepper to taste
¹/₂ pound feta cheese, crumbled
³/₄ cup cream sherry

- Sprinkle shrimp with lemon juice; set aside.
- Melt butter in large skillet.
- Sauté garlic, green onion tops, and tomato wedges.
- Add shrimp; season with oregano, salt, and pepper to taste.
- Check shrimp frequently and sauté until pink.
- Add feta cheese and sherry.
- Bring to a boil and cook 3-4 minutes.
- Serve over rice.

Mrs. Warren (Kelly) McAlpine, Hickory, NC

Junior Charity League of Marlboro County, Inc.

Shrimp and Rice Casserole

A wonderful dish for dinner parties!

Preparation time: 1 hour
Oven temperature: 325
Freezes well

Cooking time: 40 minutes
Prepare ahead

2	pounds shrimp	3	cups cooked rice
1/2	onion, chopped	1/2	cup sour cream
1/2	tablespoon lemon juice	4	ounces water chestnuts
1	dash garlic salt	1 1/2	10 3/4 ounce cans cream of
	salt and pepper to taste		mushroom soup
1 1/2	cups cheddar cheese		

- Cook shrimp for 2 minutes, then peel.
- Cook onion with oil about 3 to 5 minutes.
- Add lemon juice and seasonings.
- Add cream of mushroom soup.
- Fold rice, shrimp, and 1/2 cup of cheese in sauce.
- Add sour cream and water chestnuts.
- Place in greased dish and put remaining cheese on top.
- Bake.

Mrs. Mark (Melissa) Joye, Mt. Pleasant, SC

Easy Shrimp Creole

Serves: 4
Cooking time: 15 minutes

Preparation time: 30 minutes

2	pounds shrimp, medium-sized, fresh preferably	2	cloves minced garlic
1	medium green pepper, seeded and chopped	2	tablespoons olive oil
1	medium red pepper, seeded and chopped	2	14 1/2 ounce cans Cajun-style stewed tomatoes (undrained) garnish-chopped green onions

- Peel shrimp and devein if desired; set aside.
- Cook pepper and garlic in oil in large skillet over medium-high heat, stirring constantly, until peppers are tender.
- Add tomatoes; bring to a boil.
- Reduce heat and simmer 8 minutes.
- While tomatoes are simmering, bring 6 cups of water to a boil. Add shrimp and cook 3-5 minutes until shrimp turn pink.
- Drain well and rinse with cold water.
- Add the shrimp to the tomatoes; cook until thoroughly heated.
- Garnish if desired.
- Serve over rice.

Mrs. Charles Paul (Heather) Midgley, Bennettsville, SC

Creole Shrimp

Time for shelling/cleaning shrimp not included in preparation time.

Serves: 4
Cooking time: 20 - 30 minutes
Freezes well (if exclude rice)

Preparation time: 30 minutes
Prepare ahead

3	slices bacon	1	pound boiled shrimp, shelled
1/4	cup onion, chopped	1	cup rice, cooked
1/2	bell pepper, chopped		can use uncooked shrimp (add to
2	cups stewed tomatoes		vegetable mixture about 10 minutes
1/4	cup chili sauce		after seasonings, etc.)
	salt, pepper, and Worcestershire		

- Fry bacon in large (or deep) frying pan.
- Remove bacon, add onion and bell pepper to sauté.
- Drain off most of the grease.
- Add tomatoes, chili sauce, and seasonings.
- Cook until thick; then add the shrimp and crumbled bacon long enough to heat through.
- Serve hot over rice.

Mrs. Henry (Frances) Burroughs, Jr., Conway, SC

Shrimp Scampi

Serves: 12
Oven temperature: 300

Cooking time: 5 minutes

1	pound shrimp, cooked with 1 teaspoon vinegar added to water for 3 minutes, shelled and devein.	2	tablespoons Parmesan cheese
		1	recipe garlic butter sauce
4	slices lemon, cut up, for garnish		

- Combine garlic sauce and Parmesan cheese in a saucepan.
- Heat until cheese melts.
- Place shrimp in baking dish and pour sauce over them.
- Bake.

Garlic Butter Sauce:

1/2	cup butter	1/4	teaspoon minced chives
4	cloves garlic put through garlic press		

- Combine all ingredients and cook one minute.

The late Mrs. Charles R. (Mildred) May, Jr., Bennettsville, SC

Entrees

Junior Charity League of Marlboro County, Inc.

Breakfast Casserole

Excellent when served with fresh fruit.

Serves: 6 - 8
Cooking time: 45 minutes
Prepare ahead

Preparation time: 20 minutes
Oven temperature: 350

4	slices of bread	2	cups milk
1	pound sausage, cooked and drained	1	teaspoon dry mustard
1	cup sharp cheese, grated		salt and pepper
6	eggs, beaten		

- Cut 2 slices of bread into small cubes.
- Layer bread cubes in bottom of 9 x 13 casserole.
- Layer half of cooked sausage over bread.
- Layer half of cheese.
- Repeat with remaining ingredients.
- Mix eggs, milk, and mustard.
- Pour over top.
- Refrigerate overnight.
- Cook uncovered.

Mrs. Donald (Marty) Rankin, Bennettsville, SC

Cheese-Sausage Breakfast Casserole

Serves: 10 - 12
Cooking time: 45 minutes
Prepare ahead

Preparation time: 15 minutes
Oven temperature: 350

1	pound sausage	1	teaspoon salt
1	cup cheddar cheese, grated	$^1/_2$	teaspoon pepper
2	cups milk	2	slices torn bread
6	eggs, beaten		

- Cook and drain sausage.
- Mix all ingredients together.
- Pour into greased 9 x 12 baking dish.
- Refrigerate overnight.
- Bake.

Mrs. Hubert (Christi) Meggs, Jr., Bennettsville, SC

Sausage and Egg Casserole

Serves: 4 - 6
Oven temperature: 350
Freezes well

Cooking time: 30 - 45 minutes
Prepare ahead

¹/₂	pound mild sausage
¹/₂	pound hot sausage
¹/₂	pound sharp cheddar cheese, grated
6	slices of bread

4	eggs
2	cups of milk
1	teaspoon salt
¹/₂	teaspoon Worcestershire sauce

- Cook sausage until done.
- Drain.
- Crumble bread in the bottom of a casserole dish.
- Sprinkle sausage over bread.
- Add cheese on top.
- Mix eggs, milk, salt, and Worcestershire sauce.
- Pour over the sausage and cheese.
- Refrigerate overnight or for at least 1 hour.
- Bake.

Mrs. Jim (Jennie) Weatherly, Bennettsville, SC

Stew Beef

Serves: 6
Oven temperature: 300
Freezes well

Preparation time: 15 minutes
Cooking time: 3 hours

1	pound stew beef
1	tablespoon canola oil
1	medium onion, sliced
3	small carrots, sliced

1	cup celery, chopped
1	10³/₄ ounce can beef broth
¹/₂	cup Burgundy wine

- Brown beef on top of stove in oil. Place beef in casserole and add onion, carrots, celery, broth, and wine.
- Bake.

Mrs. Harvey (Barbara) McCants, Laurinburg, NC

Junior Charity League of Marlboro County, Inc.

Jan's Old-Fashioned Beef Stew

Low Fat ! This stew can be cooked, refrigerated overnight and finished the next day.

Serves: 10   **Preparation time: 25 minutes**
Cooking time: 2 hours

2½   pounds lean beef top round, cut into   1   teaspoon thyme leaves
      1 inch cubes   ½   teaspoon ground black pepper
2   teaspoons canola oil   2   large carrots, peeled and cubed
½   cup dry sherry or red wine   1   large sweet potato, peeled and
1   large onion, chopped   cubed
½   teaspoon garlic puree   3   red skin potatoes, peeled and cubed
2   14 ½ ounce cans beef broth   2   tablespoons flour
2   cups water   2   tablespoons water
2   bay leaves

- In a large pot, set over medium-high heat, heat the canola oil.
- When hot, add the beef cubes and brown them on all sides. (You may have to do this in batches.)
- The meat may stick to the pan, but it will cook free later.
- When all the meat is brown, add the sherry or wine, stirring vigorously to loosen meat stuck to the pot.
- Add the onion, garlic, beef broth, 2 cups water, bay leaves, thyme leaves, and pepper.
- Bring the liquid to a simmer and cook over low heat for 1½ hours.
- Add the carrots, sweet potato, and red-skinned potatoes and cook for 30 minutes longer.
- About 10 minutes before serving, mix the flour and 2 tablespoons of water to form a paste.
- Stir this into the simmering stew and allow this to cook until gravy thickens.

Ms. Jan Weaver, Bennettsville, SC

No Peek Oven Stew (or No Peek Venison Stew)

This makes a delicious brown gravy!

Serves: 6
Oven temperature: 300
Prepare ahead

Preparation time: 5 - 10 minutes
Cooking time: 3 hours
Freezes well

2   pounds stew beef or venison stew
1   1.3 ounce envelope dry onion-
    mushroom soup
1   10³/₄ ounce can cream of mushroom
    soup

10³/₄ ounces water
6   carrots, chopped
1   large onion, chopped
2   potatoes, cut into large cubes

- Mix all ingredients in 2 quart casserole dish.
- Bake covered.

Mrs. Hubert (Christi) Meggs, Jr., Bennettsville, SC

Beef Stroganoff

Serves: 4-6
Cooking time: 30 minutes

Preparation time: 20 minutes
Prepare ahead

2   tablespoons butter
¹/₄ cup onion, minced
1¹/₂ pounds ground beef
1   10³/₄ can beef consommé
2¹/₂ tablespoons ketchup

2   tablespoons garlic, minced
1   teaspoon salt
3   tablespoons flour
1   16 ounce carton sour cream

- Melt butter in pan.
- Add onions.
- Cook until tender 4-6 minutes.
- Add beef and brown.
- Reserve ¹/₃ cup beef consommé.
- Add remaining consommé to beef and stir.
- Add ketchup, garlic, and salt, and stir.
- Cover and simmer 15 minutes
- Add remaining consommé and flour, then stir.
- Heat to bubbling, stirring constantly for one minute.
- Reduce heat to low.
- Stir in sour cream.
- Serve over noodles.

Mrs. Atley (Sherrye) Jackson, Bennettsville, SC

Entrees

Junior Charity League of Marlboro County, Inc.   **133**

Quick Stroganoff

Serves: 4 - 5
Cooking time: 15 minutes

Preparation time: 20 minutes
Prepare ahead

1	pound ground beef
1	onion, chopped
1	clove garlic, minced
1	10³/₄ ounce can cream of mushroom soup
1	8 ounce carton sour cream
2	tablespoons ketchup
2	teaspoons Worcestershire sauce

- Brown ground beef.
- Drain grease.
- Add 1 onion and 1 clove of garlic.
- Cook over medium heat for 5 minutes.
- Combine cream of mushroom soup, sour cream, ketchup, and Worcestershire sauce.
- Heat through and serve over rice or noodles.

Miss Susan Turpin, Bennettsville, SC

Hot Dog Chili

Cooking time: 45 minutes

Freezes well

- 1 pound ground chuck
- 1/3 cup onions, chopped
- 1/2 teaspoon salt
- 4 1/2 teaspoons mustard
- 3/4 tablespoon chili powder
- 1/2 cup ketchup
- 1 cup water

- Brown meat.
- Add other ingredients and mix well.
- Cook on low heat.
- Makes 1 pint.

Mrs. David K. (Cathy) Lynch, Bennettsville, SC

DuPre's Chow Mein

Serves: 8 - 10
Cooking time: 45 minutes

Preparation time: 30 minutes
Freezes well

oil to cover the bottom of skillet 1 inch
1-1½ pounds ground beef
1   16 ounce can bean sprouts
1   6 ounce can sliced bamboo shoots
1   6 ounce can sliced water chestnuts
2   medium carrots
1   7 ounce can sliced mushrooms

2   bell peppers
6   onions
8 - 10 stalks celery
⅓   cup soy sauce
¼   teaspoon marjoram
¼   teaspoon oregano
1   teaspoon blended herbs and spices
    Chinese noodles

- Place meat in 4 quart heavy pot and add enough water to cover.
- Bring to a boil. Drain meat in a colander.
- Replace meat in pot.
- Open all canned goods and drain.
- Pour into pot with meat and mix thoroughly - may need to add a can of water.
- Chop onions and slice celery (slicing celery at an angle in about ⅛th of an inch thick slices).
- Cut carrots and bell peppers into small match-size strips.
- Carrots, onions, celery, and peppers should equal 2 quarts.
- Mix together.
- Sauté onions, celery, carrots, and bell peppers until onions are transparent.
- Place in colander and drain.
- Mix with other ingredients.
- Add spices, ⅓ cup of soy sauce, and enough water to make slightly soupy (Do not add too much water).
- Cook slowly for 45 minutes.
- Use a little corn starch if you want to thicken.
- Serve over Chinese noodles.

Mr. J. DuPre Miller, Bennettsville, SC

Duncan's Deer Burgers

Serves: 4
Cooking time: 20 minutes
Prepare ahead

Preparation time: 15 minutes
Oven temperature: Grill
Freezes well

1 pound ground deer meat
1 1.3 ounce envelope beefy onion soup mix

$^1/_2$ teaspoon Worcestershire sauce
slices cheddar cheese
hamburger buns

- Mix dry soup and Worcestershire sauce with the meat.
- Form patties.
- Grill and top with slices of cheese.
- Serve on hamburger buns.

Mr. Duncan McInnis, Clio, SC

Firecracker Enchilada Casserole

Serves: 8 - 10 people
Cooking time: 1 hour
Prepare ahead: 1 day

Preparation time: 30 minutes
Oven temperature: 350
Freezes well

2 pounds ground beef
1 large onion, chopped
2 teaspoons chili powder
2-3 teaspoons ground cumin
1 15 ounce can pinto beans
9 frozen corn tortillas, thawed and cut in half
$1^1/_2$ cups shredded Monterrey Jack or Mozzarella cheese

$1^1/_2$ cups shredded cheddar or American cheese
1-2 10 ounce cans tomatoes and green chiles or $7^1/_2$ ounce can tomatoes and jalapeno peppers
1 $10^3/_4$ ounce cream of mushroom soup, plus a little water

- Cook ground beef and onions in large skillet until meat is brown; drain.
- Add chili powder, cumin, and mix well.
- Cook on low heat for 10 minutes.
- Spoon half of meat mixture into 13 x 9 x 2 baking dish.
- Layer half beans, half tortillas, half cheese and pour half of tomato liquid over cheese.
- Chop tomatoes and chiles and put half over cheese.
- Layer again ending with soup over all.
- Cover and refrigerate overnight.
- Bake uncovered.

Mrs. Willliam (Anne) Caudill, Laurinburg, NC

Entrees

136   Carolina Cuisine: Nothin' Could Be Finer

Ground Beef Casserole

Serves: 6 - 8
Oven temperature: 350

Cooking time: 20 - 25 minutes

1	pound ground chuck	1	cup sour cream
1/2	stick of butter	1	cup cottage cheese
1	6 ounce can tomato sauce	1	cup spring onions, chopped
8	ounces 1/4 inch egg noodles	1 1/2	cups grated cheese

- Brown meat in butter; add tomato sauce and cook about 10 minutes.
- Cook noodles in salted water. Drain.
- Mix sour cream, cottage cheese, and spring onions with cooked noodles.
- Grease casserole dish with butter.
- In dish layer noodle mix, hamburger and top with grated cheese.
- Bake uncovered until mixture bubbles.

Miss Peggy Beaty, Bennettsville, SC

Hamburger Pie

Serves: 8 (four from each pie shell)
Cooking time: 50 minutes
Freezes well

Preparation time: 30 minutes
Oven temperature: 375

1	pound ground beef	1/4	teaspoon garlic salt
1	10 ounce package frozen chopped broccoli	1	egg, well beaten
3	ounces cream cheese, diced	1 1/4	cups milk
2	tablespoons all-purpose flour	1	small onion, chopped
1	teaspoon salt	1	cup Monterey Jack cheese, shredded
		2	9 inch frozen pie shells

- Brown meat and onion, stir in flour and salts, stir in milk and cream cheese.
- Cook until smooth. Stir in egg a little at a time.
- Stir in broccoli.
- Put in two uncooked pie shells.
- Top with cheese.
- Bake.

Mrs. Douglas (Debbie) Jennings, Jr., Bennettsville, SC

Junior Charity League of Marlboro County, Inc.

How to cook a ham

Oven temperature: 325
- Select either a whole or half ham.
- Wrap in aluminum foil.
- Bake ham 20 minutes per pound.

Mrs. R. L. (Janie) McNiel, Hamer, SC

Hash

Serves: 6
Cooking time: 20 minutes
Prepare ahead

Preparation time: 10 minutes
Oven temperature: 350

1½ pounds beef tips
1 10¾ ounce can cream of mushroom soup

1 large onion, chopped
10-12 canned biscuits

- Cook onion with beef tips in enough water to cover meat.
- Shred or cut cooked meat into small pieces.
- Add the mushroom soup and put mixture in baking dish.
- If contents are too soupy, add bits of bread to take up moisture.
- Layer top of dish with canned biscuits. (biscuits can be separated into smaller layer of dough).

Mrs. N. J. (Bernice) Broomfield, Bennettsville, SC

Carolina Cuisine: Nothin' Could Be Finer

Grandma's Famous Lasagna

This freezes well! Just put together and freeze before baking.

Serves: 8

Cooking time: 45 minutes

Preparation time: 1 3/4 - 2 hours

Oven temperature: 350

2-3 tablespoons olive oil
1 medium onion, chopped
2 cloves garlic, minced
1$\frac{1}{4}$ pounds ground chuck
1 28 ounce can tomatoes
1 6 ounce can tomato paste
2 teaspoons salt
$\frac{1}{8}$ teaspoon cayenne pepper
1 teaspoon sugar
pinch of basil

1 bay leaf
2 cups water
1 8 ounce package lasagna noodles
2 tablespoons salt
1 tablespoon olive oil
1 16 ounce carton cottage cheese
1 8 ounce package mozzarella cheese, sliced
$\frac{1}{2}$ cup Parmesan cheese

- Make meat sauce: Brown onion and garlic in olive oil; add ground chuck and cook until browned, stirring often.
- Add next 8 ingredients, cutting up tomatoes and mixing well.
- Simmer uncovered about 1$\frac{1}{2}$ hours, stirring occasionally.
- While meat sauce is cooking, cook lasagna noodles in boiling salted water until tender, stirring frequently.
- Drain and toss with 1 tablespoon olive oil.
- Grease a 9 x 13 baking dish and arrange the ingredients in the following order: cooked noodles, cottage cheese, mozzarella cheese, meat sauce and Parmesan cheese, making 2 layers of each.
- Bake.

Mrs. John I. (Carolyn) Rogers, III, Bennettsville, SC

Junior Charity League of Marlboro County, Inc.

Low-Sodium Lasagna

Good with a tossed salad and fruit for dessert.

Serves: 6
Cooking time: 30 minutes
Prepare ahead

Preparation time: 45 minutes
Oven temperature: 350

Sauce:

1/2	pound ground round	1	tablespoon Parmesan or Romano cheese, grated
1	small onion, chopped		
1	16 ounce jar spaghetti sauce, no salt added	1	8 ounce package Mozzarella cheese, shredded
1	8 ounce can tomato sauce, no salt added	8	ounces cottage cheese
		1/2	teaspoon Italian seasoning
1/2	teaspoon garlic powder	1	egg
1/2	teaspoon Italian seasoning	6	lasagna noodles

- Brown ground meat and chopped onion in large skillet until meat is brown.
- Add spaghetti sauce, tomato sauce, garlic powder, Italian seasoning, Parmesan cheese.
- Cook until thick approximately 30 minutes. Meanwhile cook pasta as directed on package.
- Mix cottage cheese, Italian seasoning and egg together and set aside.
- Put several spoonfuls of sauce in bottom of baking dish. Add layers of noodles, mozzarella cheese, spaghetti sauce, and noodles topped with all of the cottage cheese mixture.
- Then add noodles, mozzarella cheese, and sauce ending with Mozzarella cheese.
- Bake in oven until bubbly.
- Serve with grated cheese.

Mrs. John T. (Margaret) Geisel, Bennettsville, SC

Elaine's London Broil

Easy and Good!

Serves: 2 - 4
Cooking time: 15 minutes
Freezes well

Preparation time: 8 minutes
Oven temperature: Broil

2	pounds flank steak	8	tablespoons soy sauce
	Marinade:	1	teaspoon garlic salt
2	tablespoons vegetable oil	1	teaspoon oregano
2	tablespoons ketchup	3/4 -1	teaspoon pepper

- Prepare marinade.
- Pour over meat and let sit for 30 to 45 minutes.
- Broil in oven 7 minutes on each side and slice diagonally to serve.

Mrs. Duncan (Cindi) McInnis, Clio, SC

Carolina Cuisine: Nothin' Could Be Finer

Baked Meatballs in Mushroom Sauce

Serves: 8
Oven temperature: 325

Cooking time: 1½ - 1¾ hours

1 pound ground beef	½ cup hot milk
1 medium onion, chopped	1 10¾ ounce cream of mushroom
½ cup rice, uncooked	soup
1 egg, beaten	1 cup water
1½ teaspoons salt	½ teaspoon pepper
¼ teaspoon pepper	¼ teaspoon salt
1 cup bread crumbs	½ teaspoon Worcestershire sauce

- Mix first 8 ingredients.
- Make into small meatballs and place in a casserole dish.
- Mix last ingredients together and pour over meatballs.
- Bake.

Mrs. Merritt (Hazel) King, Jr., McColl, SC

Ann Landers' Meat Loaf

Always does a quick disappearing act!

Serves: 8
Cooking time: 1 hour
Prepare ahead

Preparation time: 15 minutes
Oven temperature: 350
Freeze well

2 pounds ground beef	½ cup warm water
2 eggs, beaten	1 1.3 ounce package dry onion soup
1½ cups bread crumbs	mix
¾ cup ketchup	3 strips bacon
1 teaspoon seasoned salt	1 8 ounce can tomato sauce

- Mix first seven ingredients and place in a greased loaf pan.
- Cover with bacon and tomato sauce.
- Bake.

Ms. Dempcy Rowe, Florence, SC

Marlboro Meat Loaf

Serves: 6
Cooking time: 50 minutes
Prepare ahead

Preparation time: 20 minutes
Oven temperature: 350
Freezes well

2 eggs
$^3/_4$ cup milk
$^1/_2$ cup dry bread crumbs
$^1/_4$ cup onion, finely chopped
2 tablespoons snipped parsley
1 teaspoon salt

$^1/_2$ teaspoon sage
$^1/_8$ teaspoon pepper
$1^1/_2$ pounds ground beef
$^1/_2$ cup ketchup
2 tablespoons brown sugar
1 teaspoon dry mustard

- Combine eggs and milk.
- Stir in crumbs, onion, parsley, salt, sage, and pepper.
- Add beef; mix well.
- Pat into a $5^1/_2$ cup ring mold; unmold and place in a shallow baking pan.
- Bake in a 350 degree oven for 50 minutes.
- Spoon off excess fat.
- Combine ketchup, sugar and mustard.
- Spread over meat.
- Return to oven for 10 minutes.

Mrs. Curt (Deanne) Hinson, Bennettsville, SC

Extra Special Meat Loaf

Serves: 6 - 8
Cooking time: $1^1/_4$ - $1^1/_2$ hours

Preparation time: 15 minutes
Oven temperature: 350

$1^1/_2$ pounds extra lean ground beef
1 cup herb-seasoned stuffing
1 cup tomato sauce

$^1/_2$ cup onion, chopped
$^1/_2$ cup green pepper, chopped
1 egg

- Preheat oven to 350 .
- Combine all ingredients.
- Mix thoroughly.
- Shape into loaf.
- Place in baking pan.
- Bake uncovered.

Miss Joye Breeden, Bennettsville, SC

Entrees

142 Carolina Cuisine: Nothin' Could Be Finer

Dutch Meat Loaf

Tastes great!
Serves: 6 generously
Cooking time: 1 hour 15 minutes
Prepare ahead

Preparation time: 25 minutes
Oven temperature: 350
Freezes well

1 1/2 pounds lean ground beef
1   cup fresh bread crumbs
1   medium onion, chopped
1   8 ounce can tomato sauce
1   egg, beaten

1   teaspoon salt
1/4   teaspoon pepper
2   tablespoons brown sugar, packed
2   tablespoons prepared mustard
1   tablespoon vinegar

- In medium sized bowl lightly mix beef, bread crumbs, onion, 1/2 can tomato sauce, egg, salt and pepper.
- Shape into loaf in shallow baking pan.
- Combine remaining tomato sauce with rest of ingredients.
- Pour over loaf.
- Bake.

Mrs. Willadean W. Flowers, Henderson, NC

Sweet and Sour Meat Loaf

This recipe has been a favorite with my family. It was given to me by a dear friend, the late Mary Rose Berry. She was a past president of the Junior Charity League, and an active member at the time of her death in 1967.

Serves: 8
Cooking time: 1 1/2 hours
Prepare ahead

Preparation time: 20 minutes
Oven temperature: 350
Freezes well

1 1/2 pounds ground beef
1   egg, beaten
1 1/2 teaspoons salt
1 1/2 cups bread crumbs
1   medium onion, chopped
1/4   teaspoon pepper
1   3 ounce can tomato paste

Sauce:
1   3 ounce can tomato paste
1   can water
2   tablespoons brown sugar
2   tablespoons prepared mustard
2   tablespoons vinegar

- Combine ingredients and mix lightly to form loaf.
- Place in shallow pan.
- Flatten the top to retain sauce during baking.
- Combine sauce ingredients and blend well.
- Pour half over meat loaf.
- Baste with remaining half the last 30 minutes of baking.

Mrs. James M. (Frances) Townsend , Bennettsville, SC

Junior Charity League of Marlboro County, Inc.

Sicilian Meat Roll

Serves: 6
Cooking time: 1 hour 15 minutes

Preparation time: 15 minutes
Oven temperature: 350

1   egg, beaten
1   slice bread, toasted and crumbled
¹/₄ cup tomato juice
1   tablespoon parsley
¹/₄ teaspoon oregano
¹/₄ teaspoon salt

¹/₄ teaspoon pepper
¹/₂ clove garlic, minced
1   pound lean ground beef
4   thin slices boiled ham
3   ounces mozzarella cheese, shredded
     or sliced

- Combine egg, crumbs, tomato juice, parsley, oregano, salt, pepper, and garlic.
- Stir into ground beef and mix well.
- Pat mixture into a 8 x 10 rectangle on wax paper.
- Arrange ham on top of meat mixture leaving small 2 inch margin around edges.
- Sprinkle shredded cheese (or use slices) over ham.
- Roll up meat and seal edges (like a jelly roll).
- Place in pan with seam side down.
- Bake.

Mrs. Henry (Gerry) Capps, Bennettsville, SC

Tasty Mexican Chicken Casserole

Men love this!
Serves: 6-8
Cooking time: 30 minutes

Preparation time: 45 minutes
Oven temperature: 350

1   15 ounce package 4-5 inch flour
     tortillas
6   chicken breasts, cooked
1   10 ounce can tomatoes and peppers

1   10³/₄ ounce can cream of mushroom
     soup
1   10³/₄ ounce can chicken broth
8   ounces sour cream
1¹/₂ cups sharp Cheddar cheese, grated

- Preheat oven.
- Grease 9 x 13 casserole dish and place tortillas folded in quarters to form triangles in bottom of casserole.
- Remove meat from chicken breasts and place on top of tortillas.
- Mix tomatoes, soup, and chicken broth.
- Layer on top of chicken.
- Place tortillas folded in triangles and layer covering casserole.
- Spread sour cream over tortillas.
- Sprinkle with cheese.
- Bake until bubbly.

Miss Ivy L. Pope, Dillon, SC

Mexican Casserole

Good for a crowd!

Serves: 6
Oven temperature: 350
Freezes well

Cooking time: 35 minutes
Prepare ahead

1½ pounds ground beef
1   16 ounce can tomatoes, drained and chopped
1   large onion, chopped
½   bell pepper, chopped
1   1½ ounce package taco seasoning mix
10-12 corn tortillas
1   14 ounce can chicken broth or chicken bouillon dissolved in water

1   10¾ ounce can cream of chicken soup
1   14½ ounce can garbanzo beans (if unavailable you can substitute pinto beans)
1   teaspoon seasoned salt
1   teaspoon parsley flakes
½   teaspoon oregano
1½ teaspoons cumin
1   teaspoon chili powder
1   8 ounce cheddar cheese, grated

- Cook ground beef in skillet until meat is done.
- Set aside and sauté bell pepper and onion.
- Combine with meat and add tomatoes and seasoning mix.
- Soak tortillas in warm chicken broth until soft. They won't soften unless the broth is warm.
- Coat 9 x 13 casserole dish with non-stick cooking spray.
- Add cream of chicken soup and garbanzo beans to meat mixture.
- Line tortillas in bottom of casserole.
- Add remaining seasonings to meat mixture and pour over tortillas. Bake for 25 minutes. Add grated cheese and bake another 10 minutes or until cheese melts. (Freezes well. If you add the cheese before freezing, bake with foil over it for the first 15 - 20 minutes to keep cheese from getting tough and hard).

Mrs. Steve (Beverly) Thompson, Bennettsville, SC

Jennie's Mexican Casserole

Can use taco chips instead of flour tortillas. Line dish with chips - can also add throughout the mixture.

Serves: 6 - 10

Cooking time: 30 minutes

Oven temperature: 350

1    $10^3/4$ ounce cream of chicken soup
1    $10^3/4$ ounce cream of mushroom soup (optional)
1   8 ounce jar taco sauce
1   10 ounce can enchilada sauce (optional)

5-10 flour tortillas
$1/2$-1 pound cheddar cheese, grated
1   pound ground beef
2   small onions, chopped
$1/2$ 4 ounce can green chile peppers, drained and chopped (optional)

- Cook meat and onions together, stirring often.
- Drain.
- Add all other ingredients except tortillas and cheese.
- Grease a 9 x 13 dish.
- Cut tortillas into fourths.
- Line dish with tortillas.
- Add layer of meat mixture and a layer of cheese.
- Repeat layering until ingredients are gone.
- Bake.

Mrs. Jim (Jennie) Weatherly, Bennettsville, SC

Easy Stuffed Peppers

Serves: 4

Cooking time: 30 minutes

Prepare ahead

Preparation time: 45 minutes

Oven temperature: 350

Freezes well

4   large green bell peppers
12   ounces ground beef
1   cup onions, finely chopped
1   teaspoon dried oregano

$1^1/2$ cups rice, cooked
$1/4$ cup Parmesan cheese, grated
$1/4$ cup fat-free egg substitute
1   cup tomato sauce

- Cut the peppers in half lengthwise.
- Remove and discard the stems and seeds.
- Blanch the peppers in boiling water for 3 minutes.
- Drain and set aside.
- Brown beef and onions in a non-stick frying pan.
- Add oregano.
- Stir in rice, Parmesan cheese, egg, and $1/2$ cup tomato sauce.
- Divide the mixture among the pepper halves.
- Arrange in a baking dish, top with the remaining tomato sauce, and cover with foil.
- Bake.

Mrs. J. T. (Betty) Martin, Jr., Bennettsville, SC

Carolina Cuisine: Nothin' Could Be Finer

Pork Chop and Rice Casserole

Preparation time: 25 minutes
Oven temperature: 350

Cooking time: 1 hour

1   cup rice
4-6 pork chops
1   10³/₄ ounce can beef consommé
     soup

1   10³/₄ ounce can onion soup

- Pour rice in greased casserole dish.
- Brown pork chops on each side (not completely done but brown).
- Place chops on rice.
- Cover rice and chops with soups.
- Cover dish and bake.

Mrs. Martin (Gladys) Kinard, Bennettsville, SC

Grilled Pork Tenderloin

Wonderful when served with mint jelly.
Serves: 6
Prepare ahead

Preparation time: 24 hours

1   pork tenderloin
     string
Marinade:
¹/₂ cup light brown sugar
¹/₂ cup Dijon mustard

¹/₄ cup bourbon
¹/₄ cup soy sauce
1   clove garlic, minced
2   teaspoons Worcestershire sauce
     salt and pepper to taste

- Tie tenderloin with string every 1 - 1¹/₂ inches apart.
- Mix all marinade ingredients and pour over tenderloin in reclosable bag.
- Refrigerate for 24 hours.
- Grill for 45 - 50 minutes or until done with cover closed.
- Rotate regularly.
- Remove string, slice, and serve.

Mrs. David K. (Cathy) Lynch, Bennettsville, SC

Junior Charity League of Marlboro County, Inc.

How to cook a Roast

Preparation time: 20 minutes
Prepare ahead

Cooking time: 2 - 3 hours
Freezes well

	rump roast or round roast	onion powder
3	tablespoons canola oil or margarine	sugar
	salt	water
	pepper	
	celery salt	

- Rub salt, pepper, celery salt, onion powder or onion on beef.
- Brown meat in pan on top of stove with oil or margarine.
- Turn roast and brown on all sides.
- Rub several fingers of sugar into roast.
- Cook in heavy pan on top of stove.
- Add water to pan to avoid burning beef.
- Cook slowly.
- Drain excess fat before serving.

The late Mrs. K. B. (Bess) Hodges, Bennettsville, SC

"Eye of Round" Roast

Serve hot the first day; makes good sandwiches when cold.

Cooking time: 2 hours
Prepare ahead

Oven temperature: 350
Freezes well

1	4 or 5 pound beef roast	$1/2$	teaspoon garlic powder
$1/4$	cup coarsely ground black pepper	1	teaspoon paprika
$1/2$	tablespoon ground cardamon	1	cup soy sauce
1	8 ounce can tomato paste	$3/4$	cup vinegar

- On a piece of waxed paper, mix pepper and cardamon together.
- Roll roast in it until coated on all sides and press in firmly.
- In a shallow baking dish, large enough to fit roast, mix tomato paste, garlic powder and paprika - gradually add soy sauce and vinegar - blend thoroughly.
- Marinate roast on all sides for at least 24 hours in refrigerator, turning occasionally.
- Remove from marinade and wrap in heavy foil with a little sauce.
- Bake. The marinade makes delicious gravy and can be used with other roasts.

Mrs. J. Maxwell (Martha) Gregg, Bennettsville, SC

Carolina Cuisine: Nothin' Could Be Finer

Standing Rib Roast

Preparation time: 5 minutes   **Oven temperature: Broil**

standing rib roast   pepper
salt

- Preheat broiler to 500 .
- Place in roaster uncovered after being rubbed with salt and pepper.
- To cook medium-medium rare, broil six (6) minutes per pound.
- Turn oven off and let sit in oven for two (2) hours. Do not open oven.
- For additional doneness, add one (1) minute per pound to cooking time.

Mrs. David K. (Cathy) Lynch, Bennettsville SC

Sausage Casserole

Serves: 4   **Preparation time: 20 minutes**
Cooking time: 1 hour   **Oven temperature: 350**
Prepare ahead   **Freezes well**

1	pound hot sausage	$^1/_2$	teaspoon salt
2	1.3 ounce envelopes chicken soup	3	stalks celery, chopped
1	cup rice, uncooked	1	large bell pepper, chopped
5	cups hot water	2	medium onions, chopped

- Brown sausage and drain well. Combine rice, chicken soup, and water.
- Cook 5 minutes in pot.
- Add pepper, celery, onions, and sausage.
- Pour into greased casserole dish and bake covered.

Mrs. James (Fannie) Chappelear, Bennettsville, SC

Junior Charity League of Marlboro County, Inc.

St. Paul's Casserole

Serves: 8
Oven temperature: 350
Prepare ahead

Preparation time: 20 Minutes
Cooking time: 1 hour
Freezes well

1 pound hot sausage	4^1/$_2$ cups water
^{1}/$_2$ pound mild sausage	1 stalk celery, chopped
^{1}/$_2$ cup rice, uncooked	1 bell pepper, chopped
2 1.3 ounce envelopes chicken noodle soup	1 onion, chopped

- Brown sausage and drain well.
- In a pan, boil rice, chicken noodle soup, and water for seven minutes. Add celery, bell pepper, and onion.
- Mix all ingredients.
- Bake covered.

Mrs. James (Nancy) Brogdon, Bennettsville, SC

Stuffed Shells

May use lowfat cheese and egg substitute for healthier meal.

Serves: 6 - 8
Oven temperature: 375
Prepare ahead

Preparation time: 40 minutes
Cooking time: 45 minutes
Freezes well

1 16 ounce box large pasta shells	1 egg
1 tablespoon olive oil	^{1}/$_2$ cup Parmesan cheese
1 small onion, chopped	1 teaspoon Italian seasoning
2-3 cloves garlic, minced	^{1}/$_4$ teaspoon ground nutmeg
1 10 ounce package frozen spinach, thawed and squeezed dry	1 28 ounce jar prepared spaghetti sauce (chunky garden style extra
15 ounces ricotta cheese	tomatoes and garlic)
1 cup provolone or mozzarella cheese, shredded	

- Cook shells according to package directions until not quite done. Drain and place on paper towels in single layer.
- Meanwhile, heat oil in large skillet.
- Sauté onion and garlic until onion is translucent.
- Add spinach and cook one minute.
- Remove from heat.
- Mix together in large bowl cheese, egg, Italian seasoning and nutmeg.
- Mix in spinach mixture. Stuff shells with mixture and place in single layer in 13 x 9 x 2 baking dish.
- Carefully pour spaghetti sauce over shells.
- Cover and bake.

Mrs. Brian (Dena) Kett, Huntington, WV

Newton Spaghetti Casserole

Serves: 8 - 10
Oven temperature: 350

Preparation time: 30 minutes
Cooking time: 30 - 40 minutes

1	pound lean ground beef	1	28 ounce jar or can of your favorite
1	8 ounce package spaghetti noodles		spaghetti sauce
1	egg	1	medium onion
1	tablespoon margarine	10	ounces mozzarella cheese,
1/4	cup Parmesan cheese		shredded
		1	3 ounce package pepperoni slices

- Brown ground beef and drain.
- Cook spaghetti noodles and drain.
- Finely chop onion.
- Layer bottom of 9 x 12 casserole with a mixture of spaghetti noodles, beaten egg, margarine, and Parmesan cheese.
- Mix sauce with chopped onion and ground beef and layer over noodle mixture.
- Sprinkle mozzarella cheese as next layer.
- Top with pepperoni slices placed in rows on top of casserole. Bake until bubbly.

Mrs. Larry (Mary K.) Newton, McColl, SC

Swiss-Ham Kabobs

Serves: 6
Cooking time: 4 minutes
Prepare ahead

Preparation time: 15 minutes
Oven temperature: Barbecue grill
Freezes well

1	20 ounce can unsweetened	1/4	teaspoon ground cloves
	pineapple chunks	1	pound fully-cooked ham
1/2	cup orange marmalade	1/2	pound Swiss cheese
1	tablespoon prepared mustard		

- Drain pineapple, reserving 2 tablespoons juice.
- Combine juice, marmalade, mustard, and cloves; mix well.
- Cut ham and cheese into 1 1/2 x 1/2 x 1/2 inch pieces.
- Thread ham, cheese, ham, then pineapple on 12 inch skewers. (Cheese must be between and touching two pieces of ham to prevent rapid melting.)
- Repeat procedure until all ingredients are used.
- Place kabobs 4 to 5 inches from grill coals.
- Brush with sauce; grill 3 to 4 minutes until cheese is partially melted and ham is lightly browned, turning and brushing frequently with sauce.

Mrs. Samuel (Adrienne) Thomas, III, Bennettsville, SC

Coleman's Barbecued Turkey Breast

Serves: 15
Prepare ahead

Oven temperature: 350

1	turkey breast	1	slice bacon
	celery tops		Barbecue sauce, to taste

- Place a few sprigs of celery tops and one slice of bacon on washed and salted turkey breast.
- Bake, covered tightly in heavy foil, for 25 minutes per pound.
- Turn off oven, leave turkey breast in oven for 1 hour.
- Let cool and pull meat off in finger sizes.
- Put meat in shallow dish, pour barbecue sauce over turkey pieces (just enough to cover).
- Let stand for 2 - 3 hours in refrigerator.
- May serve hot or cold with small party rolls.

Mrs. J. P. (Virginia) Hodges, Bennettsville, SC

Pledger's Favorite Barbecue Sauce

Often used with chicken.

Yields: 1 1/4 cups
Prepare ahead

Preparation time: 15 minutes

1	teaspoon cornstarch	1/4	cup brown sugar
1/4	teaspoon dry mustard	1/2	teaspoon onion salt
1/4	cup cider vinegar	1/2	teaspoon celery salt
1	cup ketchup		salt and pepper to taste

- Dissolve corn starch and mustard in vinegar.
- Add remaining ingredients.
- Cook, stirring constantly until thick on top of stove.

Mrs. J. P. (Virginia) Hodges, Bennettsville, SC

Billie's Barbecue Sauce

Preparation time: 15 minutes

Cooking time: 20 minutes

1/4	cup vinegar	1/2	stick margarine
1/2	cup water	1	medium onion, sliced
1	tablespoon prepared mustard	1	cup ketchup
2	tablespoons brown sugar	2	tablespoons Worcestershire sauce

- Mix first six ingredients in a pot.
- Simmer for 20 minutes.
- Add ketchup and Worcestershire sauce.
- Use over chicken or pork chops.

Mrs. Billie M. Beaty, Bennettsville, SC

Carolina Cuisine: Nothin' Could Be Finer

Drawing by: Margaret Singletary

Margaret Strong Singletary

"Santee Ducks"

Margaret Strong Singletary, a native of Williamsburg County, South Carolina, today enjoys retirement living on Lake Marion near Santee, South Carolina, which inspires her artwork. Mrs. Singletary began pursuing her desire to create art late in life with the assistance of Mary Anderson of Lake City, South Carolina, where she resided many years.

Mrs. Singletary also enjoys painting and creating ceramics as gifts for friends and family in addition to painting on canvas. She currently studies art at Shaw Air Force Base in Sumter, South Carolina.

A graduate of Flora McDonald College in Red Springs, North Carolina, with a degree in Elementary Education, Mrs. Singletary taught school in Lake City for 30 years. She and her husband, Jack, have four children, five grandchildren and five great-grandchildren.

Mrs. Hubert (Christi Singletary) Meggs, Jr., a granddaughter, is a current member of the Junior Charity League of Marlboro County, Inc.

Baked Asparagus Casserole

A great holiday dish!
Serves: 4
Cooking time: 20-25 minutes

Preparation time: 20 minutes
Oven temperature: 400

1   $10^3/_4$ ounce can condensed cream of
     chicken soup, undiluted
1   teaspoon prepared mustard
4   hard boiled eggs, sliced
1   16 ounce can asparagus spears,
     drained

$^1/_2$ cup almonds, chopped
1   2 ounce can pimento
$^3/_8$ cup bread crumbs
$^1/_4$ stick butter, melted

- Combine soup, mustard, almonds, and pimento.
- In 1-quart casserole, alternate layers of eggs, asparagus, and soup.
- Combine butter and crumbs; sprinkle over top.
- Bake.

Mrs. Mackie (Laurie) Norton, McColl, SC

Quick Asparagus Casserole

Can be cooked in microwave for 10 minutes.
Serves: 4
Cooking time: 20 - 25 minutes

Preparation time: 5 minutes
Oven temperature: 350

2   cups cheese crackers, crushed
1   cup Cheddar cheese, shredded
1   16 ounce can asparagus
2   tablespoons butter

2   tablespoons self-rising flour
1   cup milk
     salt and pepper to taste

- Cover bottom of baking dish with crackers, then layer cheese and asparagus.
- Make a mixture of white sauce using butter, flour, milk, salt, and pepper.
- Cook until thick, approximately 5-10 minutes.
- Pour over casserole and bake.

Mrs. John P. (Ruby) Driscoll, Bennettsville, SC

Sunday Asparagus Casserole

Serves: 6-8
Cooking time: 30 minutes

Preparation time: 5 minutes
Oven temperature: 350

1   sleeve buttered crackers, crushed
1   16 ounce can asparagus
1   10³/₄ can cream of mushroom soup

2   boiled eggs, cubed
     grated cheese

- Sprinkle layer of crackers on bottom of small baking dish.
- Put a layer of asparagus, layer cubed eggs, and a layer of mushroom soup that has been diluted with water from can of asparagus.
- Repeat layers.
- Put cracker crumbs and grated cheese on top.
- Bake.

Mrs. Glenn (Janice) Allen, Bennettsville, SC

Marinated Asparagus

Excellent and easy!
Serves: 4
Cooking time: 3 - 4 minutes

Preparation time: 10 minutes
Prepare ahead

¹/₃   cup red wine vinegar
¹/₄   cup water
¹/₄   cup sugar
¹/₄   teaspoon salt

3   whole cloves
¹/₂   teaspoon celery seed
1   cinnamon stick
1   16 ounce can asparagus spears

- Put all ingredients, except asparagus, in a small, pint size pan.
- Stir once to mix.
- Boil gently for 3-4 minutes.
- Without straining, pour over spears.
- Let sit 5 or 6 hours or overnight in the refrigerator.

Mrs. Charles (Susan) Midgley, Bennettsville, SC
Mrs. William. A. (Mary Hope) Rogers, Bennettsville, SC

Baked Beans

Serves: 16 - 18
Cooking time: 2 - 3 minutes
Prepare ahead

Preparation time: 35 minutes
Oven temperature: 250
Freezes well

1   pound mild sausage
1   medium onion
3   28 ounce cans baked beans
4   tablespoons mustard

4   tablespoons ketchup
4   tablespoons brown sugar
8   strips of bacon

- Cook the sausage and onion in a frying pan until done.
- Drain well and put in the bottom of a large baking dish.
- Put the beans on top of the sausage.
- Add mustard, ketchup, and brown sugar.
- Mix well.
- Cut bacon strips into thirds and layer over beans.
- Cook uncovered.

Mrs. Jack (Margaret) Corry, Bennettsville, SC

Patio Beans

Very good.
Serves: 8
Cooking time: 60 minutes

Preparation time: 25 minutes
Oven temperature: 350

5   strips of bacon
3   medium onions, chopped
1   1 pound can pork and beans
1   1 pound can kidney beans
1   8$^1/_2$ ounce can butter beans
$^1/_2$ teaspoon garlic powder

1   teaspoon dry mustard
$^1/_2$ teaspoon salt
$^1/_4$ cup brown sugar, firmly packed
$^1/_4$ cup vinegar
$^1/_2$ cup ketchup
$^1/_2$ teaspoon black pepper

- Fry bacon until crisp, remove from pan.
- Sauté onions in bacon drippings.
- Combine all ingredients, except bacon, and place in 3 quart deep dish casserole.
- Cook uncovered for 45 minutes.
- Cover with bacon and cook 15 minutes.

Mrs. Kenneth (Nancy) Klug, Hickory, NC

Crock Pot Baked Beans

Serves: 6
Cooking time: 8 hours

Preparation time: 15 minutes
Prepare ahead

2	pounds ground beef
1	large onion
3	16 ounce cans pork and beans
1	12 ounce jar chili sauce
3	teaspoons dry mustard

3	teaspoons Worcestershire sauce
1	cup brown sugar
1	8 ounce can crushed pineapple, drained
6	strips of bacon, cooked and chopped

- Brown meat and onion until done.
- Drain and add other ingredients.
- Place in crock pot at medium heat.
- Stir occasionally.

Ms. Hope Weatherly, McColl, SC

Quick Dried Beans

Guaranteed to be the best and easiest dried beans ever eaten. Healthy nutrients are not lost in cooking process.

Serves: 10 - 12
Cooking time: 2 -2$^1/_2$ hours
Prepare ahead

Preparation time: 5 - 10 minutes
Oven temperature: 350

1	16 ounce package dried beans, any kind
$^1/_8$	teaspoon sugar

salt and pepper to taste
water, to cover
seasoning of your choice

- Wash beans and place in Dutch oven or covered casserole, not necessary to soak or fast boil.
- Add sugar, salt, pepper, and seasoning.
- Cover with water.
- Place in oven and cook.
- Check every 45 minutes and add more water as needed.
- Water will be absorbed and has to be continually added.

Mrs. Doug (Karen) Funderburk, Bennettsville, SC

Carolina Cuisine: Nothin' Could Be Finer

Best Casserole

Serves: 10 - 12
Oven temperature: 350

Cooking time: 30 minutes

- 1   16 ounce can French cut green beans
- 1/2 cup sour cream
- 1/2 cup celery, chopped
- 1/2 cup onion, chopped
- 1   11 ounce can shoepeg white whole corn
- 1/2 cup sharp cheese, shredded
- 1/2 cup green pepper
- salt, pepper, and Accent to taste
- 1   7 ounce box cheese crackers
- 1   stick butter, softened

- Combine ingredients except crackers and butter.
- Let stand in refrigerator.
- Make a topping of crackers and butter.
- Spread over the top of casserole mixture.
- Bake.

Mrs. Forrest (Betty Lou) Fowler, Bennettsville, SC

Broccoli Casserole

Cooking time: 20 minutes

Oven temperature: 350

- 2   10 ounce packages frozen broccoli spears
- 1/2 cup mayonnaise
- 1   10 3/4 ounce can cream of mushroom soup
- 1   medium onion, chopped
- 1/2 cup cheese, shredded
- 1/4 cup cracker crumbs

- Mix broccoli, mayonnaise, soup, and onion together.
- Pour into a casserole dish.
- Top with shredded cheese then cracker crumbs.
- Dot with margarine.
- Bake.

Ms. C. J. Jones, Bennettsville, SC

Junior Charity League of Marlboro County, Inc.

Broccoli Quiche

Great for luncheons when served with fresh fruit.

Serves: 3 - 4
Cooking time: 50 - 60 minutes

Preparation time: 15 minutes
Oven temperature: 350

1	10 ounce package frozen chopped broccoli	$^1/_8$	teaspoon pepper
8	ounces Swiss cheese, cubed	$^1/_2$	teaspoon salt
2	tablespoons all-purpose flour		dash of nutmeg
1	cup milk	1	9 inch uncooked pie shell
3	eggs, beaten		

- Cook broccoli and drain.
- Mix cubed cheese with flour.
- Beat together milk, eggs, pepper, salt, and nutmeg.
- Stir in broccoli and cheese.
- Pour into pie shell and bake.
- Let sit about 15 minutes before serving.

Mrs. John I. (Carolyn) Rogers, III, Bennettsville, SC

Broccoli and Ham Quiche

Serves: 6
Cooking time: 40 minutes
Prepare ahead

Preparation time: 20 minutes
Oven temperature: 400

1	9 inch deep pie shell at room temperature	1	cup half and half
1	bunch fresh broccoli	3	eggs, beaten
$^1/_4$	pound cooked ham, diced	1	teaspoon salt
$^1/_4$	pound Swiss cheese, grated	$^1/_2$	teaspoon dry mustard
		$^1/_2$	teaspoon cayenne pepper

- Preheat oven to 400.
- Bake pie shell for 5 minutes.
- Cook or steam broccoli until tender and drain.
- Layer broccoli, ham, and cheese in pie shell.
- Mix cream, eggs, salt, and mustard.
- Pour mixture over cheese and sprinkle with cayenne pepper.
- Bake to a golden brown.

Mrs. David K. (Cathy) Lynch, Bennettsville, SC

Broccoli and Mushroom Casserole

Serves: 6 - 8
Cooking time: 20 minutes
Prepare ahead

Preparation time: 15 minutes
Oven temperature: 375
Freezes well

1   20 ounce package frozen chopped broccoli
1   10³/₄ ounce can cream of mushroom soup
1   4 ounce can or jar mushroom slices

1   egg, beaten
1   tablespoon onion, finely chopped
4   ounces Cheddar cheese, grated
1¹/₂ cups crushed butter flavored crackers
2   tablespoons butter, melted

- Preheat oven.
- Cook broccoli and drain.
- Mix broccoli, soup, mushrooms, egg, onion, and cheese.
- Place in a buttered 2 quart casserole.
- Mix crackers and melted butter.
- Sprinkle on top of casserole.
- Bake.

Mrs. Daniel E. (Elisabeth) McNiel, Bennettsville, SC

Broccoli-Rice Casserole

Super for a crowd!
Serves: 12
Cooking time: 30 minutes
Prepare ahead

Preparation time: 30 minutes
Oven temperature: 350
Freezes well

1   medium onion, chopped
1   cup celery, chopped
2   tablespoons butter
3   cups rice, cooked
2   10 ounce packages frozen chopped broccoli, cooked and drained

1   10³/₄ ounce can cream of chicken, or cream of mushroom, soup
1   8 ounce jar processed cheese spread
    salt and pepper to taste

- In a large skillet, over medium heat, sauté onion and celery in butter for 3-5 minutes.
- Mix with other ingredients and put in a well greased 2 quart casserole.
- Bake.

Mrs. Billie M. Beaty, Bennettsville, SC

Junior Charity League of Marlboro County, Inc.

Broccoli-Squash Casserole

Serves: 6
Cooking time: 30 minutes
Prepare ahead

Preparation time: 30 minutes
Oven temperature: 350
Freezes well

2	10 ounce packages frozen broccoli spears
2	pounds yellow crookneck squash
1/2	cup green peppers, chopped
1/2	cup sweet red peppers, chopped
1	10 3/4 can reduced fat cream of mushroom soup

1 tablespoon reduced fat processed cheese sauce
2 cups reduced fat saltine cracker crumbs
margarine

- Place broken broccoli spears in 2 cups boiling water.
- Cut squash into 1/2 inch slices and add to broccoli.
- Bring to second boil.
- Reduce heat and cook for 8 minutes.
- Add chopped peppers and cook 3-5 more minutes, then pour into colander and drain.
- Chop mixture and place in casserole, after adding soup and cheese sauce.
- Top with crackers and dot with margarine.
- Bake.

Miss Joye Breeden, Bennettsville, SC

Broccoli Cheese Sauce

Better than plain melted cheese!
Yields: 1 cup
Cooking time: 8 minutes

Preparation time: 10 minutes

2 tablespoons butter
2 tablespoons flour
1/4 teaspoon salt

1 cup milk
3/4 cup sharp Cheddar cheese, shredded

- Place butter in a 2 cup glass measuring cup and microwave on until melted.
- Blend in flour and salt.
- Stir well and microwave on high 2 1/2 minutes.
- Stir well and add milk.
- Microwave on high 2 1/2 - 3 minutes, while stirring at 1 minute intervals.
- When thickened, add cheese and stir until melted.

Miss Susan Turpin, Bennettsville, SC

Carolina Cuisine: Nothin' Could Be Finer

Cabbage and Onion Stir-fry

Serves: 4-6
Cooking time: 10-12 minutes

Preparation time: 15 minutes
Prepare ahead

1	tablespoon vegetable oil	1	teaspoon salt
3	green onions, chopped	1	teaspoon pepper
1	medium size cabbage, chopped		

- Wash cabbage, cut into small pieces and let drain.
- Repeat steps with onion.
- Heat oil in large skillet over medium heat.
- Add cabbage, onion, salt, and pepper.
- Stir and cover for 10 to 12 minutes.
- Turn off heat and let stand for 5 minutes.

Mrs. Lucius (Ella) Miles, Bennettsville, SC

Carrots Lyonnaise

This can easily be prepared the day before.

Serves: 4 - 6
Cooking time: 15 - 18 minutes

Preparation time: 30 minutes
Prepare ahead

8	carrots, sliced	1	tablespoon parsley, chopped
3	tablespoons butter	1/2	teaspoon salt
1	green onion, chopped	1	teaspoon sugar
1/2	green pepper, chopped	1/8	teaspoon pepper

- Cook carrots until almost tender and drain.
- Melt butter in saucepan, add onion, green pepper, and parsley.
- Cook over low heat until soft.
- Add carrots to butter mixture.
- Add seasonings and cook 10 minutes more.

Mrs. Ray (June) Rogers, Bennettsville, SC

Vegetables

Junior Charity League of Marlboro County, Inc.   163

Cheese Fondue

Good side dish to serve with meat.

Serves: 6
Cooking time: 45 minutes

Preparation time: 12 minutes
Oven temperature: 350

6 slices stale bread	$^1/_4$ teaspoon salt
2 eggs, beaten	pinch of red pepper
1 cup milk	1 cup sharp cheese, grated

- Trim crust and slice bread into finger-sized slices.
- Arrange in a greased baking dish.
- Mix the other ingredients and pour over the bread.
- Set in a pan of water.
- Bake and serve immediately.

Mrs. Forrest (Betty Lou) Fowler, Bennettsville, SC

Copper Pennies

Award winning recipe!
Preparation time: 45 minutes

Prepare ahead

2 pounds carrots	salt
1 medium green bell pepper	pepper
3 medium onions	

Dressing:
1 $10^3/_4$ ounce can cream of tomato soup	$^3/_4$ cup vinegar
$^3/_4$ cup sugar	1 teaspoon prepared mustard
$^1/_2$ cup canola oil	1 teaspoon Worcestershire sauce

- Cook carrots until just tender. Peel and slice.
- Dice bell pepper or cut into slender strips.
- Peel onion, slice, and break apart into rings.
- Layer vegetables in large dish or jar, sprinkling each layer with salt and pepper.
- Mix dressing ingredients and pour over vegetables.
- Cover tightly and refrigerate.
- Let stand at least 12 hours before serving.
- Drain vegetables and serve as a side dish and use dressing for salad.

Mrs. E. LeRoy (Florence) Powell, Florence, SC

Carolina Cuisine: Nothin' Could Be Finer

Frozen Sweet Corn

Yields: 8 pints
Cooking time: 6 minutes

Preparation time: 30 minutes
Freezes well

8 cups corn	1 tablespoon salt
1 cup water	1/4 cup butter
1 tablespoon sugar	

- Combine ingredients and bring to a boil.
- Simmer.
- Let cool, and pack in freezer bags, and freeze.

Mrs. Ray (Lydia) Smith, Bennettsville, SC

Cranberry Apple Casserole

Perfect with turkey or roast beef.
Serves: 8
Cooking time: 1 hour

Preparation time: 30 minutes
Oven temperature: 350

3 cups tart apples, uncooked	1/2 cup margarine, melted
2 cups cranberries, uncooked	1/3 cup all-purpose flour
3/4 cup sugar	1/2 cup brown sugar
1 cup oats	1/2 cup nuts

- Put apples and cranberries in a 2 quart casserole.
- Sprinkle with sugar.
- In a bowl, combine oats, butter, flour, brown sugar, and nuts.
- Spread over fruit and bake.

Mrs. Merritt (Lee) King, III, McColl, SC

Cooked Cranberries

A Thanksgiving tradition!
Preparation time: 35 minutes
Prepare ahead

Cooking time: 25 minutes

2 cups sugar	1/8 teaspoon salt
1 cup water	4 cups raw cranberries

- Boil water, sugar, and salt in saucepan until syrupy, about 15 minutes.
- Add cranberries to boiling syrup and boil 10 more minutes.
- Cool and store in refrigerator.

The late Miss Annie Kinney, Bennettsville, SC

Junior Charity League of Marlboro County, Inc.

Prize-Winning Eggplant

Serves: 6
Cooking time: 30 minutes
Prepare ahead

Preparation time: 30 minutes
Oven temperature: 350

1	medium eggplant, peeled and cubed	1	cup whipping cream or half and half
1	large onion, diced	8	ounces sharp Cheddar cheese,
1	green pepper, diced		grated
2	tablespoons butter	2	cups bread or cracker crumbs
1	tablespoon all-purpose flour		

- Boil eggplant in salted water until tender, about 10 minutes.
- Sauté onion and green pepper in butter, stirring constantly.
- Add 1 tablespoon flour and keep stirring.
- Add cream and stir.
- Drain eggplant and add to above.
- Pour into greased baking dish with grated cheese.
- Garnish top with dabs of butter, bread crumbs, and more cheese.
- Bake until bubbly.

Mrs. Julian (Kay) Fowler, Bennettsville, SC

English Pea Casserole

Serves: 6
Cooking time: 30 minutes

Preparation time: 10 minutes
Oven temperature: 300

1	15 ounce can English peas, drained	1	2 ounce jar pimentos, drained
1	10³/₄ ounce can mushroom soup	1	medium onion, chopped
1	6 ounce can water chestnuts, chopped and drained	4	slices bread
		1	stick butter

- Mix first 5 ingredients in a bowl.
- Put in casserole dish.
- Butter bread and cut into cubes.
- Place in casserole and bake.

Mrs. Hal (Mary Lois) Trimmier, Bennettsville, SC

Carolina Cuisine: Nothin' Could Be Finer

Betty Searcy's English Pea Casserole

Serves: 6
Cooking time: 30 minutes
Prepare ahead

Preparation time: 10 minutes
Oven temperature: 325

2½ cups tiny green peas
1   2 ounce jar pimento pieces
2   hard boiled eggs, sliced
1   10¾ ounce can cream of mushroom
    soup

½   cup olives, sliced
2   cups potato chips, crushed
1   15 ounce can asparagus (optional)

- Combine peas, pimento, eggs, soup, and olives and place in a greased casserole.
- Add asparagus if desired.
- Bake, then cover with potato chips.

Mrs. David (Betty) Searcy, Florence, SC

Sherried Fruit

Great for holiday season.
Serves: 8
Cooking time: 30 minutes
Prepare ahead

Preparation time: 20 minutes
Oven temperature: 350

1   16 ounce can pineapple rings
1   16 ounce can pear halves
1   16 ounce can peach halves
1   14 ounce jar spiced apple rings
1   stick margarine, melted

2   tablespoons flour
½   cup or less cooking sherry
1   cup fruit juice, saved from fruit
½   cup sugar

- Drain fruit, saving 1 cup of juice.
- Arrange fruit in a 9 x 13 baking dish.
- In a pan, heat butter, flour, sherry, fruit juice, and sugar until thick.
- Pour over fruit and refrigerate overnight.
- Bake the next day.

Mrs. Shirley H. Beeson, Little River, SC

Macaroni and Cheese

Rich and delicious!

Serves: 10
Cooking time: 30 - 35 minutes

Preparation time: 15 minutes
Oven temperature: 350

1	8 ounce box macaroni		1	egg
2	cups cottage cheese		2	cups Cheddar cheese, shredded
1½	cups sour cream			salt, pepper, and paprika to taste

- Prepare macaroni according to package directions.
- Combine all other ingredients with macaroni, except ³/₄ cup shredded cheese.
- Place in a casserole and use remaining cheese for topping.
- Bake.

Mrs. Aubrey (Alison) McCormick, Jr., Laurinburg, NC

Cheese Grits Casserole

Serves: 6-8
Cooking time: 30 minutes

Preparation time: 15 minutes
Oven temperature: 350

1	cup grits		3	eggs, beaten
1	stick butter			red pepper, to taste
½	pound sharp Cheddar cheese, grated			

- Prepare grits according to package directions.
- Add butter, cheese, and eggs.
- Sprinkle with red pepper.
- Bake in casserole.

Mrs. Hubert (Christi) Meggs, Jr., Bennettsville, SC

Slow Cooker Macaroni

Very good!
Serves: 4 - 6
Cooking time: 3 hours

Preparation time: 15 minutes

1	8 ounce package elbow macaroni	$^1/_4$	cup margarine
1	13 ounce can evaporated milk	3	cups Cheddar cheese, grated
$1^1/_2$	cups milk	1	teaspoon salt
3	eggs, beaten	$^1/_4$	teaspoon black pepper

- Prepare macaroni according to package directions.
- Drain well.
- Add evaporated milk, milk, eggs, margarine, cheese, salt, and pepper.
- Mix lightly but thoroughly.
- Pour into lightly greased slow cooker.
- Cook on low setting.

Ms. Fran Lewis, Bennettsville, SC

French Onion Casserole

Serves: 6
Cooking time: 50 minutes
Prepare ahead

Preparation time: 30 minutes
Oven temperature: 375

3	medium sweet onions	1	15 ounce can evaporated milk
2	tablespoons butter	2	teaspoons soy sauce
8	ounces fresh mushrooms, sliced	6	$^1/_2$ inch thick slices French bread
8	ounces Swiss cheese, shredded	$^1/_4$	cup fresh parsley, chopped
1	$10^3/_4$ ounce can cream of mushroom soup		

- Slice onions crosswise and cut each slice in half.
- Melt butter in large skillet.
- Cook onions and mushrooms until tender.
- Spoon mixture into lightly greased 2 quart baking dish.
- Sprinkle with 1 cup cheese.
- Combine soup, evaporated milk, and soy sauce and pour over cheese.
- Top with bread slices.
- Sprinkle with 1 cup cheese and parsley.
- Refrigerate for 4 - 8 hours.
- Let stand at room temperature for 30 minutes.
- Bake for 30 minutes, covered.
- Uncover and bake 15 - 20 minutes.

Mrs. Norman (Kay) Rentz, Pickens, SC

Sweet Pepper Relish

Delicious with greens or on hot dogs!

Yields: 12 pints
Cooking time: 45 minutes

Preparation time: 1-1$^{1}/_{2}$ hours

12	green bell peppers	2	pounds sugar
12	red bell peppers	3	tablespoons celery seed
12	onions	3	tablespoons mustard seed
2	stalks celery	3	tablespoons salt
1	quart vinegar		

- Grind peppers, onions, and celery.
- Scald by pouring boiling water over peppers, onions, and celery to cover.
- Let stand 5 minutes.
- Rinse and scald again.
- Let stand 10 minutes.
- Drain.
- Add remaining ingredients.
- Cook 45 minutes.
- Put in canning jars while very hot.
- Tighten lids to seal.

Mrs. Henry (Gerry) Capps, Bennettsville, SC

Pineapple Casserole

Serves: 8
Cooking time: 30 minutes

Preparation time: 15 minutes
Oven temperature: 350

1	20 ounce can pineapple chunks	1	cup buttery cracker crumbs
3	tablespoons flour	$^{1}/_{2}$	stick margarine, melted
$^{1}/_{3}$	cup sugar		
1	cup Cheddar cheese, grated (mild or sharp)		

- Drain pineapple, saving juice.
- Mix flour and sugar in bowl.
- Add pineapple juice to this and mix well.
- Add pineapple chunks and cheese to this and stir until well mixed.
- Put into lightly greased casserole.
- Mix cracker crumbs and margarine together and sprinkle over the top of the dish.
- Bake until bubbly.

Mrs. James (Fannie) Chappelear, Bennettsville, SC
Mrs. William E. (Toni Ann) Dew, Latta, SC
Mrs. Jim (Jennie) Weatherly, Bennettsville, SC
Ms. Hope Weatherly, McColl, SC

Hash Brown Potato Casserole

Great!
Serves: 8-10
Cooking time: 45 minutes

Preparation time: 25 minutes
Oven temperature: 350

2   pounds frozen hash brown potatoes
1   stick margarine, melted
1   cup onion, chopped
1   10³/4 ounce can cream of chicken soup

1   pint sour cream
2   cups Cheddar cheese, grated
    salt and pepper to taste
2   cups corn flakes

- Defrost hash browns and mix with other ingredients.
- Top with 2 cups of corn flakes mixed with some of the margarine.
- Bake.

Mrs. Thomas P. (Mary) Davis, Georgetown, SC
Mrs. Larry (Phoebe) Howard, Bennettsville, SC
Mrs. Ron (Elizabeth) Munnerlyn, Bennettsville, SC
Mrs. Benjy (Linda) Rogers, Bennettsville, SC

Our Favorite Potato Casserole

Serves: 6 - 8
Cooking time: 1 - 1¹/2 hours
Prepare ahead

Preparation time: 15 minutes
Oven temperature: 325
Freezes well

32   ounces hash browns
1   10³/4 can cream of celery soup
1   10³/4 can cream of chicken soup
1   cup sour cream

2   cups Cheddar cheese, grated
1   2 ounce jar pimento
¹/2   cup onion
1   stick margarine

- Sauté margarine and onion.
- Add to hash browns, soups, sour cream, pimento, and ¹/2 cup of cheese.
- Top with remaining cheese and bake.

Mrs. Curt (Deanne) Hinson, Bennettsville, SC

Vegetables

Junior Charity League of Marlboro County, Inc.   171

Super Spud Casserole

Good for a crowd.

Serves: 12 - 16
Cooking time: 1½ hours
Prepare ahead

Preparation time: 30 minutes
Oven temperature: 300
Freezes well

2	pound bag frozen hash browns	salt and pepper to taste
8	ounces Cheddar cheese, shredded	¼ cup parmesan cheese
8	ounces sour cream	
2	10¾ ounce cans cream of potato soup	

- Partially thaw the hash browns.
- In a large bowl, mix together the potatoes, cheese, salt and pepper, sour cream, and soup.
- Press in greased 8 x 12 casserole dish.
- Sprinkle top with parmesan cheese and bake.

Mrs. Les (Joann) Hart , Bennettsville, SC
Mrs. James M. (Frances) Townsend, Bennettsville, SC
Mrs. Jimmy (Janis) Usher, Bennettsville, SC

Brown Rice

A Sunday dinner favorite.

Serves: 6 - 8
Cooking time: 1 hour

Preparation time: 5 minutes
Oven temperature: 350

1	cup rice, uncooked	1 4½ ounce can sliced mushrooms
1	10¾ ounce can French onion soup	¾ stick butter
1	10¾ ounce can beef consommé	2 tablespoons onion, optional
		water, as needed

- Combine all ingredients into round casserole dish.
- Stir ingredients together and bake.

Microwave option:

- Brown butter, onions, and rice, until rice turns white, in a frying pan.
- Put in a casserole and cook 10 minutes, turn and stir, then cook 10 more minutes.

Mrs. Oscar (Betty Hailey) Derrick, Bennettsville, SC
Mrs. Hubert (Christi) Meggs, Jr., Bennettsville, SC

Carolina Cuisine: Nothin' Could Be Finer

Toni Ann's Brown Rice

Serves: 6
Cooking time: 1 hour

Preparation time: 10 minutes
Oven temperature: 350

2   cups rice
1   stick margarine

2   10³/₄ ounce cans French onion soup
2   10³/₄ ounce cans beef consommé

- Mix ingredients together and bake.

Mrs. William (Toni Ann) Dew, Latta, SC

Baked Mushroom Rice

Extremely easy.
Serves: 4
Cooking time: 1 hour

Preparation time: Less than 5 min.
Oven temperature: 350

1   cup long grain rice, uncooked
1   10³/₄ ounce can condensed chicken broth
1   10³/₄ ounce can condensed French onion soup

1   2¹/₂ ounce jar sliced mushrooms, drained
¹/₄ cup butter, melted

- Combine all ingredients in an ungreased 2 quart baking dish.
- Bake covered.

Mrs. Charles Paul (Heather) Midgley, Bennettsville, SC

Citrus Rice

Delicious with poultry or pork!
Serves: 6

Cooking time: 20 minutes

1   cup long grain rice
2   cups water
3-4 tablespoons orange juice concentrate

1   teaspoon salt
1   tablespoon margarine
3   tablespoons golden raisins
2   tablespoons slivered almonds

- Put all ingredients in a pot and bring to a boil.
- Cover tightly and simmer 20 minutes.
- Remove from heat and let stand covered until all water is absorbed.
- If not enough orange flavor, you can stir in more concentrate after rice is cooked.

Mrs. Daniel E. (Elisabeth) McNiel, Bennettsville, SC

Junior Charity League of Marlboro County, Inc.

Oriental Rice

A picnic favorite!

Serves: 12
Cooking time: 40 minutes

Preparation time: 20 minutes
Oven temperature: 350

3/4 cup butter
1   large onion, diced
1   large bell pepper, diced
5   cups rice, cooked
1/2 cup almonds, chopped

1   cup pimento, drained and chopped
1/4 cup soy sauce
2   8 ounce cans mushrooms, drained
     and chopped
1   teaspoon garlic powder

- Sauté butter, onion, and bell pepper in a skillet.
- Add the remaining ingredients and rice.
- Mix well and put into a 3 quart casserole.
- Bake.

Mrs. Shirley H. Beeson, Little River, SC

Papa's Favorite Red Rice

Serves: 6
Cooking time: 15 - 20 minutes

Preparation time: 10 minutes

1   tablespoon bacon grease
1   onion, chopped
1   bell pepper, chopped
2   cups instant rice

1   teaspoon salt
1   15 ounce can tomato sauce
4   ounces water

- In a saucepan, sauté onion and pepper in bacon grease until onions are slightly clear and peppers are bright green.
- Add rice and salt, stirring quickly to absorb grease.
- Add tomato sauce and water and bring to a boil.
- Stir well and simmer 5-10 minutes covered.
- Check once or twice.
- Remove from heat and let stand 10 minutes, covered.

Mrs. James (Nancy Ruth) Raines, Bennettsville, SC

Carolina Cuisine: Nothin' Could Be Finer

Wild Rice With Oysters

Serves: 4
Cooking time: 30 - 40 minutes

Preparation time: 20 - 30 minutes
Oven temperature: 350

1 box wild/white rice	$^1/_2$ teaspoon salt
$^1/_2$ pint oysters, cooked slightly	$^1/_4$ teaspoon pepper
$^1/_4$ stick butter	$^1/_4$ cup almonds
$^1/_4$ cup evaporated milk	1 teaspoon curry
$^1/_2$ $10^3/_4$ can mushroom soup	

- Prepare rice according to package directions.
- Mix oysters, milk, and butter, and add to rice.
- Add soup, almonds, salt, pepper, and curry.
- Bake.

Mrs. Eugene (Mary) Crosland, Bennettsville, SC

Sausage Quiche

Serves: 6
Cooking time: 45 minutes
Prepare ahead

Preparation time: 20 minutes
Oven temperature: 350

1 9 inch pie shell, at room temperature	1 cup Cheddar cheese, grated
8 ounces hot bulk sausage	2 eggs
4 ounces fresh mushrooms	1 cup half and half
3 tablespoons butter	salt, pepper, garlic powder, and
1 cup Swiss cheese, grated	onion salt to taste

- Preheat oven.
- Bake pie shell for 8 minutes.
- Cook and drain sausage.
- Sauté mushrooms in butter.
- Layer sausage, mushrooms, and cheese in pie shell.
- Sprinkle with seasonings.
- Add cream to eggs and beat well.
- Pour mixture over cheeses and bake.

Mrs. David K. (Cathy) Lynch, Bennettsville, SC

Spinach-Artichoke Casserole

A wonderful dish!
Serves: 6 - 8
Oven temperature: 350

Cooking time: 30 minutes
Prepare ahead

2   10 ounce packages frozen chopped spinach
1   8 ounce package cream cheese
1   stick butter
1   tablespoon lemon juice
2   7 ounce cans artichokes, sliced

1   8 ounce can water chestnuts, chopped
    salt and pepper to taste
    Cheddar cheese, grated, to taste
    bread crumbs

- Boil spinach 3 minutes and drain very well.
- While hot, add cream cheese, butter, lemon juice, salt and pepper.
- Allow cheese and butter to melt.
- Add artichokes and water chestnuts.
- Pour into a 9 inch baking dish and top with cheese and bread crumbs.
- Bake.

Mrs. Charles (Susan) Midgley, Bennettsville, SC

Squash Casserole

Good!
Serves: 8
Oven temperature: 350

Cooking time: 30 minutes
Freezes well

$1^1/_2$ pounds fresh squash OR
3   $14^1/_2$ ounce cans squash
1   2 ounce jar diced pimento
1   small onion, chopped
1   8 ounce package herbed stuffing mix

1   cup sour cream
1   $10^3/_4$ ounce can cream of chicken soup
1   stick margarine, melted

- Slice, cook, and drain and mash squash.
- Add pimento, onion, sour cream, and soup.
- Mix stuffing and melted butter.
- Line bottom of casserole with $^1/_2$ of the crumbs, reserving some for top.
- Pour in squash mixture and sprinkle rest of the crumbs on top.
- Bake.

Mrs. Thomas P. (Mary) Davis, Georgetown, SC

Carolina Cuisine: Nothin' Could Be Finer

Squash Soufflé

Serves: 8
Cooking time: 20 - 30 minutes
Prepare ahead

Preparation time: 15 minutes
Oven temperature: 350
Freezes well

2	cups squash, cooked		3	tablespoons butter
1	cup dry bread crumbs		1	cup cheese, grated
1	cup milk		2	eggs, well beaten
1	small onion, grated			salt and pepper to taste

- Melt butter in hot milk, pour over crumbs, add to squash.
- Add seasonings and eggs.
- Stir into squash mixture.
- Pour into greased casserole and bake.

Mrs. J. T. (Betty) Martin, Jr., Bennettsville, SC

Scrumptious Squash Soufflé

A family favorite!
Serves: 6
Cooking time: 30 - 40 minute
Prepare ahead

Preparation time: 30 minutes
Oven temperature: 375

2	cups squash, cooked and drained		1	cup milk
$1^1/_2$	teaspoons salt		2	eggs, separated
$^1/_8$	teaspoon pepper		$^3/_4$	cup cracker crumbs
2	tablespoons all-purpose flour		2	teaspoons onion, chopped
4	tablespoons margarine		$^1/_2$ - $^3/_4$	cup sharp cheese, grated

- Make white sauce by heating flour, margarine, and milk in saucepan until thick.
- Mix squash, salt, pepper, egg yolks, crumbs, onion, cheese, and white sauce.
- Stiffly beat egg whites and fold into mixture.
- Place in buttered 1 quart casserole.
- Bake.

Mrs. R. L. (Janie) McNiel, Hamer, SC

Vegetables

Junior Charity League of Marlboro County, Inc.

Glazed Sweet Potatoes

Very easy and looks fancy.
Serves: 12   **Cooking time: 20 minutes**
Oven temperature: 350

12   medium sweet potatoes, cooked, $^1/_2$ cup packed brown sugar
     peeled, and halved lengthwise   2   tablespoons margarine
1   cup dark corn syrup

- Bring corn syrup, sugar, and margarine to a boil.
- Simmer 5 minutes.
- Pour half of mixture into shallow baking dish, add potatoes.
- Pour remaining mixture on top.
- Bake.

Mrs. Merritt (Hazel) King, Jr., McColl, SC

Baked Tomatoes with Spinach

Serves: 6   **Preparation time: 25 minutes**
Cooking time: 15 minutes   **Oven temperature: 350**

6   tomatoes   2   tablespoons walnuts
$^1/_2$ cup spinach   1   clove garlic
2   tablespoons olive oil   salt, pepper, and parsley
2   tablespoons parmesan cheese

- Peel and core tomatoes, place each in a muffin tin.
- Blend all other ingredients in food processor until well blended.
- Put 2 tablespoons of the pesto in each tomato.
- Sprinkle with a little parmesan.
- Bake.

Mrs. Smith C. (Helen) Breeden, Bennettsville, SC

Baked Vegetable Medley

Excellent family meal.

Serves: 6 - 8
Cooking time: 45 minutes - 1 hour

Preparation time: 30 minutes
Oven temperature: 350

2	large yellow squash		3	medium onions
4	large tomatoes		1	cup mozzarella cheese, grated
2	large zucchini			parmesan cheese

- Butter or spray 2 quart casserole.
- Layer vegetables, sprinkling with salt, pepper, and parmesan cheese after each layer.
- Dot each layer with butter.
- Bake.
- Sprinkle the mozzarella over the top and bake again until the cheese is melted and starts to turn brown.

Mrs. William G. (Mary) Tatum, Bennettsville, SC

Marinated Vegetables

Serves: 8
Prepare ahead

Preparation time: 30 minutes

Marinade:

1	cup vegetable oil
2	cups sugar
2	cups vinegar
2	tablespoons salt
2	tablespoons water
	dash cayenne

Vegetables:

1	15 ounce can green peas
3	14.5 ounce cans whole green beans
1	cup green pepper, diced
1	cup celery, diced
1	cup onions, thinly sliced
$1/4$	cup pimento

- Blend marinade ingredients.
- Let stand for 1 hour.
- Combine vegetables.
- Pour marinade over the vegetables.
- Marinate overnight in refrigerator.
- To serve, drain marinade and save for future use.

Mrs. Jack (Melba) Hamilton, Bennettsville, SC

Vegetables

Junior Charity League of Marlboro County, Inc.

Vegetable Casserole

Serves: 8 - 10
Cooking time: 45 minutes
Prepare ahead

Preparation time: 45 minutes
Oven temperature: 350

$^1/_2$ cup celery, chopped
2 tablespoons oil
1 16 ounce can mixed vegetables
2 boiled eggs, chopped
1 $10^3/_4$ ounce can cream of chicken soup

1 8 ounce can sliced water chestnuts
1 2 ounce jar pimento
1 sleeve crackers, crushed
1 stick margarine, melted

- Sauté onions and celery in oil.
- Add mixed vegetables, eggs, and chicken soup.
- Mix well.
- Add water chestnuts, pimento, and stir.
- Pour into 3 quart casserole.
- Top with crushed crackers and pour margarine over it.
- Bake.

Mrs. Walker (Sophia) Jackson, Bennettsville, SC

Vegetable Pie

Serves: 6 - 8
Cooking time: 30 - 40 minutes

Preparation time: 30 minutes
Oven temperature: 350

1 9 inch pie crust
1 small bell pepper, cut into strips
1 small Vidalia onion, cut into strips
$^1/_2$ pound fresh mushrooms, sliced
1 yellow squash, thinly sliced

2 tablespoons olive oil
2 tablespoons mayonnaise
6 ounces mozzarella cheese, grated
2 tomatoes

- Bake pie shell 10 minutes at 300 degrees and let cool.
- Sauté bell pepper, vidalia onion, mushrooms, and squash in 2 tablespoons of olive oil, until tender.
- Slice tomatoes and place in bottom of cooled crust.
- Spread vegetables on top of tomatoes.
- Thinly spread mayonnaise on top of vegetables.
- Top with mozzarella cheese.
- Bake.

Mrs. Gene (Mildred) Moore, Bennettsville, SC

Italian Zucchini Pie

Good with barbecued chicken. Vegetables can be prepared several hours before using.

Serves: 8

Cooking time: 20 minutes

Preparation time: 30 minutes

Oven temperature: 375

4	cups zucchini, sliced	1/4	teaspoon basil
1	cup onion, chopped	1/2	teaspoon oregano
1/2	cup margarine	2	eggs, beaten
1/2	teaspoon salt	2	cups mozzarella cheese, grated
2	tablespoons parsley flakes	1	8 ounce can crescent rolls
1/2	teaspoon black pepper	2	teaspoons Dijon mustard
1/4	teaspoon garlic powder		

- Preheat oven.
- Sauté zucchini and onion in margarine until tender.
- Add the seasonings.
- In a large bowl, blend the eggs and cheese.
- Stir in the vegetable mixture.
- Make a dough crust by pressing cresent rolls into an ungreased pie plate.
- Pour in the vegetable mixture.
- Bake.
- After baking, let stand 10 minutes before serving.

Mrs. DuPre (Mary) Miller, Bennettsville, SC

Notes:

Sweet Endings

Drawing by: Bobby Avent

Henry E. Avent
"Marlboro County Confederate War Memorial"

Henry E. " Bobby" Avent, a native of Jonesboro, North Carolina, has resided in Bennettsville since the age of five. Upon graduation from Bennettsville High School, Mr. Avent attended Clemson University, where he received a Bachelor of Science degree in Architecture. While there he also was commissioned as a Second Lietenant in the United States Army Reserve.

During World War II, Mr. Avent was a Flying Tiger with the 14th Air Force. The experience gained then has enabled him to be the capable chairman of the Marlboro County Airport Commission today. Upon return from the Korean Conflict, he purchased the Pepsi-Cola, Dr. Pepper Bottling Company of Bennettsville and presently serves as the president of that corporation. He also serves as Chairman of the Board of Carolina Canners, Inc., in Cheraw, South Carolina, where he previously served as president.

An architect by profession, Mr. Avent has found the analytical architectural training he recieved in college to be quite beneficial in each business endeavor he has pursued. Training in various art techniques have proven an asset in hobby art.

He and his wife, the former Nancy Slade, have three sons and several grandchildren.

Apple Cobbler

Easy and healthy too!

Serves: 6

Cooking time: 45 minutes

Prepare ahead

Preparation time: 10 minutes

Oven temperature: 350

1 15 ounce can apple slices	¹/₂ cup walnuts or pecans, chopped
1 15 ounce jar escalloped apples	(optional)
³/₄ cup graham cracker crumbs	¹/₄ cup margarine or butter
¹/₄ cup sugar	

- Mix apple slices and escalloped apples in bottom of greased 8 inch casserole dish.
- Combine crumbs, sugar, and nuts (optional).
- Sprinkle mixture over apples.
- Dot with margarine or butter.
- Cover and bake.
- Uncover for a few minutes for crunchier topping.
- This cobbler can be made with any fruit combination desired (fresh, pie filling, canned fruits). Topping can be spread thinly or thickly. To make a la mode, use whipped cream, ice cream, or a dollop of vanilla yogurt sprinkled with brown sugar.

Mrs. Charles G. (Janice) Vaughan, Jr., Bennettsville, SC

Banana Pudding

1 6 ounce box instant vanilla pudding	6 ounces whipped topping
3 cups milk	4- 5 large bananas
4 ounces sour cream	1 11 ounce box vanilla wafers

- Mix pudding and milk according to directions on the package.
- Add sour cream and 3 ounces of whipped topping.
- Mix with an electric mixer.
- Layer a 9 x 12 dish with wafers, sliced bananas, and pudding mixture.
- Repeat.
- Top with remaining whipped topping.
- Sprinkle wafer crumbs on top.

Mrs. Tony (Becky) Clark, Bennettsville, SC

Junior Charity League of Marlboro County, Inc.

Blueberry Buckle

Serves: 9

Cooking time: 45 minutes

Prepare ahead

Preparation time: 20 minutes

Oven temperature: 375

Freezes well

Bottom Layer:

$^1/_2$ cup margarine	$1^1/_2$ teaspoons baking powder
$^1/_2$ cup sugar	$^1/_4$ teaspoon salt
1 egg, beaten	$^1/_2$ cup milk
1 cup all-purpose flour	2 cups fresh or frozen blueberries, thawed

- Preheat oven to 375.
- Spray cooking oil on 9 inch square baking pan.
- Using electric mixer, cream $^1/_2$ cup margarine with $^1/_2$ cup sugar.
- Add egg and beat 1 minute.
- Combine flour, salt, and baking powder. (Add this in 4 batches to margarine mixture, alternating with milk.)
- Turn into prepared pan, spreading evenly.
- Top with blueberries.

Topping:

$^1/_2$ stick margarine	$^1/_2$ cup all-purpose flour
1 cup sugar	$^1/_2$ teaspoon cinnamon

- Cream remaining margarine, flour, sugar, and cinnamon.
- Sprinkle over blueberries.
- Bake until golden brown and bubbly.
- Serve with whipped cream or vanilla ice cream.

Mrs. Bill (Gloria) Ward, Bennettsville, SC

Buster Bars

Serves: 12
Prepare ahead

Preparation time: 30 minutes
Freezes well

1   1½ pound package cream filled
    chocolate cookies, crushed
½   cup margarine, melted
½   gallon vanilla ice cream

1 ½ cups salted nuts (pecans, peanuts,
     or Spanish)

- Mix cookies and margarine.
- Press into 9 x 13 inch pan.
- Slice ice cream over crust.
- Spread nuts over ice cream.
- Place in freezer while preparing sauce.

Sauce:
1   cup chocolate chips
1½   cups evaporated milk
2   tablespoons butter

2   cups confectioners sugar
1   teaspoon vanilla extract (add last)

- Prepare sauce by mixing ingredients and cook 10 to 12 minutes stirring constantly.
- Add vanilla and remove from heat to cool.
- Pour over nut layer and freeze until firm.
- Before serving, remove from freezer for 10 minutes and cut into squares.

Mrs. Bill (Gloria) Ward, Bennettsville, SC

Easy Cobbler

Excellent made with blueberries or peaches.
Cooking time: 30-40 minutes

Oven temperature: 350

¾   stick butter or margarine
1   cup flour
1   cup sugar

¾   cup milk
2   cups fruit (blueberries or peaches
    are good)

- Melt butter in baking dish.
- Mix flour, sugar, and milk together.
- Pour over melted butter.
- Add fruit to top — just dump in dish.
- Cook until brown.

Mrs. Ron (Elizabeth) Munnerlyn, Bennettsville, SC

Congo Bars

Serves: 24
Cooking time: 32 minutes
Prepare ahead

Preparation time: 20 minutes
Oven temperature: 350
Freezes well

1 stick butter
$^{1}/_{3}$ stick margarine
1 16 ounce box light brown sugar
1 6 ounce package chocolate bits

$2^{2}/_{3}$ cups self-rising flour
3 eggs, slightly beaten
1 teaspoon vanilla flavoring
1 cup pecans, chopped

- Melt butter and margarine in a saucepan and add the brown sugar, folding together.
- Add remaining ingredients, folding together until everything is mixed well. (Batter will be stiff.)
- Pour into a greased 9 x 14 pan.
- Bake.
- Remove pan from oven and cool on wire rack.
- Cut into bars.

Mrs. William B. (Frances) Belcher, Bennettsville, SC
Mrs. Brian (Dena) Kett, Huntington, WV

Baked Custard

Light, delicious dessert!
Serves: 6
Cooking time: 30-35 minutes
Prepare ahead

Preparation time: 15 minutes
Oven temperature: 325

2 eggs, well beaten
$^{1}/_{4}$ cup sugar
2 cups cold milk

dash salt
1 teaspoon vanilla

- Beat eggs with sugar and salt.
- Add cold milk and vanilla.
- Pour into custard cups.
- Place cups in pan of hot water and bake until firm.
- Serve warm or chill and serve.

Mrs. John R. (Penny) Nobles, Bennettsville, SC

Carolina Cuisine: Nothin' Could Be Finer

Old-fashioned Boiled Custard

Preparation time: 10 minutes
Prepare ahead

Cooking time: 1 hour

1	quart whole milk	8	ounces half and half cream
4	eggs	1	teaspoon almond extract
4	tablespoons sugar		

- Place milk in double boiler.
- Beat eggs and sugar together and add to milk, stirring constantly.
- Keep on heat for a long time.
- Heat until mixture coats a tablespoon, then remove from heat and cool.
- After cooling, add half and half and almond extract.
- Serve warm or chilled.

The late Miss Annie Kinney, Bennettsville, SC

Death By Chocolate

Serves: 8-10

Preparation time: 30 minutes

1	18.5 ounce box brownie mix, cooked as directed for cake-like brownies	2	3.4 ounce boxes chocolate flavor instant pudding (4 serving size)
1	12 ounce whipped topping	5-6	toffee candy bars, crumbled
		3	cups milk

- Crumble half of brownies in 9 x 13 pan.
- Layer half of toffee bars.
- Mix pudding with milk and layer half of this.
- Layer half of whipped topping.
- Repeat layers.

Mrs. Arlo (Judy) Hill, Bennettsville, SC

Junior Charity League of Marlboro County, Inc.

Chocolate Surprise

Serves: 12-15
Cooking time: 15 minutes
Prepare ahead

Preparation time: 45 minutes
Oven temperature: 375

1 cup flour	2 cups whipped dessert topping
1/2 cup nuts, finely chopped	1 cup powdered sugar
1 stick butter, melted	2 3 ounce packages chocolate pudding mix
1 8 ounce package cream cheese, softened	3 cups milk

- Put flour and nuts in a 9 x 13 pan.
- Pour butter on top of mixture.
- Press into all corners, making sure entire bottom of pan is covered.
- Bake.
- Cool 1 hour; set aside.
- Mix cream cheese, 1 cup whipped dessert topping, and powdered sugar.
- Spread over crust.
- Mix pudding and milk about two minutes.
- Pour over cream cheese.
- Refrigerate for 1 hour.
- Before serving cover with remaining whipped dessert topping.

Mrs. Reid (Deanie) Hensarling, Bennettsville, SC

Quick Peach Cobbler

Can substitute other fruit for peaches if you desire.
Cooking time: 1 hour

Oven temperature: 350

1 stick butter	3/4 cup self-rising flour
3 cups sliced peaches	3/4 cup milk
1 1/4 cups sugar	

- In deep baking dish or pan, melt stick of butter in oven or microwave.
- Mix 3/4 cup sugar, flour, and milk, then pour on top of butter.
- Do not stir.
- Mix 1/2 cup sugar with peaches.
- On top, add sugared peaches.
- Do not stir.
- Bake.

Mrs. Aubrey (Alison) McCormick, Jr., Laurinburg, NC

Pumpkin Bars

Cooking time: 30 minutes

Oven temperature: 350

4	eggs
1²/₃	cups sugar
1	cup cooking oil
1	16 ounce can pumpkin
2	cups all-purpose flour

2	teaspoons baking powder
2	teaspoons cinnamon
1	teaspoon salt
1	teaspoon baking soda

Icing/Frosting:
1   3 ounce package soft cream cheese
¹/₂ cup butter or margarine, softened

1   teaspoon vanilla
2   cups sifted powdered sugar

- Combine first nine ingredients and bake in an ungreased 15 x 10 x 1 baking pan.
- Cool in pan and frost.

Mrs. Marty (Rhonda) McIntyre, Bennettsville, SC

Strawberry Trifle

This is a great low-fat dessert that is easy to prepare.

Serves: 8-10

Preparation time: 30 minutes

¹/₂ angel food cake
1   2.8 ounce whipped topping mix
    skim milk
2   6 ounce containers nonfat
    strawberry yogurt

1   pint strawberries, sliced
3   kiwi fruit, sliced (optional)
¹/₄ cup slivered almonds, toasted
    (optional)

- Tear cake into bite-sized pieces.
- Prepare topping mix according to package directions using skim milk.
- Mix strawberry yogurt with whipped topping.
- Layer half of cake pieces in a tall glass bowl.
- Pour half of yogurt mixture over cake pieces.
- Add half of sliced strawberries.
- Repeat layers, ending with strawberries on top.
- Sprinkle almonds over top.
- Garnish each serving with a slice of kiwi fruit.
- May need to sweeten strawberries to suit your taste.

Mrs. Andy (Mary Alice) Burroughs, Bennettsville, SC

Junior Charity League of Marlboro County, Inc.

Angel Bavarian Cake

This recipe was given me 30 years ago by my sister-in-law, Mrs. Norman Parks of Columbia, SC. It is the best dessert I've ever tasted. You will always get compliments when you serve it.

Prepare ahead

4	egg yolks	1	teaspoon almond flavoring
1	pint milk	4	egg whites
1	tablespoon all-purpose flour	1	angel food bar cake
1	cup sugar	½	pint whipping cream (can use whipped topping)
	pinch salt		
1	envelope unflavored gelatin	1	coconut, grated (can use frozen coconut)
½	cup cold water		

- In top of double boiler, combine egg yolks, milk, flour, sugar, and salt.
- Place over simmering water and stir constantly until mixture thickens to a custard.
- Dissolve gelatin in cold water and add to the hot mixture.
- Add almond flavoring.
- Whip the egg whites until stiff and fold (do not beat) into above mixture.
- Cut angel food cake into five slices (long way).
- Place 2 ½ slices in the bottom of a pan and pour half of the custard over this.
- Place remaining slices on top of custard and pour custard over this.
- Let stand in refrigerator 4 hours or overnight.
- One hour before serving spread cream over top.
- Sprinkle with grated coconut and cut into squares.

Mrs. Frank (Teenie) Parks, Bennettsville, SC

Fresh Apple Cake

Ashley cooked this cake for my birthday! So-o good!!

Serves: 12
Cooking time: 1 hour

Preparation time: 30 minutes
Oven temperature: 350

1½ cups vegetable oil
2 cups sugar
4 eggs
2½ cups all-purpose flour
2 teaspoons baking powder
1 teaspoon cinnamon

1 teaspoon salt
3 cups Red Delicious apples, peeled and chopped
1 cup pecans, chopped
1 teaspoon vanilla extract

- Preheat oven.
- Mix oil and sugar.
- Add eggs one at a time, beating well after each addition.
- Sift together dry ingredients and add to egg mixture.
- Stir in apples, pecans, and vanilla extract.
- Pour into greased and floured 10 inch tube pan.
- Bake.
- Remove from pan when slightly cool.

Mrs. David K. (Cathy) Lynch, Bennettsville, SC

Sauce for Fresh Apple Cake

Sauce was great!

Nice to serve as optional sauce for Fresh Apple Cake. Not everyone likes this on their cake.
Preparation time: 15 minutes

4 tablespoons butter
2 cups light brown sugar
1½ teaspoons cinnamon
2 cups boiling water

4 tablespoons all-purpose flour
1 teaspoon salt
2 teaspoons vanilla extract

- Bring all ingredients to a boil in medium saucepan.
- Stir constantly.
- Serve over cake when warm.

Mrs. David K. (Cathy) Lynch, Bennettsville, SC

Sweet Endings

Junior Charity League of Marlboro County, Inc.   193

Apple Cake

This was given to me while we lived in Stuttgart, Germany. It makes a small cake and can be cut in squares or used like cookies, if put in larger pan.

Cooking time: 50 to 55 minutes   **Oven temperature: 350**

2	medium apples, peeled	1/2	teaspoon allspice
1	cup sugar	1/2	cup margarine, melted
1 1/2	cups all-purpose flour	1	egg
1	teaspoon baking soda	1/2	cup raisins (optional)
1	teaspoon cinnamon	1/2-1	cup walnuts or pecans
1/2	teaspoon nutmeg		

- Coarsely chop apples, 1 3/4 cups into bowl.
- Add sugar — let stand 10 minutes — sift flour and dry ingredients.
- Blend melted butter and egg into apple-sugar mixture.
- Add flour and fold in nuts and raisins.
- Put in greased pan and bake (less time if larger pan is used).
- I suggest using a 9 inch square pan or 9 x 12 inch pan.

Mrs. Harry R. (Mary Kay) Easterling, Bennettsville, SC

Blackberry Wine Cake

Preparation time: 15 minutes   **Cooking time: 45 minutes - 1 hour**
Oven temperature: 350   **Freezes well**

3/4	cup pecans, chopped	1/2	cup oil
1	18.25 ounce box white cake mix	1/2	cup sour cream
3	eggs	1	cup blackberry wine
1	3 ounce box blackberry gelatin		

- Spray bundt pan with cooking oil.
- Sprinkle pecans in bottom of pan.
- Mix all ingredients together and pour on top of pecans.
- Bake.

Glaze:

1	cup powdered sugar (10X)	1/2	cup butter or margarine
		1/2	cup blackberry wine

- Mix all ingredients together and boil 1 minute.
- Pour 3/4 of mixture over cake while still hot, let set in pan for 30 minutes.
- Turn out of pan and pour balance of glaze on top of cake.

Mrs. Jackie (Virginia) Williamson, Bennettsville, SC

Carolina Cuisine: Nothin' Could Be Finer

Blueberry Cake

A scrumptious dessert! This is also good with cherry pie filling.

1	18.25 ounce box yellow cake mix	1	8 ounce package cream cheese
½	cup sugar	1	12 ounce whipped topping
½	cup powdered sugar	1	16 ounce can blueberry pie filling

- Mix cake mix as directed on box and pour into four thin layer pans.
- Cook as directed.
- Mix sugar, powdered sugar, cream cheese, and whipped topping.
- Put filling between layers and spread with pie filling.

Mrs. William (Ruth) Therrell, Bennettsville, SC

Texas Butter Cake

Cooking time: 1 hour **Oven temperature: 350**

1	18.5 ounce box butter cake mix	4	eggs
1	3.4 ounce package instant vanilla pudding	1	cup sour cream
		1	teaspoon vanilla
½	cup oil	1	teaspoon butter flavoring

- Mix together ingredients in the order given — eggs one at a time.

Mix separately:

½	cup sugar	2	teaspoons ground cinnamon
½	cup pecans, chopped finely		

- Pour ⅓ part of cinnamon mixture in bottom of a greased tube pan.
- Then pour ½ of the batter — then cinnamon mixture again.
- Then pour remaining batter over this.
- Lastly, put remaining cinnamon mixture on top.
- Bake.
- Allow the cake to cool 5 to 10 minutes before removing from the pan.

Mrs. Charles (Mary Alice) McColl, Bennettsville, SC

Caramel Cake

Delicious!
Freezes well

1   18.5 ounce box butter cake mix

- Mix cake mix according to directions on box.
- Pour batter into 3 well greased and floured, 8 or 9 inch, layer pans.
- Cook according to recipe on box.
- Cool.

Caramel Icing:

$^2/_3$ cup milk	$2^1/_8$ sticks of butter
$1^1/_2$ cups light brown sugar	$2^1/_4$ teaspoons vanilla extract
$1^1/_2$ cups sugar	

- Bring first 4 ingredients to a rolling boil and boil for 5 minutes.
- Take off heat and beat until smooth and creamy.
- Add vanilla extract.
- Spread frosting between layers, on top and sides of cooled cake.
- Decorate top with chopped pecans.

Mrs. Billie M. Beaty, Bennettsville, SC

Carrot Cake

Serves: 10-12   **Cooking time: 35 minutes**
Oven temperature: 325

2	cups sugar	2	teaspoons baking soda
$1^1/_2$	cups vegetable oil	1	teaspoon salt
4	eggs	2	teaspoons vanilla extract
2	cups all-purpose flour	3	cups carrots, grated
$^3/_4$	teaspoon cinnamon		

- Mix sugar, oil, and eggs.
- Sift flour, cinnamon, baking soda, and salt.
- Add to sugar mixture.
- Mix in vanilla and carrots.
- Bake.

Icing:		1	16 ounce box confectioners sugar
1	stick butter, softened	1	teaspoon vanilla extract
1	8 ounce package cream cheese, softened	1	cup pecans, chopped

- Mix butter and cream cheese, then other three ingredients.
- Spread over cake.

Mrs. Michael (Bonnie) Winburn, Bennettsville, SC

No Bake Cheese Cake

Serves: 8-10 generously   **Preparation time: 15 minutes**
Prepare ahead

1	stick butter or oleo	1	cup sugar
2	tablespoons powdered sugar	1	8 ounce package cream cheese
30	graham crackers, crushed	1	12 ounce can MILNOT (no substi-
1	6 ounce box lemon gelatin		tute), chilled
1	cup boiling water	1	teaspoon vanilla extract

- Melt butter, add graham crackers and powdered sugar.
- Press into a 9 x 13 pan.
- Mix gelatin and boiling water and set aside.
- Mix sugar and cream cheese until smooth and mix with gelatin mixture.
- Whip Milnot until thick, add vanilla extract.
- Blend mixtures together.
- Pour into graham cracker crust and refrigerate at least 4 hours.

Mrs. Les (Joann) Hart, Bennettsville, SC

Chocolate Sheet Cake

Serves: 20-24   **Preparation time: 1 hour**
Cooking time: 20 minutes   **Oven temperature: 400**
Prepare ahead

2	cups sugar	$^1/_2$	cup buttermilk
2	cups all-purpose flour	2	eggs, beaten
2	sticks margarine	1	teaspoon soda
4	tablespoons cocoa	1	teaspoon vanilla extract
1	cup water	1	teaspoon cinnamon

- Stir sugar and flour together.
- Boil the margarine, cocoa, and water.
- Pour over the flour and sugar mixture.
- Mix and add buttermilk, eggs, soda, vanilla, and cinnamon.
- Pour into a greased and floured 9 x 13 pan and bake.

Icing:

1	stick margarine	1	16 ounce box powdered sugar
4	tablespoons cocoa	1	teaspoon vanilla
6	tablespoons milk	1	cup pecans

- 5 minutes before the cake is done, melt margarine, cocoa, and milk.
- Remove from heat and add powdered sugar, vanilla, and nuts.
- Beat and pour over cake when it comes out of the oven.
- Cool (preferably overnight).

Mrs. Jimmy (Janis) Usher, Bennettsville, SC

Junior Charity League of Marlboro County, Inc.

Chocolate Syrup Cake

Wonderful!

Cooking time: 45 minutes

Oven temperature: 300-325

1 cup all-purpose flour
1 cup sugar
1½ teaspoons baking powder

4 eggs
1 16 ounce can chocolate syrup
1 stick butter

- Cream sugar and butter.
- Add eggs.
- Stir together flour and baking powder then add to other mixture.
- Add chocolate syrup.
- Pour in 9 x 13 pan and bake.
- Poke holes in cake so icing can go through.

Icing:

½ can milk
1 6½ ounce can evaporated milk
1 stick butter

1 cup sugar
chopped nuts

- Put all ingredients except nuts in pan and heat.
- Stir constantly and boil about 7 minutes (or until just becoming thick).
- Pour over cake and top with a few nuts.

Miss Peggy Beaty, Bennettsville, SC

Christmas Cake

Preparation time: 30-45 minutes
Oven temperature: 325

Cooking time: 1 hour

1 8 ounce package cream cheese
2 sticks butter
1½ cups sugar
1½ teaspoons vanilla
4 eggs

2 cups all-purpose flour
1½ teaspoons baking powder
½ cup red cherries
½ cup green cherries
1 cup pecans, chopped

Glaze:

1½ cups powdered sugar

¼ cup milk

- Cream together cream cheese, sugar and butter until fluffy.
- Add vanilla then add eggs — one at a time..
- Combine flour and baking powder — add gradually..
- Combine cherries and pecans with extra ¼ cup flour and fold into batter.
- Pour batter into tube pan.
- Bake.
- Glaze, combine 1½ cups powdered sugar and ¼ cup milk and pour over cake.
- Garnish with cherries and pecans.

Mrs. Robert (Mildred) Hillstrand, Bennettsville, SC

Coconut Layer Cake

A family favorite!
Cooking time: 30-35 minutes   **Oven temperature: 375**
Freezes well

1/2	pound butter, softened	3	cups cake flour, sifted
2	cups sugar	3	teaspoons baking powder
5	eggs	1	cup milk
1	teaspoon vanilla		

- Cream butter, add sugar, and beat until fluffy.
- Add eggs, one at a time, beating thoroughly after each addition.
- Add vanilla and beat 5 minutes.
- Measure flour and add baking powder, sift together 4 times.
- Add dry ingredients alternately with milk, folding in each time.
- Pour into 3 greased layer cake pans and bake.

Frosting:

2	cups sugar	1/4	teaspoon cream of tartar
1	cup water	6	ounces coconut, grated
3	egg whites, stiffly beaten		

- Dissolve sugar in water and boil until it spins a thread.
- Pour syrup gradually over egg whites.
- Add cream of tartar.
- Beat until stiff and fluffy and spread between layers.
- Add grated coconut each time between layers.
- Ice with frosting and more coconut.

Mrs. Daniel E. (Elisabeth) McNiel, Bennettsville, SC

Devil's Food Cake

A tasty and pretty cake!
Serves: 10-12   **Cooking time: 40 minutes**
Oven temperature: 350

3	squares unsweetened chocolate	1	teaspoon salt
1/2	cup butter	2	eggs
1	cup water	1	cup sour cream
2	cups all-purpose flour	2	cups sugar
1 1/4	teaspoons baking soda	1 1/2	teaspoons vanilla

- Combine chocolate, butter, and water in top of double boiler until chocolate is melted.
- Let cool.
- Sift flour, baking soda, and salt.
- Beat eggs and blend with sour cream.
- Beat in sugar and vanilla.
- Stir in cooled chocolate mixture.
- Beat into flour mixture, one-half at a time (batter will be thin).
- Pour into 2 cake pans and bake.

Mrs. Shirley H. Beeson, Little River, SC

Earthquake Cake

Serves: 16

Oven temperature: 350

Cooking time: 45 minutes

1 cup pecans, chopped	$^1/_2$ cup margarine
1 6 ounce bag coconut	1 8 ounce package cream cheese
1 18.25 ounce box German chocolate cake mix	1 16 ounce box powdered sugar

- Sprinkle nuts and coconut in bottom of a greased 13 x 9 x 2 inch pan.
- Prepare cake mix according to package directions.
- Pour batter over coconut and pecans.
- Combine margarine and cream cheese in saucepan.
- Cook over low heat until melted, stirring to blend.
- Add sugar and mix.
- Spoon sauce over cake batter.
- Bake.

Mrs. A. M. (Mary Frances) Hollingsworth, Fayetteville, NC
Mrs. Howard (Lillian) Hyatt, Bennettsville, SC
Mrs. Fred (Joyce) McIntyre, Dillon, SC
Mrs. Benjy (Linda) Rogers, Bennettsville, SC

Black Fruit Cake

Serves: 12-14

Cooking time: approximately 2 hours

Preparation time: 1 hour

Oven temperature: 275

1 pound pecans	$^1/_2$ pound orange peel
3 pounds raisins	4 cups all-purpose flour
1 pound citron	2 teaspoons baking powder
1 pound pineapple	3 6 ounce bags frozen coconut
1 pound cherries	1 pound butter
1 pound ginger	$2^1/_4$ cups sugar
$^1/_2$ pound lemon peel	8 eggs

- Chop fruit and nuts fairly small.
- Put in a large roasting pan and mix with one cup of flour, adding raisins and coconut last.
- Cream butter and sugar, add eggs one at a time, add flour and baking powder last.
- Pour batter into roasting pan over fruit and mix well.
- Grease and flour large cake pan, then cut out the outline of the cake pan on a brown paper bag.
- Grease the cut out and place in the bottom of the cake pan.
- Pour mixture into pan until $^3/_4$ full.
- Place any extra in loaf pans.
- Bake.

Mrs. Harry R. (Mary Kay) Easterling, Bennettsville, SC

Lib's Layer Cake

I usually freeze 4 layers for future use — putting wax paper between layers and placing in a large plastic freezer bag..

Yields: 8 layers or 72 cupcakes
Oven temperature: 325

Cooking time: 25-30 minutes
Freezes well

2	sticks butter	2	cups all-purpose flour
2	sticks oleo	1	cup milk
3	cups sugar	10	eggs
2	cups self-rising flour	1	tablespoon vanilla extract

- Cream oleo, butter, and sugar.
- Add eggs, one at a time, beat well.
- Add alternately, flour and milk until well mixed.
- Add vanilla.
- Pour batter in pans sprayed with non-stick spray.
- Bake.

Mrs. Robert E. (Lib) Thompson, Bennettsville, SC

Chocolate Icing

2	cups sugar		pinch salt
1	6 ounce can evaporated milk	1	6 ounce bag semisweet chocolate
1	stick butter		chips
12	marshmallows	1	teaspoon vanilla extract

- Put sugar, milk, butter, marshmallows, and salt in a saucepan.
- Cook on medium heat.
- Let boil 4 minutes, stirring constantly.
- Remove from heat and add chocolate and vanilla.
- Beat for a few minutes.
- Spread on 4 layers of cake (if icing becomes too stiff, add a little hot water).

Mrs. Robert E. (Lib) Thompson, Bennettsville, SC

Sweet Endings

Junior Charity League of Marlboro County, Inc.

Oatmeal Cake

May substitute self-rising flour for all-purpose flour; omit soda and salt if using self-rising flour.

Serves: 15-20   **Preparation time: 30 minutes**
Cooking time: 30 minutes   **Oven temperature: 350**

1¼ cups boiling water
1   cup quick oats
¼   cup margarine, softened
1   cup brown sugar
1   cup sugar
2   eggs

1   teaspoon vanilla
1⅓ cups all-purpose flour
1   teaspoon soda
½   teaspoon salt
1   teaspoon cinnamon

- Pour boiling water over oats.
- Cover and let stand 20 minutes.
- Mix together ¼ cup margarine, 1 cup brown sugar, and granulated sugar.
- Add to oats.
- Add eggs, vanilla, flour, soda, salt, and cinnamon.
- Beat 2 minutes.
- Pour into 13 x 9 x 2 inch pan.
- Bake.

Topping:
⅓   cup margarine, melted
½   cup brown sugar
¼   cup milk

½   teaspoon vanilla extract
1   cup coconut
½   cup pecans, chopped

- Mix margarine, brown sugar, milk, vanilla, coconut, and pecans.
- Spread over baked cake and broil until brown.

Mrs. William (Marvella) Easterling, Bennettsville, SC

Orange Sherbet

So good you might want to double or triple recipe!
Yield: 1 pint

¾   cup sugar
¾   cup water
    grated rind of 1 orange
1½ cups orange juice

1   tablespoon lemon juice
½   cup half-and-half cream
⅛   teaspoon salt

- Cook sugar and water slowly for 10 minutes.
- Add rind to syrup and continue to cook for several minutes.
- Strain.
- Add syrup to fruit juices, cream, and salt.
- Mix and freeze as directed by manufacturer of ice cream freezer.

Mrs. R. L. (Janie) McNiel, Hamer, SC

Orange Coconut Cake

This cake is best when made a day ahead!
Cooking time: 30 minutes   **Oven temperature: 350**
Prepare ahead

1	box orange cake mix	$^1/_3$ cup oil
1	3 ounce box orange gelatin	1 teaspoon vanilla flavoring
1$^1/_4$	cups water	1 teaspoon orange flavoring
3	eggs	

- Mix above ingredients and pour into 2 cake pans.
- Bake.

Filling:

1	16 ounce container sour cream	$^1/_3$ cup orange juice
1$^1/_2$	cups sugar	1 teaspoon vanilla flavoring
1	12 ounce container frozen coconut	1 teaspoon orange flavoring
	(use $^1/_2$ in filling and $^1/_2$ on cake)	1 12 ounce whipped topping

- Mix above ingredients to make filling.
- Mix whipped topping with one cup of filling and set aside.
- Split layers and stack (cut side up) layering with filling.
- Cover outside of cake with reserved filling-whipped dessert topping mixture.
- Sprinkle coconut on outside of cake.

Mrs. Larry (Phoebe) Howard, Bennettsville, SC

Peach Delight

This recipe is just as good with light whipped topping and no-fat sour cream! You can substitute strawberries or blueberries for peaches.
Serves: 10   **Preparation time: 20 minutes**
Prepare ahead

1	16 ounce whipped topping	1	16 ounce box confectioners sugar
1	8 ounce container sour cream	1	angel food cake
1	14 ounce can evaporated milk	2	15 ounce cans peach pie filling

- Mix whipped topping, sour cream, evaporated milk, and sugar.
- Break cake into small pieces.
- Mix cake in with mixture, and pour into 13 x 9 x 2 container.
- Put peach filling on top.

Ms. Jane Anne Feldner, Bennettsville, SC

Sweet Endings

Junior Charity League of Marlboro County, Inc.

Pineapple Layer Cake

Preparation time: 45 minutes   **Oven temperature: 375**

2   sticks butter, softened
2   cups sugar
4   cups self-rising flour, sifted

4   eggs
1   teaspoon lemon extract
1   teaspoon vanilla extract

- Cream butter and sugar until consistency of whipped cream.
- Mix in eggs, one at a time; add sifted flour, one cup at a time, alternating with eggs.
- Add lemon and vanilla and mix until smooth.
- If batter is too thick, add milk until desired consistency.
- Pour into greased 9 inch layer cake pans and bake until light brown.

Filling:

2   15 ounce cans crushed pineapple, undrained

1   cup sugar
$3/4$ cup milk

- Mix pineapple, sugar, and milk together and spread between layers.
- Prick each layer with fork so juice from filling is absorbed.

Mrs. Ethel Mercer, Bennettsville, SC

Pistachio Cake

Serves: 10-12   **Preparation time: 20 minutes**
Cooking time: 45 minutes   **Oven temperature: 350**

1   18.5 ounce box white cake mix
1   3 ounce box pistachio pudding
$3/4$ cup vegetable oil

$3/4$ cup milk
4   eggs
$1/2$ teaspoon almond extract

- Mix together cake mix, pudding, oil, milk, eggs, and almond extract.
- Bake in a bundt pan.

Icing:

1   stick butter, softened
1   8 ounce package cream cheese, softened

1   teaspoon vanilla extract
1   16 ounce box powdered sugar
1   cup pecans, chopped

- Cream butter and cream cheese well, then add powdered sugar, vanilla, and pecans.
- Pour over cake.

Ms. Inez Cottingham, Bennettsville, SC

Carolina Cuisine: Nothin' Could Be Finer

Cream Cheese Pound Cake

Serves: 20-24
Cooking time: 1½ hours
Prepare ahead

Preparation time: 30 minutes
Oven temperature: 325
Freezes well

3	sticks margarine, softened		dash salt
1	8 ounce package cream cheese, softened	1½	teaspoons vanilla extract
		6	large eggs
3	cups sugar	3	cups cake flour

- Cream margarine, cream cheese, and sugar until light and fluffy.
- Add salt and vanilla, then add eggs one at a time and beat well.
- Stir in flour.
- Spoon into a greased tube pan.
- Bake.

Mrs. Jimmy (Janis) Usher, Bennettsville, SC

Million Dollar Pound Cake

Delicious — melts in your mouth!!
Cooking time: 1 hour and 40 minutes   Oven temperature: 300

1	pound butter (4 sticks)	¾	cup milk
3	cups sugar	1	teaspoon almond extract
6	eggs	1	teaspoon vanilla extract
4	cups all-purpose flour		

- Cream butter, gradually add sugar, beating well at medium speed of mixer.
- Add eggs one at a time beating after each addition.
- Add flour to creamed mixture alternating with milk, beginning and ending with flour.
- Mix just until blended after each addition.
- Stir in flavoring.
- Pour into 10 inch tube pan and bake.

Mrs. James (Fannie) Chappelear, Bennettsville, SC

Half Pound Cake

Preparation time: 15 minutes
Oven temperature: 350

Cooking time: 55 minutes
Freezes well

1	stick butter, softened	2	cups all-purpose flour
$1/2$	cup butter-flavored shortening	$1/2$	teaspoon baking powder
$1^3/4$	cups sugar	5	eggs
		1	teaspoon vanilla extract

- In mixing bowl, cream butter and shortening. Gradually add sugar.
- Add baking powder to flour and sift.
- Add flour and eggs alternately to mixture, beginning and ending with flour.
- Add vanilla.
- If batter seems too stiff, add $1/4$ cup milk.
- Continue beating at medium speed until smooth and creamy.
- Bake in a small greased and floured tube pan.

Mrs. William B. (Frances) Belcher, Bennettsville, SC

Moist Pound Cake

Serves: 12
Cooking time: 1 hour 25 minutes
Freezes well

Preparation time: 30 minutes
Oven temperature: 325

3	sticks butter, softened	3	cups all-purpose flour, not sifted
3	cups sugar	$1/2$	teaspoon baking powder
5	eggs	1	teaspoon vanilla flavoring
1	cup milk	1	teaspoon lemon flavoring

- Cream butter and sugar.
- Add other ingredients alternately using an electric mixer.
- Pour in a greased and floured 10 inch tube pan.
- Place in a cold oven and bake.
- Remove from oven and cool about 20 minutes.
- Remove from pan.

Mrs. R. Glenn (Edna Earle) Locke, Bennettsville, SC

Chocolate Pound Cake

Cover the pan while the cake is in the oven — this preserves moisture..

Cooking time: 1½ hours   **Oven temperature: 350**

3	sticks butter, room temperature	1	teaspoon baking powder
3	cups sugar	5	eggs
1	teaspoon vanilla extract	½	cup buttermilk
3	cups all-purpose flour	½	cup milk
½	cup cocoa		

- Cream butter and sugar thoroughly.
- Add vanilla.
- Add eggs, one at a time, beating well after each.
- Alternately add flour mixture and milk.
- Bake in a tube pan.
- Remove from pan immediately.
- Cool thoroughly.

Mrs. William E. (Toni Ann) Dew, Latta, SC

Never Fail Chocolate Icing

You can use ½ cup of chopped nuts in icing, if desired.

12	large marshmallows	1	8 ounce package semi-sweet
1	6 ounce can evaporated milk		chocolate chips
2	cups sugar	½	teaspoon vanilla
1	stick butter or margarine		

- Combine first four ingredients over low heat.
- When it starts to boil, let boil for 4 minutes, stirring constantly.
- Take off heat and add chocolate chips and vanilla.
- Stir until chocolate chips melt.
- Spread on cake.

Mrs. William E. (Toni Ann) Dew, Latta, SC

Junior Charity League of Marlboro County, Inc.

Red Velvet Cake

Serves: 12
Cooking time: 30 minutes

Preparation time: 45 minutes
Oven temperature: 350

¹/₂ cup butter	¹/₂ teaspoon salt
1¹/₄ cups sugar	1 tablespoon vanilla extract
2 eggs	1 teaspoon baking soda
2 ounces red food coloring	1 cup buttermilk
2 tablespoons cocoa	1 tablespoon vinegar
2¹/₄ cups all-purpose flour	

- Preheat oven.
- Cream butter, sugar, and eggs.
- Make paste with food coloring and cocoa.
- Add to creamed mixture and beat.
- Sift flour and salt together.
- Blend buttermilk and vanilla.
- Alternately, add flour mixture and buttermilk mixture to creamed ingredients.
- Sprinkle baking soda over batter.
- Drop vinegar over soda and fold into batter.
- Bake in two 9 inch round cake pans greased and floured.
- Cool in pans for 5 minutes then place on wire racks to cool completely.

Mrs. Hank (Gloria) Avent, Sewickley, PA

Frosting for Red Velvet Cake

Makes frosting for one 2 layer cake
Preparation time: 15 minutes

3 tablespoons all-purpose flour	1 cup margarine, softened
1 cup milk	1 teaspoon vanilla extract
1 cup sugar	¹/₂ cup pecans, chopped

- In saucepan, put flour and add milk gradually.
- Cook over low heat until thick.
- Cool in refrigerator.
- Cream sugar, margarine, and vanilla extract until fluffy.
- Add flour mixture to creamed ingredients.
- Beat with mixer until the consistency of whipped cream.
- Spread on cool cake and sprinkle with pecans.

Mrs. Hank (Gloria) Avent, Sewickley, PA

Carolina Cuisine: Nothin' Could Be Finer

Strawberry Angel Food Cake

You can substitute fresh peaches for the strawberries.

Serves: 8-12   **Preparation time: 30 minutes**
Prepare ahead

1   8 ounce package cream cheese,   1   8 ounce whipped topping
    softened   1   carton fresh strawberries, chopped
1   14 ounce can condensed milk   (save a few whole strawberries for
1   angel food cake   top)

- Blend cream cheese and condensed milk.
- Cut a layer off the angel food cake, $^1/_3$ from the top.
- Scoop or pinch a "trough" around the bottom part of the cake.
- Mix the pieces of cake with the cream cheese mixture.
- Add strawberries and put the mixture in the "trough".
- Replace the top of the cake.
- Pour remaining mixture into the hole in the middle of the cake.
- Frost with whipped topping and place whole strawberries around the top of cake.

Mrs. B. B. (Martha) Sanders, IV, Bennettsville, SC

Ambrosia Pie

Yields: 2 pies

2   baked 9 inch pie shells   6   tablespoons flour
3   bananas $1^1/_2$ cups sugar
1   cup nuts, chopped   1   12 ounce package whipped topping
1   16 ounce can crushed pineapple   1   6 ounce package frozen coconut

- Mix flour into sugar and add pineapple.
- Cook until thick, stirring often.
- Let cool.
- Sprinkle nuts in pie shells.
- Cut up bananas and place on top of nuts.
- Add cooled pineapple mixture.
- Mix top with whipped topping with coconut.
- Pour over pineapple mixture.
- Cover and keep refrigerated.

Mrs. Fred (Joyce) McIntyre, Dillon, SC

Banana Cream Pie

Delicious during the summer months!
Serves: 6   **Preparation time: 10 minutes**
Prepare ahead

1	8 ounce package cream cheese, softened	1	9 inch graham cracker crust
1	14 ounce can condensed milk	3-4	bananas
½	cup lemon juice	1	8 ounce package whipped topping

- Blend the first three ingredients in a blender.
- Layer bananas, condensed milk mixture, bananas, and whipped topping in the pie crust.
- Serve chilled.

Mrs. Dudley C. (Sharon) Beaty, III, Bennettsville, SC

Frozen Cherry Pie

Serves: 12

1	14 ounce can condensed milk	1	cup cream, whipped (½ pint carton)
½	cup fresh lemon juice		
1	cup sugar	½	cup nuts, chopped
1	17 ounce can sour pitted cherries, drained	2	9 inch vanilla wafer pie crusts

- Mix milk, lemon juice, sugar, and cherries in mixer until cherries are well broken up.
- Fold in nuts and whipped cream.
- Pour into crusts.
- Freeze and serve frozen.

Mrs. J. P. (Virginia) Hodges, Bennettsville, SC

Cream Pie

Yields: 2 pies   **Preparation time: 15 minutes**
Cooking time: 45 minutes   **Oven temperature: 350**

¾	cup brown sugar	½	teaspoon vanilla extract
¾	cup sugar	2	cups whipping cream
3	rounded tablespoons flour	2	unbaked 9 inch pie crusts or one 9 inch deep dish
⅛	teaspoon salt		
⅛	teaspoon nutmeg		

- Mix all of the above items together and bake in pie shells.
- Cool.

Mrs. Gordon (Ruth) King, Bennettsville, SC

Sweet Endings

Carolina Cuisine: Nothin' Could Be Finer

Mary Kay and Margaret Ann's Chocolate Pie

This is without any doubt, the best chocolate pie recipe that I, or anyone else who has tasted it, has ever eaten. It is also larger and different from any other chocolate pie recipe that I've ever seen. Mrs. Charles R. May, III's mother, Mrs. S. M. Atkinson, baked this pie many times for Margaret Ann and myself when we were in high school and were neighbors. Mrs. Atkinson named her recipe Mary Kay and Margaret Ann's Chocolate Pie because we enjoyed it so much.

1	10 inch pie shell, baked	$1/4$	teaspoon salt
2	squares unsweetened chocolate OR	$1^1/3$	cups sugar
5	tablespoons cocoa	1	tablespoon butter
$1/2$	cup cake flour	1	tablespoon vanilla extract
$2^2/3$	cups milk	$1/2$	cup sugar
4	eggs, separated		

- Melt chocolate in double boiler, add sugar and flour which have been mixed together.
- Add milk slowly and cook until thick.
- Cook for 10 minutes and pour some of chocolate mixture into egg yolks, mixing while pouring.
- Add the egg yolk mixture and chocolate mixture together.
- Return mixture to double boiler and cook 2 more minutes.
- Remove from heat; add butter, vanilla and salt, then cool.
- Pour into pie shell.
- Make meringue using 4 egg whites and 1 cup sugar.

Mrs. Harry R. (Mary Kay) Easterling, Bennettsville, SC

Eggnog Bavarian

Serves: 6
Prepare ahead

Preparation time: 15 minutes
Freezes well

1	9 inch pie crust, baked and cooled	$1^1/4$	cups eggnog, canned or other
1	3.4 ounce package vanilla instant pudding	1	cup whipped topping nutmeg

- Combine pudding mix with eggnog.
- Use wire whisk and mix thoroughly.
- Add whipped topping, folding gently into pudding mix.
- Pour into cooled pie crust and dust with nutmeg.
- You may top the pie with whipped topping.
- Place in freezer.
- When ready to serve, take out of freezer a few minutes beforehand.

Mrs. Wade R. (Elaine) Crow, Bennettsville, SC

Sweet Endings

Junior Charity League of Marlboro County, Inc.

Fudge Pie

Yields: 1 pie
Cooking time: 20-22 minutes
Preparation time: 10 minutes
Oven temperature: 350

2 squares unsweetened chocolate
½ stick oleo
1 cup sugar
1 teaspoon vanilla
¼ teaspoon salt
½ cup flour
2 eggs, beaten
½-¾ cup nuts, chopped

- Melt chocolate and oleo.
- Add other ingredients.
- Bake in greased and floured pie pan.

Mrs. Shirley H. Beeson, Little River, SC

Grape Hull Pie

Yields: 1 pie
Cooking time: 40 minutes
Freezes well
Preparation time: 1 hour
Oven temperature: 400

4 cups Concord or Scuppernong grapes, washed
1 cup sugar
¼ cup all-purpose flour
¼ teaspoon salt
1 tablespoon lemon juice
1½ tablespoons margarine or butter, melted
1 9 inch unbaked pie shell (sometimes makes 2 pies)
1 9 inch unbaked pie shell for top OR crumb topping

- Slip skins from grapes, keep separate.
- Bring pulp to boil, simmer until mixture looks melted.
- Remove seeds with sieve or press through strainer.
- Add skins to pulp and gradually add combined sugar, flour, and salt.
- Simmer with lemon juice and margarine (or butter).
- Pour into pie shell(s) and top with another pie shell (cut slits in top) or top with crumb topping (see below).
- Bake.
- Top with vanilla ice cream or whipped dessert topping.

Crumb Topping:

- Combine ½ cup all-purpose flour and ¼ cup sugar.
- Cut in 6 tablespoons butter or margarine until crumbly.
- Sprinkle over pie before baking.

Mrs. William L. (Peggy) Kinney, Jr., Bennettsville, SC

Kentucky Pie

Serves: 6-8
Cooking time: 45 minutes-1 hour

Preparation time: 30 minutes
Oven temperature: 350

1	9 inch pie shell, partially baked	2	eggs, lightly beaten
	mint jelly	2	tablespoons bourbon
1	cup sugar	1	teaspoon vanilla extract
1/2	cup flour	1	cup chocolate chips
1/4	teaspoon salt	1	cup pecans, chopped
1	stick butter, melted		

- Prick pie shell all over with a fork and "paint" bottom with a thin coating of mint jelly.
- Bake for 8-9 minutes in a preheated 400 oven.
- Mix dry ingredients.
- Stir in remainder of ingredients.
- Pour into pie shell and bake until puffed and firm.

Mrs. John (Nancy) Fritschner, Cheraw, SC

Elisabeth's Key Lime Pie

Serves: 6
Cooking time: 30-40 minutes
Prepare ahead

Preparation time: 30 minutes
Oven temperature: 300

1	9 inch pie shell	1/2	cup lime juice
6	eggs	3/4	teaspoon cream of tartar
1	14 ounce can sweetened condensed milk	4	tablespoons sugar

- Preheat.
- Bake pie shell for 8 minutes.
- Separate eggs.
- Beat yolks and add milk, mix well and then add lime juice.
- Blend well and turn into pie shell.
- Beat egg whites until stiff while adding cream of tartar.
- Do not let them get dry.
- Gradually beat in sugar just until whites hold firm peaks.
- Swirl onto pie, spreading to edge of pie shell.
- Bake until meringue is pale honey-colored.
- Refrigerate until served.

Mrs. Daniel E. (Elisabeth) McNiel, Bennettsville, SC

Lemonade Pie

A light dessert!
Serves: 12

Prepare ahead

1   14 ounce can sweetened condensed milk
1   6 ounce can frozen lemonade concentrate, thawed

1   12 ounce container frozen whipped topping, thawed
2   9 inch graham cracker crusts

- Combine condensed milk, lemonade, and whipped topping, folding until well blended.
- Spread filling in crusts.
- Chill overnight.

Mrs. Benjy (Linda) Rogers, Bennettsville, SC
Mrs. Fred (Joyce) McIntyre, Dillon, SC

Easy Lemon Pie

Light and refreshing!
Serves: 6-8
Prepare ahead

Preparation time: 15 minutes
Freezes well

1   6 ounce frozen lemonade concentrate
1   pint vanilla ice cream (2 cups)

1   8 ounce container non-dairy whipped topping
1   9 inch graham cracker pie shell

- Pour lemonade concentrate into mixing bowl and beat with electric mixer for about 30 seconds.
- Slowly spoon in ice cream and beat until blended.
- Gently stir in whipped topping until smooth.
- Pour into crust and smooth with spatula.
- Freeze overnight or until firm.
- Let stand at room temperature 30 minutes before serving and garnish with fresh strawberries.

Mrs. Rhett (Gray) Covington, Bennettsville, SC

Whole Lemon Blender Pie

Very easy to prepare!
Yields: 2 pies
Cooking time: 20-30 minutes

Preparation time: 10 minutes
Oven temperature: 350

2   9 inch pie crusts, frozen
1   whole lemon, cut into pieces without seeds

1   stick margarine
4   eggs
$1^{1}/_{2}$ cups sugar

- Put all ingredients in blender and puree.
- Pour into pie crusts.
- Bake.

The late Miss Annie Kinney, Bennettsville, SC

Lemon Icebox Bisque

For tarter taste, use 12 ounce can frozen lemonade. (May substitute pink lemonade and add 1 cup or more pureed or well mashed fresh strawberries.)

Serves: 12
Freezing Time: 6 hours
Freezes well

Preparation time: 30 minutes
Prepare ahead

1   6 ounce can frozen lemonade, melted
½   gallon vanilla ice cream or ice milk, very soft

2   9 inch graham cracker pie shells
    ground cinnamon (optional)
1   12 ounce container whipped dessert topping

- Stir lemonade and ice cream toether until mixed well.
- Pour into pie shells or 9 x 13 pan of graham cracker crumb crust.
- May sprinkle cinnamon on crust and on top of ice cream filling and may sprinkle with graham cracker crumbs on top.
- Freeze until firm.
- Serve with whipped dessert topping, if desired.

Mrs. William L. (Peggy) Kinney, Jr., Bennettsville, SC

Nutty Buddy Pie

Serves: 8-10 (3 pies)
Prepare ahead

Preparation time: 20 minutes

3   9 inch chocolate pie crusts
1   8 ounce package cream cheese, softened
¾   cup crunchy peanut butter
1   cup milk

2   cups powdered sugar
1   cup peanuts, chopped
1   16 ounce container whipped dessert topping
    chocolate syrup

- Mix cream cheese, powdered sugar, milk, and peanut butter together.
- Blend in whipped topping.
- Pour into crusts and sprinkle with peanuts.
- Drizzle chocolate syrup over top.
- Cover and freeze.
- Remove from freezer 20 minutes before serving.

Mrs. James (Carole) Bowdre, Bennettsville, SC

Sweet Endings

Junior Charity League of Marlboro County, Inc.

Peanut Butter Pie

Serves: 6-8
Oven temperature: 325

- 1   9 inch baked pie shell
- 1   cup powdered sugar
- 1/2   cup peanut butter
- 1/4   cup cornstarch
- 2/3   cup sugar
- 1/4   teaspoon salt
- 2   cups scalded milk
- 3   egg yolks, beaten
- 2   tablespoons butter
- 1/4   teaspoon vanilla
- 3   egg whites for meringue

- Combine powdered sugar and peanut butter and blend to appearance of biscuit mix.
- Spread 1/2 of this on pie shell.
- Combine cornstarch, sugar and salt; add scalded milk and mix well.
- Gradually add beaten egg yolks and cook in top of double boiler until thick.
- Add butter and vanilla and pour into pie shell.
- Top with meringue and sprinkle remainder of peanut butter mixture over meringue.
- Bake until meringue is brown.

Mrs. Ralph (Emily) Kelly, Bennettsville, SC

Pecan Pie

Serves: 6
Preparation time: 10 minutes
Cooking time: 50 minutes
Oven temperature: 375
Freezes well

- 1/2   cup sugar
- 2   tablespoons butter
- 2   eggs, beaten
- 2   tablespoons all-purpose flour
- 1/4   teaspoon salt
- 1   teaspoon vanilla extract
- 1   cup white corn syrup
- 1 1/2   cups pecans, chopped
- 1   9 inch pie shell

- Preheat oven.
- Cream butter and sugar.
- Add beaten eggs, flour, salt, vanilla extract, and syrup.
- Stir and add pecans.
- Pour in crust and bake at 375 for 10 minutes.
- Then reduce heat to 350 for 40 minutes.

Mrs. Henry (Gerry) Capps, Bennettsville, SC

Sweet Endings

216   Carolina Cuisine: Nothin' Could Be Finer

Tip-Top Pecan Pie

Best served warm, a must for all southern pies, with a scoop of vanilla ice cream on top. This is a favorite from the Tip-Top Inn, Pawleys Island, South Carolina, which was destroyed by Hurricane Hugo in September, 1989.

Serves: 8   **Cooking time: 1 hour or more**
Oven temperature: 325

1	9 inch pie shell	3	eggs
4	tablespoons butter, softened	$1/4$	teaspoon salt
1	cup light brown sugar	1	teaspoon vanilla extract
1	cup light corn syrup	1	cup pecans, chopped

- Preheat oven.
- Bake pie shell for 8 minutes.
- Cream butter and sugar.
- Gradually add syrup, beating constantly.
- In a small bowl, beat eggs and salt until light and fluffy.
- Add to creamed mixture.
- Stir in vanilla and pecans.
- Pour into pie shell.
- Bake until knife inserted in center comes out clean.

The late Tip-Top Inn, Pawleys Island, SC

Strawberry Pie

Serves: 10   **Prepare ahead**

2	baked 9 inch deep dish pie shells	4	tablespoons cornstarch
3	pints strawberries	10	tablespoons strawberry gelatin
$1^{1}/_{2}$	cups sugar	1	12 ounce container whipped
$1^{1}/_{2}$	cups water		topping

- Boil sugar, water, and cornstarch.
- Remove from heat and stir in dry gelatin.
- Let cool about 2 hours until thick.
- Cut up strawberries and place in cooked pie shells.
- Pour gelatin mixture over berries.
- Refrigerate until firm.
- Top with whipped topping and serve!

Mrs. Jimmy (Janis) Usher, Bennettsville, SC

Blonde Brownies

Yields: 24 cookies
Cooking time: 45 minutes

Preparation time: 20 minutes
Oven temperature: 300

2   sticks margarine
1   cup sugar
1   cup light brown sugar
2   teaspoons baking powder
2   cups all-purpose flour, sifted then
     measured

2   teaspoons vanilla extract
2   eggs
     nuts or dates

- Melt margarine.
- Add sugar, eggs, and flour to melted margarine.
- Mix well and then add nuts.
- Bake in 9 x 12 baking tin.
- Cool before cutting or removing from pan. (You may think it is not done, but it is.)

Mrs. Donald (Marty) Rankin, Bennettsville, SC

Martin's Blonde Brownies

Cooking time: 30-35 minutes

Oven temperature: 325

2   sticks butter, softened
1   16 ounce box light brown sugar
2   eggs

2   cups self-rising flour
1   tablespoon vanilla extract
2   cups nuts, chopped

- Cream butter and sugar.
- Add eggs, flour, and vanilla, beating very well.
- Stir in nuts.
- Bake in greased and floured 10 x 15 pan.

Mrs. Martin (Gladys) Kinard, Bennettsville, SC

Charleston Squares

Cooking time: 25 minutes   **Oven temperature: 350**

1	stick butter	1	teaspoon baking powder
1	cup sugar	2	cups all-purpose flour
2	eggs (save 1 white)	1	teaspoon vanilla extract
1/4	teaspoon salt	1	teaspoon almond extract

- Mix butter, sugar, eggs, salt, baking powder, flour, vanilla, and almond.
- Spread in two pans or one 9 x 13 pan.
- Dip hands in flour and press batter in pans.

Icing:

1	egg white, beaten stiff	1	cup nuts, chopped
1/2	cup light brown sugar	1	6 ounce jar cherries, chopped
1	teaspoon of vanilla extract		

- Add brown sugar and vanilla to egg white.
- Spread over batter.
- Sprinkle nuts and chopped cherries over icing.
- Bake after completing all steps, including icing.

Mrs. John (Peggy) Culp, Bennettsville, SC

Cheesecake Cookies

Yields: 3-4 dozen   **Preparation time: 1 hour**
Cooking time: 15 minutes   **Oven temperature: 350**
Prepare ahead

2	8 ounce packages cream cheese, softened	1	teaspoon vanilla extract
		3-4	dozen vanilla wafers
3	eggs	1	15 ounce can cherry pie filling
3/4	cup sugar		

- Beat cream cheese, eggs, sugar, and vanilla with a mixer until very smooth.
- Place cup cake papers on a cookie sheet.
- Put 1 vanilla wafer in each paper.
- Put 1 tablespoon cream cheese mixture on top of vanilla wafer.
- Bake just until they start to crack.
- Let cool.
- Put a small spoonful of pie filling in center of each cooled cookie.

Mrs. Jimmy (Janis) Usher, Bennettsville, SC

Sweet Endings

Junior Charity League of Marlboro County, Inc.

Forgotten Cookies

Yields: 40 cookies
Cooking time: 8 hours
Prepare ahead

Preparation time: 30 minutes
Oven temperature: 350

2   egg whites
       pinch salt
1/4   teaspoon cream of tartar
2/3   cup sugar

1/4   teaspoon vanilla
1   cup nuts, chopped
1   cup chocolate chips

- Preheat oven.
- Beat egg whites until foamy.
- Add salt and cream of tartar and beat until stiff.
- Add sugar, 2 tablespoons at a time, beating well after each addition.
- Stir in vanilla, nuts, and chocolate chips.
- Drop by teaspoonfuls onto cookie sheet lined with aluminum foil.
- Put in oven and turn off heat immediately.
- Do not open oven for at least 8 hours.
- Carefully remove cookies from foil.

Mrs. Reid (Deanie) Hensarling, Bennettsville, SC

Crunchy Fudge Sandwiches

Yield: 30-40 cookies
Prepare ahead

Preparation time: 30-60 minutes

1   6 ounce packages butterscotch chips
1/2   cup peanut butter
4   cups toasted rice cereal
1   6 ounce package chocolate chips

1/2   cup powdered sugar
1   tablespoon water
2   tablespoons margarine, softened

- Melt butterscotch chips and peanut butter over low heat.
- Stir in the rice cereal.
- Divide and press one half in a 12 x 8 dish.
- Chill.
- Melt chocolate chips, water, and margarine over low heat.
- Stir in powdered sugar.
- Carefully spread chocolate mixture over chilled rice cereal mixture.
- Top with remaining cereal mixture, pressing gently.
- Chill 2 hours before cutting.
- Keep cool.

Mrs. Jimmy (Janis) Usher, Bennettsville, SC

Carolina Cuisine: Nothin' Could Be Finer

Tangy Lemon Bars

Cooking time: 40 minutes   **Oven temperature: 350**

1   18.25 ounce package lemon cake   1   egg
    mix with pudding   1   stick butter, melted

- Mix above ingredients and pat out in a 9 x 13 pan.
- Add topping and bake.

Topping:
1   8 ounce package cream cheese   3   eggs
1   16 ounce box confectioners sugar

- Mix topping ingredients and pour on top BEFORE baking.

Mrs. William E. (Toni Ann) Dew, Latta, SC

Lemon Cookies

So easy and good!

Cooking time: 12-15 minutes   **Oven temperature: 350**

1   18.25 ounce box lemon cake mix   2   eggs
1   8 ounce container whipped topping   1   cup confectioners sugar

- Combine the first three ingredients and roll by the spoonful in powdered sugar.
- Place cookie mixture about $1^1/_2$ inches apart.
- Bake until lightly brown.

Mrs. Walter W. (Saress) Gregg, Bennettsville, SC

Ruth Kirkwood's Mints

This is my grandmother's much used recipe!

Yields: 100-150 small mints   **Preparation time: 1 hour**

1   stick butter, softened $^1/_2$ dropper oil of peppermint
1   16 ounce box powdered sugar, 4X
    or 10X

- Mix ingredients.
- Add food coloring, if wanted (1 or 2 drops) — may need to add more powdered sugar.
- Take mixture and form small rolls of desired thickness and slice into individual mints.

Mrs. Leith (Virginia) Fowler, Bennettsville, SC

Sweet Endings

Junior Charity League of Marlboro County, Inc.   **221**

Lemon Sours

Yields: 2 dozen squares
Cooking time: 30 minutes
Prepare ahead

Preparation time: 15 minutes
Oven temperature: 350
Freezes well

$3/4$ cup all-purpose flour, sifted
$1/3$ cup butter
2 eggs
1 cup brown sugar
$3/4$ cup coconut, shredded
$1/2$ cup nuts, chopped

$1/8$ teaspoon baking powder
$1/2$ teaspoon vanilla extract
1 teaspoon lemon rind, grated
$1 1/2$ teaspoons lemon juice
$2/3$ cup confectioners sugar

- Mix flour and butter to a fine crumb.
- Sprinkle evenly in 11 x 7 pan.
- Bake for 10 minutes.
- Beat eggs, then mix in brown sugar, coconut, nuts, baking powder, and vanilla.
- Spread on first mixture as you take it from oven.
- Return to oven and bake 20 minutes.
- Mix lemon rind and juice and add confectioners sugar to make a creamy mixture.
- Spread over top as soon as pan is taken from oven.
- Cool and cut into squares.

Mrs. Ray (Lydia) Smith, Bennettsville, SC

Aunt Kay B's Peanut Butter Cookies

Yields: 3 dozen
Oven temperature: 350

Cooking time: 7-10 minutes

2 sticks butter
$1 1/4$ cups sugar
$3/4$ cup light brown sugar
2 eggs
1 teaspoon vanilla extract

1 cup peanut butter
$2 1/2$ cups all-purpose flour, sifted
2 teaspoons baking soda
$1/2$ teaspoon salt

- Cream butter.
- Add sugars and beat until light and fluffy.
- Beat in eggs and vanilla.
- Blend in peanut butter.
- Sift together flour, soda, and salt.
- Gradually add to creamed mixture.
- Drop by rounded teaspoons onto ungreased cookie sheet.
- Bake.

Miss Courtney Hodges, Bennettsville, SC

Carolina Cuisine: Nothin' Could Be Finer

Seven-Layer Cookies

Yield: 36 small squares
Oven temperature: 325

Cooking time: 30 minutes

1/2 stick butter	1 6 ounce package butterscotch chips
1 cup graham cracker crumbs	1 14 ounce can sweetened condensed
1 3 1/2 ounce can flaked coconut	milk
1 6 ounce package chocolate chips	1 cup nuts, chopped

- Melt butter in 9 x 12 pan.
- Add ingredients by layers, in order listed.
- Bake.
- Let cool in pan.
- Cut into small squares.

Mrs. Carolyn Dudley Wallace, Bennettsville, SC

World's Best Sugar Cookies

Very crisp! They melt in your mouth!

Yield: 5-6 dozen
Cooking time: 10 minutes
Prepare ahead

Preparation time: 30 minutes
Oven temperature: 350
Freezes well

1 cup butter, softened	2 eggs, beaten
1 cup vegetable oil	5 cups all-purpose flour
1 cup sugar	1/2 teaspoon salt
1 cup powdered sugar	1 teaspoon baking soda
1 teaspoon vanilla extract	1 teaspoon cream of tartar
1 teaspoon almond extract	

- Cream butter, oil, and both sugars with mixer.
- Add extracts.
- Beat in eggs one at a time.
- Sift dry ingredients and add to creamed mixture.
- Beat until combined.
- Chill dough 1-2 hours in refrigerator.
- Roll into balls the size of walnuts.
- Place on ungreased cookie sheet.
- Flatten with bottom of glass dipped in sugar.
- Bake.

Mrs. Susan McNiel Hinson, Bennettsville, SC
Mrs. Norman (Kay) Rentz, Pickens, SC

Sweet Endings

Golden Nugget Fudge

Soft and creamy!
Yields: 32 bars

- 3 cups sugar
- 1 1/2 cups milk
- 3/4 teaspoon salt
- 3 tablespoons butter
- 3 tablespoons light corn syrup
- 2 teaspoons vanilla extract
- 1/2 cup dried apricots, chopped
- 1/2 cup marshmallow creme
- 1/3 cup walnuts or pecans, chopped

- Butter sides of a three quart saucepan.
- Mix sugar, milk, syrup, and salt in saucepan.
- Stir and heat until sugar dissolves and mixture boils.
- Cook, without stirring, to soft ball stage (234 degrees on candy thermometer).
- Stir in butter and vanilla.
- Place in pan of cold water and cool to lukewarm, without stirring.
- Add apricots and beat until mixture holds shape.
- Stir in marshmallow creme and nuts.
- Beat until candy loses its gloss (about 5 minutes).
- Spread fudge in buttered 9 inch square pan.
- When set, cut in 32 bars.

Mrs. Walter W. (Saress) Gregg, Bennettsville, SC

Peanut Butter Candy

Serves: 10 **Preparation time: 10 minutes**

- 1 1/2 sticks margarine, melted
- 2 cups chunky peanut butter
- 1 16 ounce box confectioners sugar
- 7 milk chocolate candy bars, melted

- Mix the first three ingredients and press this mixture into a pan sprayed with non-stick cooking spray.
- Spread melted chocolate bars on top.
- Let sit for a few hours, then cut into squares.

Mrs. Dudley C. (Sharon) Beaty, III, Bennettsville, SC

Chocolate Sauce

Delicious over vanilla ice cream!

- 2 squares unsweetened chocolate
- 3/4 stick butter or margarine
- 1 cup sugar
- 1/2 cup milk

- Put all the ingredients in a double boiler and cook until consistency of canned syrup, not as thick as candy.
- Serve hot over ice cream.

The late Miss Annie Kinney, Bennettsville, SC

CHILDREN'S FUN

Drawing by: Demonica Covington

Domonica Covington
"Fun at the Beach"

Domonica Covington is a source of joy to her family, friends and teachers at Bennettsville Primary School where she is an honor roll student. She loves to draw beautiful pictures and has a creative imagination.

Domonica is the daughter of Calendra and James McCollum and has two brothers and a sister. She always wears a smile and loves to laugh. Her favorite subject is spelling and after school she enjoys riding her bicycle.

Fried Bananas

Wonderful way to use those too ripe bananas.

Serves: 4 - 6   **Cooking time: about 20 minutes**

6	bananas, very ripe	$1/4$	cup sugar
3	tablespoons butter	$1/2$	teaspoon cinnamon

- Melt butter in large skillet until very hot on medium high.
- Peel bananas and place in skillet whole or cut in half lengthwise.
- Cook until golden brown while constantly flipping bananas and sprinkling with sugar each time flipped.
- When bananas are brown, sprinkle with cinnamon and serve immediately.

Miss Susan Turpin, Bennettsville, SC

Circus Bagels

Great for birthday parties! Can easily be doubled.

Serves: 2   **Preparation time: 10 minutes**

1	bagel, halved	2	teaspoons sweetened coconut,
4	tablespoons crunchy peanut butter		shredded
$1/2$	banana, sliced		

- Spread toasted or untoasted plain bagel halves with peanut butter.
- Top bagel with banana slices and sprinkle with coconut.

Mrs. Mark S. (Jimmy Carol) Avent, Bennettsville, SC

Children

"Beary" Easy and Good Dessert

Serves: 6 - 8   **Preparation time: 5 minutes**
Prepare ahead

1   2^1/$_8$ ounce box animal shaped   1   8 ounce whipped dessert topping
     chocolate graham crackers

- Place crackers in mixing bowl and add the whipped topping.
- Stir well, cover, and refrigerate.
- For crunchy consistency, prepare 2 - 3 hours before serving.
- For softer consistancy, prepare one day ahead.
- Chocolate chip cookies or chocolate wafers broken into pieces may be substituted for graham crackers.

Mrs. James (Nancy Ruth) Raines, Bennettsville, SC

Bologna Sandwich Spread

This is a sandwich my mother made me when I was little. I still make it every now and then. Children like it and it comes in handy for an extra spread.

Preparation time: 15 minutes   **Prepare ahead**

1   12 ounce package bologna, sliced   mayonnaise
1   12 ounce jar sweet gherkin pickle

- Grind bologna in meat grinder, then add pickles to grinder.
- Add mayonnaise to bind.
- Keep refrigerated for several days.

Mrs. Ray (June) Rogers, Bennettsville, SC

Hole-n-One Burger

Serves: 8
Cooking time: 40 minutes
Prepare ahead

Preparation time: 10 minutes
Oven temperature: 375
Freezes well

1 egg	3 tablespoons ketchup
1/2 cup water	1 pound lean ground beef or turkey
3/4 cup oatmeal	4 bagels, halved
1 teaspoon salt	

- Mix all the ingredients, except for the bagels.
- Spread the mixture on each bagel half, leaving a hole in the middle.
- Bake until filling is fully cooked.

Mrs. Mark S. (Jimmy Carol) Avent, Bennettsville, SC

Ghoul's Hands

Yields: 5 favors
Prepare ahead

Preparation time: 30 minutes

caramel coated popcorn	5 rubber bands
75 pieces candy corn	5 plastic spider rings
5 clear industrial gloves	orange and black ribbon

- Place 3 pieces of candy corn into ends of each glove finger.
- Fill gloves tightly with popcorn.
- Close securely at wrist with rubber band, and tie ribbon over rubber bands.
- Place ring on one finger of each hand.

Mrs. Curt (Deanne) Hinson, Bennettsville, SC

Junior Charity League of Marlboro County, Inc.

Monkey Bread

Easy for children to do.
Preparation time: 25 minutes
Oven temperature: 350

Cooking time: 30 minutes

1/2 cup sugar
1/2 cup nuts, chopped
1/4 cup milk
1   stick margarine, melted

1   cup sugar
1   heaping tablespoon cinnamon
30   canned biscuits

- Mix and pour 1/2 cup sugar, nuts, and milk into a bundt pan.
- Mix 1 cup sugar and cinnamon.
- Dip biscuits in melted margarine and roll in cinnamon and sugar, coating well.
- Arrange in bundt pan and bake.
- Let cool in pan for 2 minutes and invert on plate.

Mrs. James (Carole) Bowdre, Bennettsville, SC

Beth's Cooked Play Dough

1   cup flour
1/2 cup salt
1   tablespoon vegetable oil

2   teaspoons cream of tartar
1   cup water with desired choice of
     food coloring

- Heat all ingredients together in a saucepan.
- Stir from the bottom of the pan until it sticks together and the liquid is absorbed.
- Remove from pan and knead together.
- Let dough cool and stir in air-tight containers.

Mrs. John (Pam) Napier, Pawleys Island, SC

Carolina Cuisine: Nothin' Could Be Finer

Honey Crackle Popcorn

Preparation time: 15 minutes
Oven temperature: 250

Cooking time: 1 hour
Prepare ahead

3-4 quarts freshly popped popcorn, kept
warm in oven
$^1/_2$ cup butter

1 cup light brown sugar, packed
$^1/_4$ cup honey
1 teaspoon vanilla extract

- Preheat oven.
- Melt butter over low heat in a heavy saucepan.
- Stir in brown sugar and honey.
- Over medium heat, cook, stirring constantly, and boil gently for five minutes.
- Remove from heat and add vanilla.
- Drizzle over popcorn and mix well, try to coat each piece well.
- Bake, stirring popcorn every 15 minutes.
- Cool completely and break apart.
- Store in a tightly sealed container.

Mrs. Andy (Mary Alice) Burroughs, Bennettsville, SC

Funnel Cakes

Old Tennessee recipe given by a dear friend.

$1^1/_4$ cups all-purpose flour
2 tablespoons sugar
1 teaspoon baking soda
$^3/_4$ teaspoon baking powder
$^1/_4$ teaspoon salt

1 egg
$^3/_4$ cup milk
vegetable oil, enough to fill skillet 1
inch deep
2 teaspoons powdered sugar

- Combine dry ingredients.
- Add egg and milk, beating until smooth.
- Heat oil in a deep skillet at 375 degrees.
- Cover bottom opening of a funnel with a finger.
- Pour $^1/_4$ cup batter into funnel.
- Hold funnel over center of skillet.
- Remove finger from bottom to release batter into hot oil.
- Move funnel in a slow circular motion to form cake.
- Fry until golden brown.
- Sprinkle with powdered sugar and serve with syrup.

Mrs. James (Carole) Bowdre, Bennettsville, SC

Children

Junior Charity League of Marlboro County, Inc.

Morning Mix Up

Can mix in chopped bacon, sausage, or ham for a meal.

Serves: 4　　　　　　　　　　　　　　**Preparation time: 15 minutes**
Cooking time: 15 minutes

16　ounces tater tots, cooked
8　eggs
¼　cup milk

4　ounces shredded cheddar cheese
　　salt and pepper
　　vegetable oil

- Place enough cooking oil in bottom of a frying pan to cover and heat.
- Add tater tots and mash with a fork.
- Cook until warm.
- Mix together eggs, milk, salt, and pepper.
- Pour over potatoes.
- Cook until eggs are set, add cheese and fold into mixture.
- Cook until cheese is melted and serve.

Mrs. Tim (Elaine) Seales, Bennettsville, SC

Spoonburgers

Serves: 4 - 6　　　　　　　　　　　　**Preparation time: 10 minutes**
Cooking time: 15 minutes

1　pound ground beef
2　teaspoons mustard
2　tablespoons ketchup

1　$10^3/_4$ ounce can tomato soup
　　salt and pepper
6　hamburger buns

- Brown ground beef and drain.
- Add other ingredients.
- Cover and cook.
- Serve on buns.

Mrs. Tom (Dottie) Pharr, Bennettsville, SC

Turtles

Serves: 1
Cooking time: 1 - 2 minutes

Preparation time: 5 minutes
Oven temperature: Broil

1   slice bologna
$^1/_2$ cup cooked potatoes, mashed

1   slice cheese

- Place bologna on a baking sheet under the broiler until it turns up and forms a bowl.
- Place one scoop mashed potatoes in "bowl".
- Place a slice of cheese on top of potatoes.
- Broil until cheese melts and serve immediately.

Mrs. Hubert (Christi) Meggs, Jr., Bennettsville, SC

Barbecued Wieners

Children adore these.
Serves: 4 - 6
Cooking time: 25 - 30 minutes

Preparation time: 20 minutes
Oven temperature: 350

$^1/_2$ cup onion, chopped
1   teaspoon butter, melted
1   teaspoon pepper
2   tablespoons sugar
2   teaspoons mustard

$^1/_2$ cup ketchup
8   teaspoons Worcestershire sauce
2   tablespoons vinegar
2   dozen hot dogs, sliced

- Sauté onion in butter until slightly brown.
- Add remaining ingredients, except wieners.
- Mix well and pour over hot dogs in casserole dish.
- Bake.

Mrs. Tom (Dottie) Pharr, Bennettsville, SC

Children

Junior Charity League of Marlboro County, Inc.   233

Notes:

Helpful Handfulls

Drawing by: Margaret Singletary

Margaret Strong Singletary
"Easy Living"

Margaret Strong Singletary, a native of Williamsburg County, South Carolina, today enjoys retirement living on Lake Marion near Santee, South Carolina, which inspires her artwork. Mrs. Singletary began pursuing her desire to create art late in life with the assistance of Mary Anderson of Lake City, South Carolina, where she resided many years.

Mrs. Singletary also enjoys painting and creating ceramics as gifts for friends and family in addition to painting on canvas. She currently studies art at Shaw Air Force Base in Sumter, South Carolina.

A graduate of Flora McDonald College in Red Springs, North Carolina, with a degree in Elementary Education, Mrs. Singletary taught school in Lake City for 30 years. She and her husband, Jack, have four children, five grandchildren and five great-grandchildren.

Mrs. Hubert (Christi Singletary) Meggs, Jr., a granddaughter, is a current member of the Junior Charity League of Marlboro County, Inc.

Tables of Measure

Helpful Handfuls

Measurements

1 dash	less than $1/8$ teaspoon
1 barspoon	$3/4$ teaspoon
1 tablespoon	3 teaspoons
1 tablespoon	$1/2$ fluid ounce
1 cup	16 tablespoons
1 cup	8 fluid ounces
1 gill	$1/2$ cup
1 gill	4 fluid ounces
1 pint	2 cups
1 pint	4 gills
1 quart	2 pints
1 gallon	4 quarts
1 jigger	$1 1/2$ ounces
1 pony	1 ounce
1 peck	8 quarts
1 bushel	4 pecks

Conversions

1 teaspoon	5 milliliters
1 tablespoon	15 milliliters
1 cup	240 milliliters
1 pint	480 milliliters
1 quart	960 milliliters
1 gallon	3.8 liters
1 ounce (weight)	28 grams
1 pound	454 grams

Average Can Size

No. 1	$1 1/3$ cups
No. 2	$2 1/2$ cups
No. $2 1/2$	$3 1/2$ cups
No. 3	4 cups
No. 10	13 cups

Junior Charity League of Marlboro County, Inc.

Substitutions

Helpful Handfuls

For These	You May Use These
1 whole egg, for thickening or baking	2 egg yolks. Or 2 tablespoons dried whole egg plus $2^{1}/_{2}$ tablespoons water
1 cup butter or margarine for shortening	$^{7}/_{8}$ cup lard, or rendered fat with $^{1}/_{2}$ teaspoon salt
1 square ounce chocolate	3 or 4 tablespoons cocoa plus $^{1}/_{2}$ tablespoon fat
1 teaspoon double-acting baking powder	$1^{1}/_{2}$ teaspoons phosphate baking powder.
Sweet milk and baking powder, for baking	Equal amount sour milk plus $^{1}/_{2}$ teaspoon soda per cup. (Each half teaspoon soda with 1 cup sour milk takes the place of 2 teaspoons baking powder and 1 cup sweet milk)
1 cup buttermilk, for baking	1 cup milk mixed with either: 1 tablespoon vinegar, 1 tablespoon lemon juice, or $1^{3}/_{4}$ teaspoons cream of tartar
1 cup whole milk	$^{1}/_{2}$ cup evaporated milk plus $^{1}/_{2}$ cup water
1 cup skim milk	4 tablespoons nonfat dry milk plus 1 cup water
1 tablespoon flour, for thickening	$^{1}/_{2}$ tablespoon corn starch, potato starch, rice starch or arrowroot starch. Or 1 tablespoon granulated tapioca
1 cup cake flour, for baking	$^{7}/_{8}$ cup all-purpose flour
1 cup all-purpose flour, for baking breads	Up to $^{1}/_{2}$ cup bran, whole-wheat flour, or corn meal plus enough all-purpose flour to fill cup

Oven Temperatures

very slow	250 - 275 degrees
slow	300 - 325 degrees
moderate	350 - 375 degrees
hot	400 - 425 degrees
very hot	450 - 475 degrees
extremely hot	500 - 525 degrees

Carolina Cuisine: Nothin' Could Be Finer

Quantities for Serving 25, 50 & 100 People

Helpful Handfuls

	25 Servings	50 Servings	100 Servings
Sandwiches			
Bread	50 slices or 3 1 pound loaves	100 slices or 6 1 pound loaves	200 slices or 12 1 pound loaves
Butter	$1/2$ pound	$3/4$ to 1 pound	$1 1/2$ pounds
Mayonnaise	1 cup	2 to 3 cups	4 to 6 cups
Mixed filling (meat, eggs, fish)	$1 1/2$ quarts	$2 1/2$ to 3 quarts	5 to 6 quarts
Mixed filling (sweet fruit)	1 quart	$1 3/4$ to 2 quarts	$2 1/2$ to 4 quarts
Lettuce	$1 1/2$ heads	$2 1/2$ to 3 heads	5 to 6 heads
Meat, Poultry, or Fish			
Wieners (beef)	$6 1/2$ pounds	13 pounds	25 pounds
Hamburger	9 pounds	18 pounds	35 pounds
Turkey or Chicken	13 pounds	25 to 35 pounds	50 to 75 pounds
Fish, large whole (round)	13 pounds	25 pounds	50 pounds
Fish, fillets or steaks	$7 1/2$ pounds	15 pounds	30 pounds
Salads, Casseroles			
Potato salad	$4 1/4$ quarts	$2 1/4$ gallons	$4 1/2$ gallons
Scalloped potatoes	$4 1/2$ quarts or 1 12 x 20 pan	$8 1/2$ quarts	17 quarts
Spaghetti	$1 1/4$ gallons	$2 1/2$ gallons	5 gallons
Baked beans	$3/4$ gallon	$1 1/4$ gallons	$2 1/2$ gallons
Gelatin salad	$3/4$ gallon	$1 1/4$ gallons	$2 1/2$ gallons
Icecream			
Brick	$3 1/4$ quarts	$6 1/2$ quarts	$12 1/2$ quarts
Bulk	$2 1/4$ quarts	$4 1/2$ quarts or $1 1/4$ gallons	9 quarts or $2 1/2$ gallons
Beverages			
Coffee	$1/2$ pound and $1 1/2$ gallons water	1 pound and 3 gallons water	2 pounds and 6 gallons water
Tea	$1/12$ pound and $1 1/2$ gallons water	$1/6$ pound and 3 gallons water	$1/3$ pound and 6 gallons water
Lemonade	10 - 15 lemons, $1 1/2$ gallons water	20 to 30 lemons 3 gallons water	40 to 60 lemons, 6 gallons water
Desserts			
Watermelon	$37 1/2$ pounds	75 pounds	150 pounds
Cake	1 10 x 12 sheet cake $1 1/2$ layer cakes	1 12 x 20 sheet cake 3 layer cakes	2 12 x 20 sheet cakes 6 layer cakes
Whipping Cream	$3/4$ pint	$1 1/2$ to 2 pints	3 pints

Junior Charity League of Marlboro County, Inc.

Vegetable Cooking Chart

Helpful Handfuls

	Minutes to Cook		
Vegetable	**Boiling**	**Steaming**	**Seasonings**
Asparagus	2 to 5	5 to 8	Tarragon, dill, lemon, vinaigrette
Beans, green	10 to 20	15 to 25	Basil, dill, thyme, mint, oregano, savory, tarragon
Beets (whole)	30		Allspice, ginger, orange, lemon
Broccoli			Dill, tarragon, lemon, vinaigrette
(spears)	6 to 8	10 to 15	
(flowerets)	3 to 5	8 to 10	
Cabbage			Caraway, taragon, savory, dill
(wedges)	7 to 10	15	
(shredded)	3 to 10	8 to 12	
Carrots (slices or thin strips)	5 to 8	10 to 15	Ginger, nutmeg, caraway, cinnamon, dill, lemon, mint, orange
Cauliflower (flowerets)	8 to 12	10 to 20	Caraway, dill, mace, tarragon, Parmesan cheese
Eggplant (slices or cubes)	5 to 8	10 to 15	Marjoram, sage, oregano, basil, Parmesan cheese
Greens			Basil, chives, dill, oregano, tarragon,
Spinach and beet	3 to 8		nutmeg, rosemary, Parmesan cheese, lemon
Kale and Swiss chard	10 to 15		
Mustard	20 to 45		
Arugula and watercress	1 to 3		
Peas, green	5 to 12	10 to 20	Mint, chervil, marjoram, rosemary, garlic, tarragon
Potatoes, new (whole)	10 to 15	20 to 30	Lemon, parsley, vinaigrette, chives, dill, basil, thyme
Squash (slices)	8 to 12	10 to 12	Basil, garlic, rosemary, dill, thyme, oregano

To boil: Bring a small amount of water or broth to a boil. Add vegetables, reduce heat, and cook as recommended.

To steam: Arrange vegetables in a steamer basket; place over boiling water. Cover and steam for time given or until crisp-tender.

Carolina Cuisine: Nothin' Could Be Finer

Vegetable Freezing Chart

Vegetable	Preparation	Blanching Time
Beans (butter, lima, and pinto)	Choose tender beans with well-filled pods. Wash and shell; then sort according to size.	Small beans, 2 minutes; medium beans, 3 minutes; large beans, 4 minutes
Beans (green, snap, and waxed)	Select tender young pods. Wash beans, and cut off tips. Cut lengthwise or in 1 to 2 inch lengths.	3 minutes
Corn (on the cob)	Husk corn and remove silks; trim and wash.	Small ears, 7 minutes; medium ears, 9 minutes; large ears, 11 minutes
Corn (whole kernel)	Blanch ears first. Then cut kernels from cob about $^2/_3$ depth of kernels.	4 minutes
Corn (cream-style)	Blanch ears first. Cut off tips of kernels. Scrape cobs with back of a knife to remove juice and hearts of kernels.	4 minutes
Greens (beet, chard, collards, mustard, spinach, turnip)	Select tender green leaves. Wash thoroughly; remove woody stems.	Collards, 3 minutes; other greens, 2 minutes
Okra	Select tender, green pods. Wash and sort according to size. Remove stems at end of seed cells being careful not to expose seed cells. After blanching, leave pods whole or slice crosswise.	Small pods, 3 minutes; large pods, 4 minutes
Peas	Select pods with tender, barely mature peas. Shell and wash peas; discard those that are immature, hard, or overly mature.	2 minutes for black-eyed and field peas; $1^1/_2$ minutes for green peas
Squash (summer)	Select young squash with small seeds and tender rind. Wash and cut into $^1/_2$ inch slices.	3 minutes
Tomatoes	Raw: Wash; dip tomatoes in boiling water 30 seconds to loosen skins. Core and peel. Chop or quarter tomatoes, or leave whole. Pack to 1 inch from top.	Stewed: Remove stem and core; peel and quarter. Cover; cook until tender (10 to 20 minutes). Place pan in cold water to cool. Pack pints to $^1/_2$ inch from top, quarts to 1 inch from top.

Helpful Handfuls

Junior Charity League of Marlboro County, Inc.

Helpful Hints

Helpful Handfuls

The secret in making meringues is to bring egg whites to room temperature before beating them and to always spread them on a hot filling.

Tenderize chicken by rubbing the inside and outside with lemon juice before cooking.

Clean shrimp by running an ice pick down the back towards their tails. You can then easily pull off the shell and vein.

For smooth gravy, blend a little salt into the flour or cornstarch before adding water to the thickening.

To cut down on the odor of boiling shrimp, add fresh celery leaves to the water.

Substitute corn syrup or honey for $1/2$ amount of sugar called for and use $1/4$ less liquid.

Put an apple cut in half in a cake container to keep cake fresh.

To improve the flavor of store bought French dressing, add a clove of garlic to the bottle.

Spice up seafood with a small amount of mace.

Add a little vinegar to the water when cooking cabbage, etc. It will cut down on the cooking odor.

Add 1 teaspoon salt to the water to keep egg white from escaping from a cracked shell when being boiled.

To correct too much salt added to food, add 1 teaspoon each of vinegar and sugar while cooking.

To make nut meats come out whole, soak nuts in salt water overnight before cooking.

Lemons with the smoothest skin and the least points on the end have more juice and flavor.

Add a pinch of baking powder to powdered sugar icings. This keeps the icing from getting hard and dry.

A little salt in the frying pan will keep grease from splashing.

To rid vegetables of insects, add a pinch of borax and a little vinegar to the water in which they are washed.

Wash and store parsley in a tightly covered jar in the refrigerator. This will keep it fresh for a long time.

Wrap a cloth moistened with vinegar around cheese to keep it fresh.

To keep macaroni, spaghetti, and noodles from boiling over, put a tablespoon of butter in the water.

Carolina Cuisine: Nothin' Could Be Finer

Helpful Hints

When you cook eggs in the shell, put a heaping teaspoon of salt in the water. Then the shells won't crack.

Never double the salt if you double the recipe. Use only half again as much.

When cooking rice, add a spoonful of vinegar or lemon juice, and the rice will be light, separated and fluffy.

Before frying fish, soak the fish in lemon juice for about 20 to 25 minutes, roll in meal, fry in deep fat, no odor.

Drop a lettuce leaf into a pot of homemade soup to absorb excess grease.

Perk up soggy lettuce by adding lemon juice to a bowl of cold water and soak for an hour in the refrigerator.

Lettuce and celery keep longer stored in paper bags instead of celophane.

Cream will whip faster if you first chill the cream, the bowl, and the beaters well.

If your brown sugar is brick hard, use your cheese grater to grate the amount you need.

Brown sugar will not harden if an apple slice is placed in the container with it.

For a brown crust on roasted chicken, rub mayonnaise generously on the skin before cooking.

Use greased muffin tins as molds when baking stuffed green peppers.

Do not use metal bowls when mixing salads. Use wooden, glass, or china.

To ripen tomatoes, put them in a brown paper bag in a dark pantry and they will ripen overnight.

For a smooth cake:
 a) cream butter or oil and sugar very well
 b) add eggs one at a time, beating extremely well after each addition
 c) when alternating flour and milk, always begin and end with flour

To ripen pears:
a) place in a brown paper bag
b) fold down the top
c) keep at room temperature

To give turkey gravy a good texture, add one cup of dressing, cooked or uncooked, to gravy before cooking. Also add a good splash of soy sauce.

Bake rice instead of cooking it on top of stove when baking a roast or chicken, etc. in the oven. Use same ingredients as on package, place in a casserole, cover and bake for 1 hour. Stir once. This not only saves energy, but the rice never sticks and reheats beautifully.

Never put a rubber band around silver or it will leave a permanent stain.

Junior Charity League of Marlboro County, Inc.   243

Helpful Hints

Helpful Handfuls

Spray a little spray starch on your potholders. They will stay clean longer and grease won't soak in.

Whenever a recipe calls for salt, add a pinch of sugar as well. Whenever a recipe calls for sugar, add a pinch of salt as well.

Pasta Preparations

Dry	Prepared
8 ounces medium pasta (i.e., bow ties or rigatoni)	4 cups cooked
1½ inch diameter bundle long dry pasta (i.e., spaghetti)	4 cups cooked
8 ounces dry egg noodles	2½ cups cooked

Jewelry Cleaner

1 tablespoon Mr. Clean or 409 cleaner
1 tablespoon household ammonia
1 cup water

- Soak jewelry overnight or boil for 5 minutes. Works like magic.
- Do not use on pearls!

Mrs. Eugene (Winnie) Hamer, Monroe, NC

All Purpose Cleaner

Preparation time: 15 minutes   **Prepare ahead**

| 1 | empty gallon jug | 1 | cup sudsy ammonia |
| 8 | ounces isopropyl alcohol | 1 | teaspoon Dawn |

- Place the three ingredients in gallon jug and add water to fill.
- Pour as needed and use spray bottle.
- Do not use on glass.

Mrs. Bill (Gloria) Ward, Bennettsville, SC

INDEX

Drawing by: Johnsie Stidd

Johnsie Choate Stidd
"Wise Old Tree"

Johnsie Choate Stidd grew up in Danville, Virginia, where she had art classes throughout her schooling. She also took private art lessons at a local college.

In 1961, Mrs. Stidd graduated from the University of Florida with a degree in Art Education, her major emphasis being in fine arts. She and her husband, Ray, and two daughters, Laura and Amy, moved to Marlboro County in 1968.

Mrs. Stidd began teaching art in 1970 at Clio High School and Blenheim High School. She also wrote the first art curriculum guide for the county. Her teaching career has alternated between teaching art and the elementary grades. She has now taught art at every level - from kindergarten to twelfth grade, and her students have won many awards.

Besides teaching art in the public schools, Mrs. Stidd has taught at Girl Scout meetings, Vacation Bible School, church camp, and has given private lessons. She had a one-man show of her art work at a local bank in 1973.

Mrs. Stidd enjoys drawing and painting scenes and objects from nature using watercolors, pastels and pen and ink.

A

A Different Cheese Ring	19
Adelaide's Instant Russian Tea	41
Albritain Plantation Wassail	44
Ambrosia Pie	209
Angel Bavarian Cake	192
Ann Landers' Meat Loaf	141
Another Version of	
" Hot Kentucky Brown"	89

Appetizers

A Different Cheese Ring	19
Barbecued Pecans	30
Beer Cheese	21
Cheese Ball	18
Cheese Biscuits	20
Cheese Straws	20
Cinnamon Roll-Ups	23
Coastal Shrimp Mold	34
Cocktail Sausages	33
Crab And Shrimp Delight	25
Dried Beef Dip	17
Edythe's Cheese Straws	21
Fresh Fruit Dip	25
Ham Delights	25
Hot Cheese Olives	28
Hot Oyster Cocktail A La Belle Isle	29
Jalepeno Roll-Ups	26
Kaye's Crab Dip	23
Lemon Chicken Kabobs	22
Magnolia Caviar	17
Marinated Mushrooms	27
Mark's Mess	26
Meeting St. Crab Dip	24
Mexican Dip	27
Ole' Dip	28
Onion Canapes	29
Pepper Jelly Mold	31
Petite Toast Cups	34
Pie's Sausage Pinwheels	33
Pig's Boiled Peanuts	30
Pineapple Cheese Ball (or Spread)	19
Regal Red Caviar Dip	18
Salmon Mousse	32
Sausage Dip	32
Shrimp Ball	34
Stuffed Mushrooms	28
Taco Dip	35
Taparo's Hot Chili Cheese Dip	22
Tex Mex	35
Toasted Pecans	31
Trawler Crab Dip	24
Vegetable Pizza Bake	36
Virginia's Vegetable Dip	36

Apple Cake	194
Apple Cobbler	185
Apricot Salad	57

Aunt Kay B's Peanut Butter Cookies	222
Avgholemono Soup	47

B

Baked Asparagus Casserole	155
Baked Beans	157
Baked Custard	188
Baked Meatballs in Mushroom Sauce	141
Baked Mushroom Rice	173
Baked Sandwich	95
Baked Tomatoes with Spinach	178
Baked Vegetable Medley	179
Banana Cream Pie	210
Banana Pudding	185
Banana Slush	39
Banana-Wheat Quick Bread	81
Barbecued Chicken	101
Barbecued Pecans	30
Barbecued Wieners	233
Beary Easy and Good Dessert	228
Becky's Vegetable Soup	54
Beef Stroganoff	133
Beer Bread	81
Beer Cheese	21
Best Casserole	159
Beth's Cooked Play Dough	230
Better than Ever Tomato Aspic	73
Betty's Chicken Salad	62
Betty Searcy's English Pea Casserole	167

Beverages

Adelaide's Instant Russian Tea	41
Albritain Plantation Wassail	44
Banana Slush	39
Bloody Marys for a Crowd	39
Champagne Punch	40
Cheerwine Punch	42
Christmas Spritzer	44
Instant Hot Chocolate	40
Mimosas	42
Party Punch	42
Pawley's Island Daiquiris	41
Polly's Whiskey Sour Punch	44
Rum Divine	43
Russian Tea	43
Sparkling Punch	43

Big Sis' Chicken Pie	112
Billie's Barbecue Sauce	152
Black Bean Salad	59
Black Fruit Cake	200
Blackberry Wine Cake	194
Blender French Dressing	76
Bleu Cheese Dressing	75
Blonde Brownies	218
Bloody Marys for a Crowd	39
Blueberry Buckle	186
Blueberry Cake	195
Blueberry Pancakes for Two	82

Index

Junior Charity League of Marlboro County, Inc.   247

Blueberry Salad	60
Bologna Sandwich Spread	228

Breads & Spreads

Another Version of "Hot Kentucky Brown"	89
Baked Sandwich	95
Banana-Wheat Quick Bread	81
Beer Bread	81
Blueberry Pancakes for Two	82
Breakaway Bread	84
Cannoli Bagels	79
Catherine's Bran Muffins	83
Cheese Danish	84
Cinnamon Flop	85
Corny Corn Bread	85
Crook's Corner's Black Pepper Cornbread	86
Easy Biscuits	82
Ginger Sandwich Spread	87
Honey Muffins	88
John's Island Corn Bread	86
Marmalade Sandwich Spread	89
Mayonnaise Rolls	92
Melt in Your Mouth Rolls	92
Mexican Corn Bread	87
My Favorite Rolls	93
Nancy's Little Rolls	93
Nimmy's Bagel Spread	80
Orange Cranberry Bread	90
Pear Bread	90
Pecan Muffins	91
Pineapple - Cream Bagels	79
Pumpkin Muffins	91
Raisin And Nut Spread	88
Refrigerated Rolls	94
Refrigerator Bran Muffins	83
Shrimp Sandwiches	94
Spicy Pimento Cheese	92
Squash Bread	95
Star Loaves	96
Sticky Buns	96
Strawberries-and-Cream Bagel Slimmers	80
Sweet Potato Biscuits	97
Sweet Potato Bread	97
Vegetable Sandwich Spread	98
Zucchini Nut Bread	98
Breakaway Bread	84
Breakfast Casserole	130
Broccoli and Ham Quiche	160
Broccoli and Mushroom Casserole	161
Broccoli Casserole	159
Broccoli Cheese Sauce	162
Broccoli Quiche	160
Broccoli Salad	60
Broccoli Salad Supreme	61

Broccoli-Rice Casserole	161
Broccoli-Squash Casserole	162
Brown Rice	172
Buster Bars	187

C

Cabbage and Onion Stir-fry	163
Cannoli Bagels	79
Caramel Cake	196
Carbo's "Ashland Farms" Salad	58
Carrot Cake	196
Carrots Lyonnaise	163
Catherine's Bran Muffins	83
Champagne Punch	40
Charleston Chicken Casserole	102
Charleston Squares	219
Cheerwine Punch	42
Cheese and Crab Meat	120
Cheese Ball	18
Cheese Biscuits	20
Cheese Danish	84
Cheese Fondue	164
Cheese Grits Casserole	168
Cheese Straws	20
Cheese-Sausage Breakfast Casserole	130
Cheesecake Cookies	219
Cheesy Baked Potato Soup	52
Chesapeake Bay Crab Cakes	118
Chesapeake Crab Quiche	121
Chicken and Broccoli Casserole	103
Chicken and Chip Bake	105
Chicken and Dumpling Casserole	109
Chicken and Dumplings	108
Chicken Bog	102
Chicken Crunch	106
Chicken Delights	106
Chicken Parmesan	110
Chicken Pie	111
Chicken Pot Pie	112
Chicken Pot Pie Casserole	113
Chicken Salad with Fruit	62
Chicken Stew	47
Chicken Tetrazzini	116

Children's Fun

"Beary" Easy and Good Dessert	228
Barbecued Wieners	233
Beth's Cooked Play Dough	230
Bologna Sandwich Spread	228
Circus Bagels	227
Fried Bananas	227
Funnel Cakes	231
Ghoul's Hands	229
Hole-n-One Burger	229
Honey Crackle Popcorn	231
Monkey Bread	230
Morning Mix Up	232
Spoonburgers	232
Turtles	233

Chocolate Icing	201	Easy Biscuits	82
Chocolate Pound Cake	207	Easy Chicken Casserole	105
Chocolate Sauce	224	Easy Chicken Divan	107
Chocolate Sheet Cake	197	Easy Cobbler	187
Chocolate Surprise	190	Easy Lemon Pie	214
Chocolate Syrup Cake	198	Easy Shrimp Casserole	127
Christmas Cake	198	Easy Shrimp Creole	128
Christmas Spritzer	44	Easy Stuffed Peppers	146
Cinnamon Flop	85	Edythe's Cheese Straws	21
Cinnamon Roll-Ups	23	Eggnog Bavarian	211
Circus Bagels	227	Elaine's London Broil	140
Citrus Rice	173	Elisabeth's Key Lime Pie	213
Clam Chowder	48	English Pea Casserole	166
Coastal Shrimp Mold	34	**Entrees**	
Cocktail Sausages	33	Ann Landers' Meat Loaf	141
Coconut Layer Cake	199	Baked Meatballs in Mushroom Sauce	141
Coleman's Barbecued Turkey Breast	152	Barbecued Chicken	101
Congealed Asparagus Salad	58	Beef Stroganoff	133
Congealed Corn Beef Salad	64	Big Sis' Chicken Pie	112
Congo Bars	188	Billie's Barbecue Sauce	152
Cooked Cranberries	165	Breakfast Casserole	130
Copper Pennies	164	Charleston Chicken Casserole	102
Corny Corn Bread	85	Cheese and Crab Meat	120
Country Style Chicken Kiev	110	Cheese-Sausage Breakfast Casserole	130
Crab And Shrimp Delight	25	Chesapeake Bay Crab Cakes	118
Crab Casserole	120	Chesapeake Crab Quiche	121
Crab Imperial	119	Chicken and Broccoli Casserole	103
Cranberry Apple Casserole	165	Chicken and Chip Bake	105
Cream Cheese Pound Cake OLD	205	Chicken and Dumpling Casserole	109
Cream Pie	210	Chicken and Dumplings	108
Creamed Shrimp	126	Chicken Bog	102
Creamy Frozen Salad	65	Chicken Crunch	106
Creamy Potato Soup	52	Chicken Delights	106
Creole Shrimp	129	Chicken Parmesan	110
Crisp Broccoli Salad	61	Chicken Pie	111
Crisp Chicken Casserole	104	Chicken Pot Pie	112
Crock Pot Baked Beans	158	Chicken Pot Pie Casserole	113
Crook's Corner's Curried Chicken Salad	63	Chicken Tetrazzini	116
Crook's Corner's Black Pepper		Coleman's Barbecued Turkey Breast	152
Cornbread	86	Country Style Chicken Kiev	110
Crunchy Fudge Sandwiches	220	Crab Casserole	120
D		Crab Imperial	119
Death By Chocolate	189	Creamed Shrimp	126
Delicious Bean Salad	59	Creole Shrimp	129
Delicious Seafood Casserole	126	Crisp Chicken Casserole	104
Deluxe Chicken Casserole	104	Delicious Seafood Casserole	126
Devil's Food Cake	199	Deluxe Chicken Casserole	104
Deviled Crab	121	Deviled Crab	121
Dried Beef Dip	17	Duck	117
Duck	117	Duncan's Deer Burgers	136
Duncan's Deer Burgers	136	DuPre's Chow Mein	135
DuPre's Chow Mein	135	Dutch Meat Loaf	143
Dutch Meat Loaf	143	Easy Chicken Casserole	105
E		Easy Chicken Divan	107
Earthquake Cake	200	Easy Shrimp Casserole	127
		Easy Shrimp Creole	128
		Easy Stuffed Peppers	146

Index

Junior Charity League of Marlboro County, Inc.

Elaine's London Broil	140
Extra Special Meat Loaf	142
Eye of Round Roast	148
Firecracker Enchilada Casserole	136
French Italian Chicken	109
Garides Tourkolimano (Greek Shrimp)	127
Grandma's Famous Lasagna	139
Grilled Pork Tenderloin	147
Ground Beef Casserole	137
Hamburger Pie	137
Hash	138
Heavenly Flounder or Sole	122
Hot Dog Chili	134
How to cook a ham	138
How to cook a Roast	148
Imitation Crab Meat Casserole	119
Jan's Old-Fashioned Beef Stew	132
Jean and Allen's Chicken Divan	107
Jennie's Mexican Casserole	146
Kay's Poppy Seed Chicken	114
Low Country Boil	123
Low-Sodium Lasagna	140
M.M.'s Oyster Pie	124
Marlboro Meat Loaf	142
Mexican Casserole	145
Mrs. "C's" Crab Meat and Shrimp Casserole	122
Newton Spaghetti Casserole	151
No Peek Oven Stew (or No Peek Venison Stew)	133
No-Peek Chicken	111
Oyster Pie	124
Pawley's Island Frogmore Stew	123
Piper's Chicken Pie	113
Pledger's Favorite Barbecue Sauce	152
Pork Chop and Rice Casserole	147
Quick Chicken and Dumplings	108
Quick Stroganoff	134
Rolled Chicken Breast	103
Rosemary Chicken	114
Salmon Croquettes	125
Sausage and Egg Casserole	131
Sausage Casserole	149
Seafood Casserole	125
Shrimp and Rice Casserole	128
Shrimp Scampi	129
Sicilian Meat Roll	144
Smoked Fowl	118
Soy Chicken	115
St. Paul's Casserole	150
Standing Rib Roast	149
Stew Beef	131
Stir-Fried Chicken with Vegetables	115
Stuffed Shells	150
Sweet and Sour Meat Loaf	143
Swiss Chicken Casserole	116

Swiss-Ham Kabobs	151
Tasty Mexican Chicken Casserole	144
Texas Pile-Up	117

F

Extra Special Meat Loaf	142
Eye of Round Roast	148
Firecracker Enchilada Casserole	136
Forgotten Cookies	220
French Dressing	75
French Italian Chicken	109
French Onion Casserole	169
French Onion Soup	50
Fresh Apple Cake	193
Fresh Corn Chowder	48
Fresh Fruit Dip	25
Fresh Mushroom Soup	50
Fried Bananas	227
Frosting for Red Velvet Cake	208
Frozen Cherry Pie	210
Frozen Sweet Corn	165
Fruit Compote	66
Fudge Pie	212
Funnel Cakes	231

G

Garides Tourkolimano (Greek Shrimp)	127
Ghoul's Hands	229
Ginger Sandwich Spread	87
Glazed Sweet Potatoes	178
Golden Nugget Fudge	224
Grandma's Famous Lasagna	139
Grape Hull Pie	212
Grilled Pork Tenderloin	147
Ground Beef Casserole	137

H

Half Pound Cake	206
Ham Delights	25
Hamburger Pie	137
Hash	138
Hash Brown Potato Casserole	171
Hearts of Palm Salad	67
Heavenly Flounder or Sole	122
Hole-n-One Burger	229
Honey Crackle Popcorn	231
Honey Muffins	88
Hot Cheese Olives	28
Hot Dog Chili	134
Hot Oyster Cocktail A La Belle Isle	29
How to cook a ham	138
How to cook a Roast	148

I

Imitation Crab Meat Casserole	119
Instant Hot Chocolate	40
Irene's Cranberry Salad	65
Italian Zucchini Pie	180

J

Jalepeno Roll-Ups	26	Nancy's Little Rolls	93
Jan's Old-Fashioned Beef Stew	132	Never Fail Chocolate Icing	207
Jean and Allen's Chicken Divan	107	Newton Spaghetti Casserole	151
Jennie's Mexican Casserole	146	Nimmy's Bagel Spread	80
John's Fruit Compote	66	No Bake Cheese Cake	197
John's Island Corn Bread	86	No Peek Oven Stew (or No Peek Venison	

K

		Stew)	133
Kay's Poppy Seed Chicken	114	No-Peek Chicken	111
Kaye's Crab Dip	23	Nutty Buddy Pie	215
Kentucky Pie	213		

O

L

		Oatmeal Cake	202
Lemon Chicken Kabobs	22	Old-fashioned Boiled Custard	189
Lemon Cookies	221	Ole' Dip	28
Lemon Icebox Bisque	215	Onion Canapes	29
Lemon Sours	222	Orange Coconut Cake	203
Lemonade Pie	214	Orange Cranberry Bread	90
Lentil and Brown Rice Soup	49	Orange Salad	67
Lib's Layer Cake	201	Orange Sherbet	202
Low Country Boil	123	Oriental Rice	174
Low Salt Chicken Salad	63	Our Favorite Potato Casserole	171
Low-Sodium Lasagna	140	Oyster Pie	124

M

P

M.M.'s Oyster Pie	124	Papa's Favorite Red Rice	174
Macaroni and Cheese	168	Party Punch	42
Macaroni Salad	68	Pat's Salad Dressing	75
Macaroni-Shrimp Salad	72	Patio Beans	157
Magnolia Caviar	17	Pawley's Island Frogmore Stew	123
Mandarin Orange Salad	68	Pawley's Island Daiquiris	41
Marinated Asparagus	156	Pawleys Island Frogmore Stew	51
Marinated Cole Slaw	71	Peach Delight	203
Marinated Mushrooms	27	Peanut Butter Candy	224
Marinated Steak Salad	73	Peanut Butter Pie	216
Marinated Vegetable Salad	74	Pear Bread	90
Marinated Vegetables	179	Pecan Muffins	91
Mark's Mess	26	Pecan Pie	216
Marlboro Meat Loaf	142	Pepper Jelly Mold	31
Marmalade Sandwich Spread	89	Petite Toast Cups	34
Martin's Blonde Brownies	218	Picnic Broccoli Salad	61
Mary Kay and Margaret Ann's		Pie's Sausage Pinwheels	33
Chocolate Pie	211	Pig's Boiled Peanuts	30
Mayonnaise Rolls	92	Pineapple - Cream Bagels	79
Meeting St. Crab Dip	24	Pineapple Casserole	170
Melt in Your Mouth Rolls	92	Pineapple Cheese Ball (or Spread)	19
Mexican Casserole	145	Pineapple Layer Cake	204
Mexican Corn Bread	87	Piper's Chicken Pie	113
Mexican Dip	27	Pistachio Cake	204
Million Dollar Pound Cake	205	Pledger's Favorite Barbecue Sauce	152
Mimosas	42	Polly's Whiskey Sour Punch	44
Moist Pound Cake	206	Poppy Seed Dressing	74
Monkey Bread	230	Pork Chop and Rice Casserole	147
Morning Mix Up	232	Potato Soup	51
Mountain Pot Beans	49	Pretzel Salad	69
Mrs. "C's" Crab Meat and Shrimp		Prize-Winning Eggplant	166
Casserole	122	Pumpkin Bars	191
My Favorite Rolls	93	Pumpkin Muffins	91

N

Q

Junior Charity League of Marlboro County, Inc.   **251**

Quick Asparagus Casserole	155
Quick Chicken and Dumplings	108
Quick Dried Beans	158
Quick Peach Cobbler	190
Quick Salad Dressing	76
Quick Stroganoff	134

R

Raisin And Nut Spread	88
Raspberry Salad	70
Red Velvet Cake	208
Refrigerated Rolls	94
Refrigerator Bran Muffins	83
Regal Red Caviar Dip	18
Rolled Chicken Breast	103
Rosemary Chicken	114
Rum Divine	43
Russian Tea	43
Ruth Kirkwood's Mints	221

S

Salads

Apricot Salad	57
Better than Ever Tomato Aspic	73
Betty's Chicken Salad	62
Black Bean Salad	59
Blender French Dressing	76
Bleu Cheese Dressing	75
Blueberry Salad	60
Broccoli Salad	60
Broccoli Salad Supreme	61
Carbo's "Ashland Farms" Salad	58
Chicken Salad with Fruit	62
Congealed Asparagus Salad	58
Congealed Corn Beef Salad	64
Creamy Frozen Salad	65
Crisp Broccoli Salad	61
Crook's Corner's Curried Chicken Salad	63
Delicious Bean Salad	59
French Dressing	75
Fruit Compote	66
Hearts of Palm Salad	67
Irene's Cranberry Salad	65
John's Fruit Compote	66
Low Salt Chicken Salad	63
Macaroni Salad	68
Macaroni-Shrimp Salad	72
Mandarin Orange Salad	68
Marinated Cole Slaw	71
Marinated Steak Salad	73
Marinated Vegetable Salad	74
Orange Salad	67
Pat's Salad Dressing	75
Picnic Broccoli Salad	61
Poppy Seed Dressing	74
Pretzel Salad	69
Quick Salad Dressing	76

Raspberry Salad	70
Seashell Salad	70
Seven Layer Salad	71
Sour Cream Potato Salad	69
Spaghetti Salad	72
Sparacino's Antipasto Salad	57
Spicy Chicken Salad	64
Tangy Slaw Dressing	76
Tomato Refresher	74

Salmon Croquettes	125
Salmon Mousse	32
Sauce for Fresh Apple Cake	193
Sausage and Egg Casserole	131
Sausage Casserole	149
Sausage Dip	32
Sausage Quiche	175
Scrumptious Squash Soufflé	177
Seafood Casserole	125
Seashell Salad	70
Seven Layer Salad	71
Seven-Layer Cookies	223
Sherried Fruit	167
Shrimp and Rice Casserole	128
Shrimp Ball	34
Shrimp Sandwiches	94
Shrimp Scampi	129
Sicilian Meat Roll	144
Slow Cooker Macaroni	169
Smoked Fowl	118

Soups

Avgholemono Soup	47
Becky's Vegetable Soup	54
Cheesy Baked Potato Soup	52
Chicken Stew	47
Clam Chowder	48
Creamy Potato Soup	52
French Onion Soup	50
Fresh Corn Chowder	48
Fresh Mushroom Soup	50
Lentil and Brown Rice Soup	49
Mountain Pot Beans	49
Pawleys Island Frogmore Stew	51
Potato Soup	51
Spaghetti Soup	53
Turkey Soup	53
Vegetable Soup	54

Sour Cream Potato Salad	69
Soy Chicken	115
Spaghetti Salad	72
Spaghetti Soup	53
Sparacino's Antipasto Salad	57
Sparkling Punch	43
Spicy Chicken Salad	64
Spicy Pimento Cheese	92

Spinach-Artichoke Casserole	176	Eggnog Bavarian	211
Spoonburgers	232	Elisabeth's Key Lime Pie	213
Squash Bread	95	Forgotten Cookies	220
Squash Casserole	176	Fresh Apple Cake	193
Squash Soufflé	177	Frosting for Red Velvet Cake	208
St. Paul's Casserole	150	Frozen Cherry Pie	210
Standing Rib Roast	149	Fudge Pie	212
Star Loaves	96	Golden Nugget Fudge	224
Stew Beef	131	Grape Hull Pie	212
Sticky Buns	96	Half Pound Cake	206
Stir-Fried Chicken with Vegetables	115	Kentucky Pie	213
Strawberries-and-Cream Bagel Slimmers	80	Lemon Cookies	221
Strawberry Angel Food Cake	209	Lemon Icebox Bisque	215
Strawberry Pie	217	Lemon Sours	222
Strawberry Trifle	191	Lemonade Pie	214
Stuffed Mushrooms	28	Lib's Layer Cake	201
Stuffed Shells	150	Martin's Blonde Brownies	218
Sunday Asparagus Casserole	156	Mary Kay and Margaret Ann's Chocolate	
Super Spud Casserole	172	Pie	211
Sweet and Sour Meat Loaf	143	Million Dollar Pound Cake	205
Sweet Endings		Moist Pound Cake	206
Ambrosia Pie	209	Never Fail Chocolate Icing	207
Angel Bavarian Cake	192	No Bake Cheese Cake	197
Apple Cake	194	Nutty Buddy Pie	215
Apple Cobbler	185	Oatmeal Cake	202
Aunt Kay B's Peanut Butter Cookies	222	Old-fashioned Boiled Custard	189
Baked Custard	188	Orange Coconut Cake	203
Banana Cream Pie	210	Orange Sherbet	202
Banana Pudding	185	Peach Delight	203
Black Fruit Cake	200	Peanut Butter Candy	224
Blackberry Wine Cake	194	Peanut Butter Pie	216
Blonde Brownies	218	Pecan Pie	216
Blueberry Buckle	186	Pineapple Layer Cake	204
Blueberry Cake	195	Pistachio Cake	204
Buster Bars	187	Pumpkin Bars	191
Caramel Cake	196	Quick Peach Cobbler	190
Carrot Cake	196	Red Velvet Cake	208
Charleston Squares	219	Ruth Kirkwood's Mints	221
Cheesecake Cookies	219	Sauce for Fresh Apple Cake	193
Chocolate Icing	201	Seven-Layer Cookies	223
Chocolate Pound Cake	207	Strawberry Angel Food Cake	209
Chocolate Sauce	224	Strawberry Pie	217
Chocolate Sheet Cake	197	Strawberry Trifle	191
Chocolate Surprise	190	Tangy Lemon Bars	221
Chocolate Syrup Cake	198	Texas Butter Cake	195
Christmas Cake	198	Tip-Top Pecan Pie	217
Coconut Layer Cake	199	Whole Lemon Blender Pie	214
Congo Bars	188	World's Best Sugar Cookies	223
Cream Cheese Pound Cake OLD	205		
Cream Pie	210	Sweet Pepper Relish	170
Crunchy Fudge Sandwiches	220	Sweet Potato Biscuits	97
Death By Chocolate	189	Sweet Potato Bread	97
Devil's Food Cake	199	Swiss Chicken Casserole	116
Earthquake Cake	200	Swiss-Ham Kabobs	151
Easy Cobbler	187	**T**	
Easy Lemon Pie	214	Taco Dip	35

Junior Charity League of Marlboro County, Inc.

Index

Tangy Lemon Bars	221
Tangy Slaw Dressing	76
Taparo's Hot Chili Cheese Dip	22
Tasty Mexican Chicken Casserole	144
Tex Mex	35
Texas Butter Cake	195
Texas Pile-Up	117
Tip-Top Pecan Pie	217
Toasted Pecans	31
Tomato Refresher	74
Toni Ann's Brown Rice	173
Trawler Crab Dip	24
Turkey Soup	53
Turtles	233

V

Vegetable Casserole	180
Vegetable Pie	180
Vegetable Pizza Bake	36
Vegetable Sandwich Spread	98
Vegetable Soup	54

Vegetables

Baked Asparagus Casserole	155
Baked Beans	157
Baked Mushroom Rice	173
Baked Tomatoes with Spinach	178
Baked Vegetable Medley	179
Best Casserole	159
Betty Searcy's English Pea Casserole	167
Broccoli and Ham Quiche	160
Broccoli and Mushroom Casserole	161
Broccoli Casserole	159
Broccoli Cheese Sauce	162
Broccoli Quiche	160
Broccoli-Rice Casserole	161
Broccoli-Squash Casserole	162
Brown Rice	172
Cabbage and Onion Stir-fry	163
Carrots Lyonnaise	163
Cheese Fondue	164
Cheese Grits Casserole	168
Citrus Rice	173
Cooked Cranberries	165
Copper Pennies	164
Cranberry Apple Casserole	165
Crock Pot Baked Beans	158
English Pea Casserole	166
French Onion Casserole	169
Frozen Sweet Corn	165
Glazed Sweet Potatoes	178
Hash Brown Potato Casserole	171
Italian Zucchini Pie	180
Macaroni and Cheese	168
Marinated Asparagus	156
Marinated Vegetables	179
Oriental Rice	174
Our Favorite Potato Casserole	171
Papa's Favorite Red Rice	174

Patio Beans	157
Pineapple Casserole	170
Prize-Winning Eggplant	166
Quick Asparagus Casserole	155
Quick Dried Beans	158
Sausage Quiche	175
Scrumptious Squash Soufflé	177
Sherried Fruit	167
Slow Cooker Macaroni	169
Spinach-Artichoke Casserole	176
Squash Casserole	176
Squash Soufflé	177
Sunday Asparagus Casserole	156
Super Spud Casserole	172
Sweet Pepper Relish	170
Toni Ann's Brown Rice	173
Vegetable Casserole	180
Vegetable Pie	180
Wild Rice With Oysters	175
Virginia's Vegetable Dip	36

W

Whole Lemon Blender Pie	214
Wild Rice With Oysters	175
World's Best Sugar Cookies	223

Z

Zucchini Nut Bread	98

CAROLINA CUISINE: NOTHIN' COULD BE FINER
Junior Charity League of Marlboro County, Inc.
Post Office Box 185
Bennettsville, South Carolina 29512

Please send ____ copy(ies) of CAROLINA CUISINE . . . . @$14.95 each
Shipping & Handling . . . . @$3.50 each
South Carolina residents add 6% sales tax. . . . . @$.90 each

Total enclosed. . . . . $_____.__ total

Make checks payable to the Junior Charity League of Marlboro County, Inc. or
charge to (circle one): Visa   Mastercard   Valid thru _____
Account #_____ Signature_____
Please Print:
Name: _____
Address:_____
City: _____ State:_____ Zip: _____
Telephone:_____

CAROLINA CUISINE: NOTHIN' COULD BE FINER
Junior Charity League of Marlboro County, Inc.
Post Office Box 185
Bennettsville, South Carolina 29512

Please send ____ copy(ies) of CAROLINA CUISINE . . . . @$14.95 each
Shipping & Handling . . . . @$3.50 each
South Carolina residents add 6% sales tax. . . . . @$.90 each

Total enclosed. . . . . $_____.__ total

Make checks payable to the Junior Charity League of Marlboro County, Inc. or
charge to (circle one): Visa   Mastercard   Valid thru _____
Account #_____ Signature_____
Please Print:
Name: _____
Address:_____
City: _____ State:_____ Zip: _____
Telephone:_____

CAROLINA CUISINE: NOTHIN' COULD BE FINER
Junior Charity League of Marlboro County, Inc.
Post Office Box 185
Bennettsville, South Carolina 29512

Please send ____ copy(ies) of CAROLINA CUISINE . . . . @$14.95 each
Shipping & Handling . . . . @$3.50 each
South Carolina residents add 6% sales tax. . . . . @$.90 each

Total enclosed. . . . . $_____.__ total

Make checks payable to the Junior Charity League of Marlboro County, Inc. or
charge to (circle one): Visa   Mastercard   Valid thru _____
Account #_____ Signature_____
Please Print:
Name: _____
Address:_____
City: _____ State:_____ Zip: _____
Telephone:_____

Junior Charity League of Marlboro County, Inc.

Where did you hear about this cookbook?_____

_____

What local stores would you like ot see carry CAROLINA CUISINE? _____

_____

Store Name:_____ Phone #_____

Address: _____

City: _____ State:_____ Zip:_____

Was this cookbook purchased as a gift? _____

What attracted you to this particular cookbook?_____

_____

What is your age? _____
Thank you in advance for your time and assistance.

Where did you hear about this cookbook?_____

_____

What local stores would you like ot see carry CAROLINA CUISINE? _____

_____

Store Name:_____ Phone #_____

Address: _____

City: _____ State:_____ Zip:_____

Was this cookbook purchased as a gift? _____

What attracted you to this particular cookbook?_____

_____

What is your age? _____
Thank you in advance for your time and assistance.

Where did you hear about this cookbook?_____

_____

What local stores would you like ot see carry CAROLINA CUISINE? _____

_____

Store Name:_____ Phone #_____

Address: _____

City: _____ State:_____ Zip:_____

Was this cookbook purchased as a gift? _____

What attracted you to this particular cookbook?_____

_____

What is your age? _____
Thank you in advance for your time and assistance.

Carolina Cuisine: Nothin' Could Be Finer